Ramesh Thakur is Vice Rector of the United Nations University. He was previously Head of the Peace Research Centre, Research School of Pacific and Asian Studies, at the Australian National University. Born and raised in India, he received his formal education in India and Canada, and has held full-time academic appointments in Fiji, New Zealand and Australia. He is the author or editor of numerous books on Asian politics and international relations and has published widely in both academic journals and quality newspapers.

NUCLEAR WEAPONS-FREE ZONES

Also by Ramesh Thakur

A CRISIS OF EXPECTATIONS: UN Peacekeeping in the 1990s (*editor with Carlyle A. Thayer*)

* THE GOVERNMENT AND POLITICS OF INDIA

IN DEFENCE OF NEW ZEALAND: Foreign Policy Choices in the Nuclear Age

INTERNATIONAL CONFLICT RESOLUTION (*editor*)

INTERNATIONAL PEACEKEEPING IN LEBANON: United Nations Authority and Multinational Force

*PAST IMPERFECT, FUTURE *UN*CERTAIN: The United Nations at Fifty (*editor*)

PEACEKEEPING IN VIETNAM: Canada, India, Poland and the International Commission

THE POLITICS AND ECONOMICS OF INDIA'S FOREIGN POLICY

RESHAPING REGIONAL RELATIONS: Asia Pacific and the Former Soviet Union (*editor with Carlyle A. Thayer*)

* THE SOUTH PACIFIC: Problems, Issues and Prospects (*editor*)

* SOVIET RELATIONS WITH INDIA AND VIETNAM (*with Carlyle A. Thayer*)

THE SOVIET UNION AS AN ASIAN PACIFIC POWER: Implications of Gorbachev's 1986 Vladivostok Initiative (*editor with Carlyle A. Thayer*)

* *From the same publishers*

Nuclear Weapons-Free Zones

Edited by

Ramesh Thakur
Vice Rector (Peace and Governance)
United Nations University
Tokyo, Japan

First published in Great Britain 1998 by
MACMILLAN PRESS LTD
Houndmills, Basingstoke, Hampshire RG21 6XS and London
Companies and representatives throughout the world

A catalogue record for this book is available from the British Library.

ISBN 0-333-73980-9

 First published in the United States of America 1998 by
ST. MARTIN'S PRESS, INC.,
Scholarly and Reference Division,
175 Fifth Avenue, New York, N.Y. 10010

ISBN 0-312-21745-5

Library of Congress Cataloging-in-Publication Data
Nuclear weapons-free zones / edited by Ramesh Thakur.
p. cm.
Includes bibliographical references and index.
ISBN 0-312-21745-5 (cloth)
1. Nuclear-weapon-free zones. I. Thakur, Ramesh Chandra, 1948–
.
JZ5725.N83 1998
341.7'34—dc21   98-23639
                                                                  CIP

Selection, editorial matter and Introduction © Ramesh Thakur 1998
Text © Macmillan Press Ltd 1998

All rights reserved. No reproduction, copy or transmission of this publication may be made without written permission.

No paragraph of this publication may be reproduced, copied or transmitted save with written permission or in accordance with the provisions of the Copyright, Designs and Patents Act 1988, or under the terms of any licence permitting limited copying issued by the Copyright Licensing Agency, 90 Tottenham Court Road, London W1P 9HE.

Any person who does any unauthorised act in relation to this publication may be liable to criminal prosecution and civil claims for damages.

The authors have asserted their rights to be identified as the authors of this work in accordance with the Copyright, Designs and Patents Act 1988.

This book is printed on paper suitable for recycling and made from fully managed and sustained forest sources.

10 9   8   7   6   5   4   3   2   1
07 06 05 04 03 02 01 00 99 98

Printed and bound in Great Britain by
Antony Rowe Ltd, Chippenham, Wiltshire

Contents

Notes on Contributors	vii
Abbreviations	xi
Map	xiv

PART ONE: INTRODUCTION		1
1	Stepping Stones to a Nuclear-Weapon-Free World *Ramesh Thakur*	3
PART TWO: THE FOUR ESTABLISHED ZONES		33
2	Latin America – The Treaty of Tlatelolco *Monica Serrano*	35
3	The South Pacific – The Treaty of Rarotonga *Michael Hamel-Green*	59
4	Southeast Asia – The Treaty of Bangkok *Carolina G. Hernandez*	81
5	Africa – The Treaty of Pelindaba *Julius O. Ihonvbere*	93
PART THREE: FOUR PROSPECTIVE ZONES		121
6	A Northeast Asian Nuclear-Weapon-Free Zone: A Korean Perspective, *Bon-Hak Koo*	123

7	A Northeast Asian Nuclear-Weapon-Free-Zone: A Japanese Perspective, *Naoko Sajima*	140
8	The Case for a South Asian Nuclear-Weapon-Free Zone, *Samina Yasmeen*	152
9	The Obstacles to a South Asian Nuclear-Weapon-Free Zone, *Dipankar Banerjee*	173
10	The Case For a Nuclear-Weapon-Free Zone in the Middle East, *Ibrahim A. Karawan*	184
11	The Obstacles To A Middle East Nuclear-Weapon-Free Zone, *Gerald M. Steinberg*	194
12	A Nuclear-Weapon-Free Southern Hemisphere *Terence O'Brien*	210

Index   223

Notes on Contributors

Major-General Dipankar Banerjee AVSM took early retirement after 36 years of active combat service in the India Army. In the last four years of his service, he was the Deputy Director of the Institute for Defence Studies and Analyses, New Delhi. His particular areas of interest include nuclear strategy, arms control and disarmament issues; China's military potential; and aspects of Indian security policies. He has authored four books, edited four and written about twenty chapters in books. He is a regular contributor to the debate on security in India and the Asia–Pacific. Currently he is the Co-Director of the Institute of Peace and Conflict Studies, New Delhi.

Michael Hamel-Green is Associate Professor in the Department of Social and Community Studies at Victoria University of Technology in Melbourne. Active in peace, disarmament and environmental movements in Melbourne since the 1960s, he became involved in the campaign for a Nuclear Free and Independent Pacific in the 1980s. He subsequently completed a doctoral thesis and monograph on the South Pacific Nuclear Free Zone, and more recently has been engaged in comparative studies of nuclear-weapon-free zones.

Carolina G. Hernandez is the Carlos P. Romulo Professor of International Relations at the University of the Philippines and President of the Institute for Strategic and Development Studies in Manila. In January 1998 Prof. Hernandez will assume the Lopez Chair in Asian Studies at the Virginia Military Institute. Dr. Hernandez is associated with several international bodies including the ASEAN Institutes for Strategic and International Studies (ASEAN-ISIS), Asia–Australia Institute and the Asia Society. She obtained her Ph.D. in Political Science at the State University of New York, Buffalo.

Julius O. Ihonvbere took his Ph.D. from the University of Toronto in Canada. He has taught at the universities of Ife and Port Harcourt in Nigeria, Toronto in Canada and Texas at Austin in the US. He has published extensively on diverse third world issues. His recent books include *Nigeria: The Politics of Adjustment and Democracy* (Transaction, 1994) and *Economic Crisis, Civil Society and Democratization: The Case of Zambia* (Africa World Press, 1996). His forthcoming books include *Africa and the New World Order* (Peter Lang, 1998) and *The Illusions of Power: Nigeria in Transition* (Africa World Press, 1998). A recipient of the First Mario Zamora Memorial Award, he is currently Program Officer in the Peace and Social Justice Program of the Ford Foundation in New York.

Ibrahim A. Karawan is Associate Professor of Political Science at the University of Utah, Salt Lake City, where he teaches Middle Eastern and international politics. A former Research Fellow at the Al-Ahram Centre for Political and Strategic Studies, Cairo, he wrote the chapter for this book while Senior Fellow for the Middle East at the International Institute for Strategic Studies (IISS) in London. His most recent publication is *The Islamist Impasse* (Oxford University Press for the IISS, Adelphi Paper 314, 1997).

Bon-Hak Koo is a Research Fellow at the Korea Institute for Defense Analyses (KIDA). He was educated at Yonsei University, Seoul and received his Ph.D. from the University of Cincinnati, Ohio. His research interests centre on North Korean politics, US-South Korea security relations and international relations in Northeast Asia. He is the author of *The Political Economy of Self-Reliance: Juche and Economic Development in North Korea, 1961–1990* (1992) and an editor of *The Korean Peninsula: Prospects for Peace and Reunification* (1997). He is currently the head of research cooperation at KIDA and the managing editor of the *Korean Journal of Defense Analysis*.

Terence O'Brien has been the foundation Director of the Centre for Strategic Studies in Wellington since September 1993. A career diplomat with the New Zealand Ministry of Foreign Affairs and Trade, he served as New Zealand Permanent Representative to the United Nations in Geneva and concurrently Ambassador to the General Agreement on Tariffs and Trade (GATT) (1980–3); Ambassador to the European Community, Belgium and Denmark (1983–6); and

Permanent Representative to the United Nations (1990–3). He was the New Zealand representative on the UN Security Council in 1993 and President of the Security Council for March 1993.

Naoko Sajima is a Research Professor at the National Institute for Defense Studies, Japan. After graduating from Sophia University in Tokyo, she spent ten years in the Japan Defense Agency, where from 1989 to 1992 she was a Protocol Specialist in the Foreign Relations Office. Concurrently, she got a Master's degree in International Politics from Aoyama Gakuin University in Tokyo. Her areas of interest include alliance management policies and international relations in the Asia–Pacific region. Among her publications in English is *Japan and Australia: A New Security Partnership?* (Canberra: Australian National University, Strategic and Defence Studies Centre, Working Paper No. 292, 1995).

Monica Serrano received her undergraduate degree from El Colegio de Mexico and her D.Phil. in International Relations from the University of Oxford. She has also attended the US-European School on Global Security and Arms Control at the University of Sussex and the Hague Academy of International Law. A Senior Lecturer at El Colegio de Mexico, Dr Serrano has also lectured at the Institute of Latin American Studies of the University of London, and been Research Associate/Fellow there as well as at the International Institute for Strategic Studies (IISS) in London. She has published extensively on nuclear arms control and non-proliferation and other security studies with respect to Latin America.

Gerald M. Steinberg is Professor of Political Studies and Director of Arms Control and Non-Proliferation Research at the Begin-Sadat Center for Strategic Studies, Bar Ilan University, Israel. He received his Ph.D. in International Relations from Cornell University. He has published widely on Israeli and Middle East foreign and defence policy, arms control and proliferation. He is also a participant in the 'Track Two' discussions on the multilateral working group on regional security arms control, a consultant to the Israeli Ministry of Foreign Affairs and a participant in the Mediterranean Dialogue activities of the Organisation for Security and Cooperation in Europe (OSCE). Prof. Steinberg's most recent publications include *Strategy, Deterrence and Arms Control in the Nuclear Age* (in Hebrew) (Israeli

Open University, 1997)); 'Deterrence and Middle East Stability: An Israeli Perspective', *Security Dialogue* (1997) and 'The 1995 NPT Extension and Review Conference and the Arab-Israeli Peace Process', *Nonproliferation Review* (1996).

Ramesh Thakur is Professor and Head of the Peace Research Centre at the Australian National University in Canberra. Educated at the University of Calcutta and Queen's University in Canada, he was formerly Professor of International Relations and Director of Asian Studies at the University of Otago in New Zealand. In April 1998 he will become the Vice Rector (Peace and Governance) of the United Nations University in Tokyo. Professor Thakur is a member of the National Consultative Committee on Peace and Disarmament in Australia, having previously been a member of the Public Advisory Committee on Arms Control and Disarmament in New Zealand. Dr Thakur is the author/editor of over a dozen books and more than 100 articles and book chapters, and the editor of the *Australian Journal of International Affairs*. He also writes for the quality national and international press, including *The Asian Wall Street Journal, The International Herald Tribune* and *Newsweek* (Japan).

Samina Yasmeen, educated at the universities of Punjab and Quaid-i-Azam in Pakistan and the Australian National University and Tasmania in Australia, is Senior Lecturer in International Politics at the University of Western Australia. She works on political and strategic developments in South Asia, Pakistani politics and Islamic studies. Her publications include 'Democracy in Pakistan', *Asian Survey* (1994); 'Pakistan's Cautious Foreign Policy', *Survival* (1994); and *Confidence Building Measures in South Asia* (with Aabha Dixit) (Henry L. Stimson Center, Occasional Paper No. 23, 1995).

Abbreviations

ABACC	Argentina-Brazil Accounting and Control Commission
ABM	anti-ballistic missile
ACRS	Arms Control and Regional Security (Middle East)
AFCONE	African Commission on Nuclear Energy
AFTA	ASEAN Free Trade Area
ANC	African National Congress
ANWFZ	African Nuclear-Weapon-Free Zone
APEC	Asia–Pacific Economic Cooperation
ARF	ASEAN Regional Forum
ASEAN	Association of South-east Asian Nations
BWC	Biological and Toxin Weapons Convention (1972)
CBM	confidence building measure(s)
CD	UN Conference on Disarmament (Geneva)
CFE	Conventional Forces in Europe
COCOM	Coordinating Committee on Export Controls
COPREDAL	*Comisión Preparatoria para la Desnuclearización de América Latina* (Preparatory Commission for the Denuclearisation of Latin America)
CPSU	Communist Party of the Soviet Union
CTBT	Comprehensive Test Ban Treaty (1996)
CWC	Chemical Weapons Convention (1993)
DMZ	Demilitarised Zone
DPRK	Democratic People's Republic of Korea (North Korea)
ECA	Economic Commission for Africa
ECOWAS	Economic Community of West African States
EEZ	exclusive economic zone
EIF	entry into force
EU	European Union
Euratom	European Atomic Energy Community
FPDA	Five Power Defence Arrangements

FSM	Federated States of Micronesia
G7	Group of Seven industrialised countries—Canada, France, Germany, Italy, Japan, the UK and the US
HEU	highly enriched uranium
IAEA	International Atomic Energy Agency
ICBM	intercontinental ballistic missile
ICJ	International Court of Justice
ICRC	International Committee of the Red Cross
IMF	International Monetary Fund
INF	Intermediate-range Nuclear Forces
KEDO	Korean Energy Development Organisation
LPA	Lagos Plan of Action (1980)
MENWFZ	Middle East nuclear-weapon-free zone
MTCR	Missile Technology Control Regime
NATO	North Atlantic Treaty Organisation
NEANWFZ	Northeast Asian nuclear-weapon-free zone
NGO	non-government organisation
NPT	Nuclear Non-Proliferation Treaty (1968)
NPTREC	NPT Review and Extension Conference (New York, April–May 1995)
NWFZ	nuclear-weapon-free zone(s)
NWS	nuclear-weapons state(s)
OAS	Organisation of American States
OAU	Organisation of African Unity
OPANAL	Agency for the Prohibition of Nuclear Weapons in Latin America and the Caribbean
OPEC	Organisation of Petroleum Exporting Countries
OSCE	Organisation for Security and Cooperation in Europe
P5	the five permanent members of the Security Council (China, France, Russia, the UK and the US)
PNE	peaceful nuclear explosion
PrepCom	NPT preparatory committee meetings
RMA	the revolution in military affairs
ROK	Republic of Korea (South Korea)
SALT	Strategic Arms Limitation Treaty
SDI	Strategic Defence Initiative
SANWFZ	South Asian nuclear-weapon-free zone
SAARC	South Asian Association for Regional Cooperation
SEANWFZ	Southeast Asian Nuclear-Weapon-Free Zone

SPF	South Pacific Forum
SPNFZ	South Pacific Nuclear Free Zone
START	Strategic Arms Reduction Treaty
SWAPO	South West African People's Organisation
TAC	[ASEAN] Treaty of Amity and Cooperation
UDI	Unilateral Declaration of Independence (by Rhodesia)
UK	United Kingdom
UN	United Nations
UNCLOS	United Nations Convention on the Law of the Sea (1982)
UNIDIR	United Nations Institute for Disarmament Research
UNSCOM	UN Special Commission (Iraq)
UNSSOD	United Nations Special Session on Disarmament
US	United States
USSR	Union of Soviet Socialist Republics
WMD	weapons of mass destruction (chemical, biological and nuclear weapons)
ZOPFAN	zone of peace, freedom and neutrality

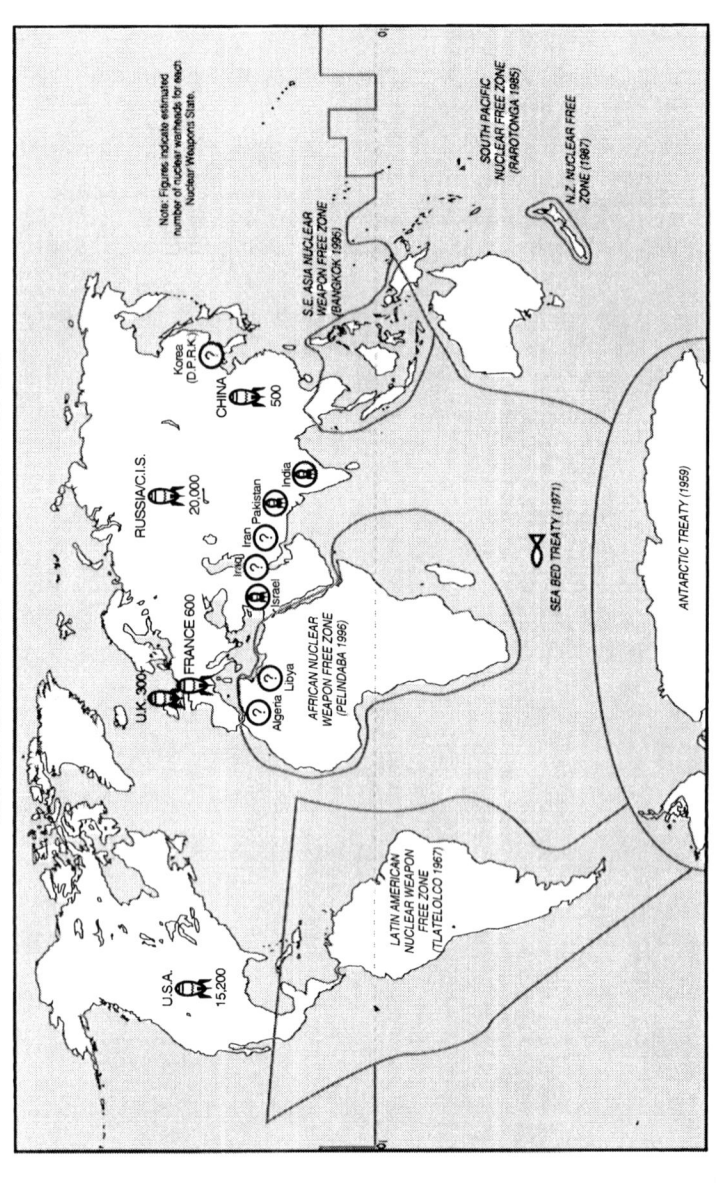

PART ONE
Introduction

1
Stepping Stones to a Nuclear-Weapon-Free World

Ramesh Thakur

The nuclear arms control agenda has two interlinked components: non-proliferation and disarmament. Nuclear-weapon-free zones (NWFZ) are legal mechanisms for the former and political stepping stones towards the latter. The worldwide outrage and disbelief provoked by the French decision to resume nuclear testing in 1995 confirmed both the public revulsion against nuclear weapons and their associated infrastructure, and the general belief that they are problems left over from the history of the Cold War. There is a growing strategic disconnect between the unaltered theology of nuclear deterrence, on the one hand, and, on the other, the military and political reality of reduced nuclear stockpiles and increasing normative constraints on the usability of nuclear weapons. The barriers against the use of these weapons include the fact of their non-use for over fifty years.

The five nuclear-weapons states (NWS) are trapped in the fundamental paradox that while they justify their own nuclear weapons in *national security* terms, they seek to deny such weapons to anyone else for reasons of *global security*. They must assess the security gains of their nuclear weapons against the costs, risks and alternatives, and weigh the costs of the political chain reaction of nuclear-weapons status against the likelihood of the usability of nuclear weapons.

We are at an interesting crossroads on the international strategic landscape. The past decade has seen great progress in nuclear disarmament. The threat of nuclear war between Moscow and

Washington has receded. Yet the United States continues to deploy over 8000 nuclear weapons and Russia over 11 000. The two erstwhile Cold War enemies have reduced nuclear delivery vehicles, but have not yet agreed to dismantle nuclear warheads. France, China, Britain, Israel, India and Pakistan too have active nuclear-weapons programmes. The gravest nuclear danger now is not war between Russia and the United States, but the spread of nuclear-weapons technology and materials beyond the five NWS. The danger of horizontal proliferation cannot be contained indefinitely by maintaining the status quo of five NWS.

In other words, the existing balance of nuclear-weapons status is a dynamic equilibrium, not a static equation. The world cannot accept forever a power hierarchy frozen in terms of the nuclear-weapons divide of 1968. Without concrete disarmament on the part of the NWS, the world will slip back into real dangers of horizontal proliferation. So the choice is between progress and reversal, not between progress and the status quo. 'Minimal deterrence' will not do. The two policy options are a progression down to zero for the existing NWS, or the spread of nuclear weapons to many other states.

NWFZ, meant to forestall the latter eventuality, signify 'disarmament before the fact'. They are undertaken by those who do not possess nuclear weapons but fear being ensnared in outsiders' nuclear webs. The concept predates and supplements the Nuclear Non-Proliferation Treaty. Ten years before the NPT, Poland's Foreign Minister Adam Rapacki proposed the establishment of a NWFZ in Central Europe (Poland, Czechoslovakia, East and West Germany) as a means of forestalling the nuclearisation of West Germany and the deployment of Soviet nuclear weapons on the territory of Warsaw Pact allies. As well as manufacture, the stationing and stockpiling of nuclear weapons and delivery vehicles would be prohibited in the zone.[1] Ironically, even though a NWFZ has yet to be established in Central or any other part of Europe, it has been established in many other parts of the world and the meaning of the concept has been greatly clarified and refined since the Rapacki Plan of 1958.

The Antarctic Treaty of 1959 denuclearised the uninhabited continent; the Outer Space Treaty (1967) and Moon Agreement (1979) denuclearised the heavens, while the Seabed Treaty (1971) did the same with the ocean floor. The first NWFZ in a populated region was set up in Latin America by the Treaty of Tlatelolco in 1967. This was followed by the Treaty of Rarotonga in the South Pacific in 1985, the Treaty of Bangkok in Southeast Asia in 1995 and the Treaty of Pelindaba in Africa in 1996. The number of states parties to have signed and ratified the four zones, and details of NWS signature of the zonal protocols, are shown in Table 1.1. The total number of countries that have signed NWFZ spread across four continents has reached 108. The Bangkok Treaty has been signed by all eligible regional countries. Martinique and Madagascar are the only eligible regional countries not to have signed Tlatelolco and Pelindaba respectively. The status of the Federated States of Micronesia (FSM), Marshall Islands and Palau with respect to the Treaty of Rarotonga is discussed below. The treaties of Tlatelolco, Rarotonga and Bangkok have just one state each that have signed but not ratified (as of 1 September 1997), namely Cuba, Tonga and the Philippines respectively. The last is a matter of course. By contrast, only 3 of the 52 signatories of the Treaty of Pelindaba have so far ratified it.

Table 1.1: The Four Established NWFZ

	Tlatelolco	Rarotonga	Bangkok	Pelindaba
Date signed	14 Feb 1967	6 Aug 1985	15 Dec 1995	11 Apr 1996
Date in force	22 Apr 1968	11 Dec 1986	27 Mar 1997	
No. of articles	32	16	20	22
No. of annexes	0	4	1	4
No. of protocols	2	3	1	3
No. eligible	34	16	10	53
No. signed	33	13	10	52
No. ratified	32	12	9	3

Protocol Signatories

China	21 Aug 1973	10 Feb 1987	–	11 Apr 1996
France	18 Jul 1973	25 Mar 1996	–	11 Apr 1996
UK	20 Dec 1967	25 Mar 1996	–	11 Apr 1996
USA	1 Apr 1968	25 Mar 1996	–	11 Apr 1996
USSR/Russia	18 May 1978	15 Dec 1986	–	11 Apr 1996

Sources: Department of Foreign Affairs and Trade, Australia, September 1997; Monterey Institute of International Studies, September 1997.

NWFZ have developed cumulatively. The South Pacific Nuclear Free Zone (SPNFZ) built on and adapted the Latin American zonal provisions to suit the conditions and circumstances of the South Pacific. Southeast Asia and Africa in turn borrowed from both models available to them, namely Tlatelolco and Rarotonga. Like Rarotonga, for example, Bangkok and Pelindaba extend their proscription not just to nuclear weapons but to 'nuclear explosive devices' that release nuclear energy, irrespective of peaceful or aggressive purposes.

The authors of the following chapters describe the nature and elements of each of the four established zones in Latin America, the South Pacific, Southeast Asia and Africa in chronological order. The obligations and responsibilities of the states parties to each zonal arrangement are also spelt out, as are the verification and control machinery. Effort is made to locate each zone within the context of the national security policies of the most significant military powers in each region, including impact on the politics of alliance relationships. Often the call for the establishment of regional NWFZ arrangements has been led by peace movements and non-government organisations (NGOs). That being the case, to what extent can any zone be said to be cooptive rather than responsive to the anti-nuclear distemper of its time and place? The question of whether NWFZ enhance national security and/or build regional confidence is also examined.

In many ways the more interesting case studies are those regions for which NWFZ have been proposed but without success. Why does the idea of NWFZ for the Middle East, South Asia and Northeast Asia continue to attract some policy analysts or academic commentators? Conversely, why does it fail to attract key groups of players in each of these regions? The Korean peninsula was in fact denuclearised in 1991, while an authoritative UN report on a NWFZ for the Middle East was published in 1990.[2] Between them, the eight authors who examine these four zones of conflict point to the range of technical, geographical, historical, domestic, regional and global obstacles to the attainment of NWFZ in these troubled theatres.

Nature and Goals of NWFZ

A NWFZ denotes an area established by a group of states by a treaty which defines the status of the absence of nuclear weapons from the zone and sets up a system of verification and control to guarantee compliance. A NWFZ is characterised by 'four Noes': no possession, testing, deployment or use of nuclear weapons. Thus it differs from the NPT in one crucial respect. The latter permits the stationing of nuclear weapons on the territory of states parties as long as they do not exercise jurisdiction and control over them; a NWFZ prohibits such stationing. A NWFZ goes beyond the NPT also in requiring commitments from the NWS not to use nuclear weapons against zonal members – unlike unilateral declarations of non-use, treaty commitments are legally binding on the NWS; and in setting up regional verification machinery to complement the work of the International Atomic Energy Agency (IAEA) in preventing cheating.

All NWFZ share the elements of prohibiting forever the acquisition, deployment, use and testing of nuclear weapons on territorial land, sea and airspace; requiring no-use assurances from the nuclear powers; setting up verification systems; and obtaining the endorsement of the international community through a UN General Assembly resolution. They differ on whether the scope of the prohibitions extends to peaceful nuclear explosions (permitted by Tlatelolco but prohibited by the others), delivery systems (none), nuclear facilities and research and development (Pelindaba), and the disposal of radioactive wastes (Rarotonga and Pelindaba);[3] on whether the area of application includes exclusive economic zones (EEZ) (Bangkok) and the high seas (Tlatelolco); on the entry-into-force and denunciation provisions; and on subjecting protocol obligations of the NWS to compliance procedures (Pelindaba) and linking the latter to international mechanisms like the IAEA and the UN Security Council (all except Rarotonga). In the main the differences reflect disparate geostrategic circumstances. The Treaty of Pelindaba, for example, contains a provision for the dismantling and destruction of nuclear explosive devices, and the destruction and conversion of facilities for their manufacture (Article 6). This clearly reflects the persisting worry about South Africa's clandestine nuclear-weapons programme under the apartheid regime.

Article 7 of the NPT accepts that 'Nothing in this Treaty affects the right of any group of states to conclude regional treaties in order to assure the total absence of nuclear weapons in their respective territories'. The article implicitly acknowledged that the NPT itself had failed 'to assure the total absence of nuclear weapons' in the territories of states parties. It further acknowledged that one regional treaty had been negotiated more or less simultaneously with the NPT, namely

Tlatelolco. When the NPT was indefinitely extended in 1995, the 'Principles and Objectives for Non-proliferation and Disarmament' adopted by the NPT Review and Extension Conference (NPTREC) expressed the conviction of the participants that regional denuclearisation, including NWFZ, enhance global as well as regional security.[4] The Principles and Objectives have been described as 'politically binding' by NPTREC President Jayantha Dhanapala, reflecting the political bargain and encapsulating the political will of the conference participants.[5] They 'comprise a rolling text with a program of action geared towards eventually achieving total nuclear disarmament'.[6]

Regional disarmament campaigns are spurred by lack of visible progress in universal disarmament. While comprehensive disarmament remains a long-range goal of the international community, the conviction has grown that immediate and partial measures, which would increase confidence and create a more favourable atmosphere for overall disarmament, should be pursued. Arms control efforts look too much to the past, and are reactive and curative. For a region which seeks to perpetuate the status quo of isolation from nuclear-weapons strategy and deployment, the greater need is for measures that are anticipatory: prophylactic, not therapeutic.

NWFZ proposals concentrate on nuclear weapons rather than the underlying causes of conflicts and the impossibility of reversing scientific knowledge and technological capability. The ostensible goal is to insulate a region totally from the destructive effects of nuclear warfare in general, and nuclear-weapons deployment and testing in particular. Subsumed within this broad objective are subsidiary goals of lowering the costs and burdens of the nuclear arms race, reducing the probability of war, and decreasing the harmful effects if war should nevertheless occur.

There is no consensus on the requirements of a NWFZ. The closest approximation to a widely acceptable articulation of the criteria and nature of NWFZ are contained in two comprehensive expert studies under UN auspices in 1975 and 1985.[7]

Regional Initiative

First, the initiative should come from the countries of the region. This avoids charges of an outside power imposing its preferences on regional actors. In Latin America, the South Pacific, Southeast Asia and Africa the initiative was pursued through the appropriate regional organisations. In April 1963 five Latin American countries (Bolivia, Brazil, Chile, Ecuador and Mexico) announced their willingness to sign a multilateral agreement making Latin America a NWFZ. The Treaty of Tlatelolco (named after a suburb of Mexico City) was signed at the regional meeting of Latin American countries in 1967. The South Pacific Forum (SPF) first considered a NWFZ for the region in 1975. The idea was revived in 1983, a negotiating group was set up in 1984 and the treaty was adopted at the annual meeting of the SPF in August 1985. The idea has long histories in Southeast Asia and Africa, and was pursued through the major regional organisations to successful conclusion in December 1995 and April 1996 respectively.

Monica Serrano argues that the attainment of a NWFZ in Latin America was facilitated by the continent's experience of multilateralism. The same is true of the South Pacific, Southeast Asia and Africa. Conversely, the Middle East, South Asia and Northeast Asia are seriously lacking in inclusive experiences of multilateralism. The Middle East and Northeast Asia lack the formal institutions, while the South Asian Association for Regional Cooperation (SAARC) lacks the history and experience of successful regional cooperation on major items. The obstacle could potentially be circumvented in Northeast Asia by nesting security explorations in the ASEAN Regional Forum (ARF), and in the Middle East by nesting NWFZ discussions in the Arms Control and Regional Security multilateral working group. SAARC has neither the status nor unifying role of a major regional organisation similar, for example, to the Association of South-east Asian Nations (ASEAN), the Organisation of American States (OAS), the Organisation of African Unity (OAU) or the SPF which set up NWFZ in Southeast Asia, Latin America, Africa and the South Pacific respectively.

Regional organisations have the advantages of closeness to the conflicts, deeper familiarity with the issues underlying the conflict and the social and political contexts encasing them, and awareness of the urgency to deal with the crisis to hand. The handicaps under which regional arrangements operate include local rivalries, partisanship, the tendency to replicate local power imbalances within the regional organisations and the fear of establishing precedents for intervention in the internal affairs of member countries.[8]

In order to take on the role of initiating zonal talks, regional organisations would need to overcome an obstacle and resolve a paradox. First, they would need to possess the requisite financial, institutional and military capacity to play a regional conflict management role. Second, they would need to be synchronous with the regional security complexes which emphasise the 'interdependence of rivalry as well as that of shared interests'.[9] That is, for regional arrangements to have real meaning, all the parties that are central to a regional security complex must be included. Thus subregional organisations like ASEAN cannot play regional conflict management roles because they do not coincide with the regional security complex. But third, if all relevant regional actors are included, then the regional arrangements can be rendered impotent because of the refusal of the parties to permit security discussions for fear of derailing regional cooperation on non-security issues, as is the case with SAARC.[10] As Dipankar Banerjee notes, India rejects Pakistan's efforts at the UN for a South Asian NWFZ (SANWFZ) in part on the procedural objection that there is no authority of a regional organisation behind them.

The question of China-Taiwan relations could play a similar spoiling role in Northeast Asia. Taiwan remains one of the most likely flashpoints in Asia. But, insisting that it is an internal affair and not a regional or international problem, China will not permit any discussion of the Taiwan issue in any regional or international, inter-governmental or second track forum.

Treaty

Second, the specific provisions of the NWFZ should be codified in a multilateral treaty establishing the zone in perpetuity. This ensures that the zone is established in a legally binding form, the commitments of zonal members are transparent, and outsiders as well as members can have reasonable confidence in the value and durability of the zone. All four zones have been established by treaty, with Rarotonga being the shortest and Tlatelolco the longest. All four have been established in perpetuity and none is subject to any reservations. Bangkok is the only one that contains a provision for a review, to be conducted ten years after the treaty has entered into force (Article 20).

The entry-into-force clauses are the simplest for Rarotonga and Bangkok, requiring eight and seven ratifications respectively. Pelindaba needs 28 ratifications to come into force, while Tlatelolco was the most complex. It was contingent upon certain conditions (adherence by all regional and protocol states, and conclusion of safeguards agreements with the IAEA), but these could be waived by the states parties and were waived by most. Tlatelolco and Pelindaba permit withdrawal upon three and 12 months' notice respectively when the supreme interests of a party are jeopardised by extraordinary events. Rarotonga and Bangkok are more restrictive in limiting denunciation to material breaches of the NWFZ treaties themselves and requiring 12-month periods of notice.

Membership

Third, adherence to a treaty by sovereign states has to be voluntary. In order to reflect the adherence of the English-speaking Caribbean states, the official title of the Latin American zone was formally amended in 1990 with the addition of the words 'and the Caribbean' after 'Prohibition of Nuclear Weapons in Latin America'. By September 1997, Tlatelolco had 33 states parties, with only Martinique not having signed. Pelindaba too has just one non-signatory, Madagascar, from among the 53 eligible parties. Bangkok is the only one to have achieved 100 per cent signature by all eligible states parties. In the case of Rarotonga, all who were eligible in 1985, when the treaty was concluded, had signed by 1997. Three countries – the FSM, Marshall Islands and Palau – joined the SPF after 1985. All three have been self-governing in compacts of free association with the US since 1986 which leaves the latter in charge of their defence and security.

Therein lies the problem. The compacts permit the United States to transit territory and overfly airspace with nuclear weapons, and to store nuclear weapons on these territories in times of national emergency, state of war or as necessary to defend against actual or impending attack (sec. 314.b of compact). The application of SPNFZ obligations would be inconsistent with these US rights. Compact obligations can be reviewed and modified by the US Congress. The FSM at least has expressed, from time to time, the desire to accede to the Treaty of Rarotonga, but has not done so because of fears that the Congressionally-mandated assistance package could be jeopardised.

Even if all relevant regional states were supportive of a zone in principle, the difficulty would remain of how best to convert support for a NWFZ in the abstract into signature of a NWFZ treaty in the particular. Regional countries will have different approaches in respect of the content of a treaty. Conservatives will want to reject measures which impact upon existing security policies and practices; they might prefer to leave open the option of the stationing of nuclear weapons of a protector-NWS in the region at a future date. Radicals might favour banning all types of nuclear involvement in the region – port calls, transit facilities for nuclear-capable aircraft, command, control, computer and intelligence (C4I) facilities, movement of nuclear-capable warships in regional waterways – and extending the zonal boundary to bring contiguous NWS within its scope.

A NWFZ deepens and extends the NPT. What happens then in a region where important local actors are not party to the NPT, like Israel in the Middle East and India and Pakistan in South Asia? All the potential signatory states to a Northeast Asian nuclear-weapon-free zone (NEANWFZ) are already members of the NPT.[11] Yet the international community has been suspicious of the fidelity of North Korea to its NPT obligations. The Korean case illustrates just how difficult it is to implement a NWFZ successfully when proliferation risks are high, political relationships are strained, verification procedures are both critically important yet difficult to agree on, and no patient process of treaty negotiation has been undertaken by an expert working group. What this means is that progress towards a NEANWFZ will require the prior resolution of the issue of North Korea's nuclear-weapons programme. Similarly, a SANWFZ cannot precede but must follow the renunciation of the nuclear-weapons option by India and Pakistan. Efforts to use SANWFZ as the instrument of renunciation would thus be misguided. A NWFZ is not the means but the symbol of forswearing nuclear weapons, and of precluding any future departure from the non-nuclear status.

To be credible, a NWFZ must include all militarily significant states in the region. This immediately raises the question of how the determination is to be made as to which states are 'militarily significant' for any particular zone. In the case of a NEANWFZ, for example, this would mean the inclusion of the two Koreas, Japan and Taiwan. But what of China and Russia? And should China be included or excluded from a SANWFZ? Should it be subject to the restrictions of any future South or Northeast Asian NWFZ as a full-fledged state party, or should it be a protocol, de facto extra-regional NWS whose zonal obligations are not subject to monitoring and verification mechanisms? China argues that it is a global NWS and should be involved in discussions alongside the other four NWS, not as a regional member of the relevant zone. One of the most important incidents driving the symbolic politics of keeping the nuclear option open in India was the dispatch of the *USS Enterprise* to the Bay of Bengal during the 1971 Bangladesh War. How can India's renunciation of the option of strategic defiance *vis-à-vis* the United States be compensated for by binding US obligations with respect to the core integrity of a South Asian NWFZ? In other words, how can we square the familiar circle of a NWFZ symbolising non-proliferation to the NWS but disarmament to the threshold NWS?

Existing Security Arrangements

Fourth, a NWFZ must satisfy the principle of undiminished security for all countries in the region as well as the global powers. States will become parties to a NWFZ only if convinced that it will, on balance, advance rather than threaten their security interests. Countries of Latin America, the South Pacific, Southeast Asia and Africa agreed to zonal arrangements when so convinced. Conversely, zonal proposals for the Middle East and South and Northeast Asia have not borne fruit so far because important states in these regions suspect that a NWFZ would seriously degrade their security. For example, government spokesmen insist that India cannot give up its nuclear option when such weapons are deployed across its borders on land and around its waters.

Similarly, states are unlikely to enter into NWFZ arrangements if their existing treaty relationships will be jeopardised by zonal obligations. This is why it is accepted that security treaty relationships within a zone should not be disturbed. In South Asia, many Indian analysts believe Pakistan to be a de facto nuclear ally of China, and some even suspect that China has conducted one or more nuclear tests as a proxy for Pakistan. In Northeast Asia, the most critical security relationships are Seoul-Washington, Tokyo-Washington, and possibly Pyongyang-Beijing. In the Middle East, the problem may lie in the de facto and non-reciprocal US security guarantee of Israel. In the Middle East, Gerald Steinberg points to the example of Turkey which is a member of the North Atlantic Treaty Organisation. The possession and deployment of nuclear weapons are integral to NATO doctrine and command structure. How can this be reconciled with Turkey's membership of a Middle East NWFZ? Alternatively, how meaningful would be a Middle East NWFZ if Turkey was not included? The dynamic and interactive relationship between structural, locational and perceptual determinants of security undergo many transformations over time. Structurally, the transcendental and pervasive ideological rivalry of the Cold War is gone, and the power distribution has changed from a bipolar military order to a unipolar military-cum-multipolar economic distribution of capabilities and influence. The end of the Cold War was simultaneously the triumph of liberalism, market economics and democratisation. The collapse of the Soviet Union hastened and deepened scepticism of the utility of nuclear weapons, heightened suspicions of the role of military budgets in bankrupting the national economy and raised awareness of the increased prominence of economic success as the major element of national power.

Of the four existing NWFZ, two (Latin American and South Pacific) were established during the Cold War and two (Southeast Asian and African) after the end of the Cold War. This affects the dynamics of the interaction between the regional NWFZ and the NWS. During the Cold War, the most important motivating factor behind confidence-building measures (CBM) like NWFZ was to reduce the prospect of a war between the superpowers. The two zones of that era reflected concerns among regional countries of being ensnared in the devastating consequences of a nuclear war. For this reason, NWS endorsement of the NWFZ through relevant protocols was fundamental to their credibility and practical utility.

By contrast, zones established since the Cold War reflect frustration with the NWS' failure to engage in genuine nuclear disarmament more than anxieties about being caught in the effects of a nuclear war. Because the latter fears have abated, and because part of the new motive is to send a message to the NWS about the growing illegitimacy of nuclear weapons, formal endorsement of the new NWFZ by the NWS may be less crucial, if still important. Perhaps regional NWFZ established after the end of the Cold War can be more ambitious and courageous in the scope and coverage of their clauses, and less intimidated by and deferential towards the NWS major powers.

On the other hand, the prospects of establishing NWFZ in the Middle East, South Asia and Northeast Asia may have become more difficult in the 1990s because of several interlinked and overlapping processes that are underway and render the strategic environments in all three regions very fluid. There is no stable regional geostrategic environment that can be 'frozen' in a NWFZ. The election of Binyamin Netanyahu arrested and diverted the flow of Israeli-Palestinian relations after the Oslo accords. The collapse of the Soviet Union in 1991, the indefinite extension of the NPT in 1995 and the adoption of the Comprehensive Test Ban Treaty (CTBT) in 1996 have fundamentally impacted on India's security calculations in South Asia. In Northeast Asia, the collapse of the Soviet Union, the passing of Kim Il Sung, the status of China as the emergent superpower and the outwards reinterpretation of the US-Japan security alliance have unsettled the basic parameters of the regional order. Precisely because NWFZ are CBM, that is stability *enhancing* measures, they are inappropriate instruments for use in fluid geopolitical environments.

As with so much else in human society, timing can be critical with respect to the catalyst that propels regional countries towards a NWFZ and determines success or failure of zonal negotiations. Initiatives, negotiations and the terms of NWFZ cannot be divorced from the regional and international political environment, including the number, identity and state of major power relations; the state of arms control; and the prospect of deployment of nuclear weapons in new and sensitive areas. In such circumstances, a NWFZ can institute a safe corridor between the nuclear weapons of contending rivals. The threat of having Soviet missiles based in Cuba, which led to the 1962 missile crisis, was critical in concentrating the minds of the people and governments of Latin America on the realisation that they could have been the victims of a nuclear war despite no country in the continent possessing any nuclear weapons.

In the South Pacific, French nuclear testing provided the focal point of coordination of anti-nuclear concerns, and the tensions of the second Cold War in the 1980s concentrated the minds of nations on the merits of a NWFZ. The absence of the appropriate conjunction of regional interests aborted the NWFZ initiative in 1975 but vested it with success in 1985. The anti-nuclear coalition was galvanised by New Zealand's determination to shed its previous security identity that had tied it firmly to the ANZUS alliance. New Zealand accepted being cast into the security wilderness by the US rather than permit ship visits under the ambiguous formula of neither confirming nor denying the presence of nuclear weapons on board.[12] The way in which the regional zone was drafted avoided the stark choice between irreconcilable alternatives that New Zealand had drifted into in its national policy. Michael Hamel-Green notes that SPNFZ was crafted in such a way as to harmonise its obligations with existing ANZUS practice. Australia was able to sign SPNFZ and remain an active defence partner of the US with no curtailment of any existing security interactions.

Julius Ihonvbere notes that the attainment of the African NWFZ was delayed for several decades pending the right political conditions and balances needed for the continent's denuclearisation. The twin developments of black majority rule and ex post facto revelations of white South Africa having been an undeclared NWS were powerful boosts to the NWFZ campaign. Carolina G. Hernandez explains why the two decades-old dream of a NWFZ for Southeast Asia suddenly became attainable in the mid-1990s.

Also important is the timing and sequencing of changes in the local nuclear dynamics. Australia was lukewarm, if not opposed, to the South Pacific initiative in 1975 but actively led the zonal movement in 1984–5. The rise of a powerful domestic anti-nuclear movement in the interim was not coincidental. Some of the authors argue that while the programmes of nuclear-weapons capability may have made sense originally, for example for Israel, their rationale has in many cases been overtaken by regional and global transformations. Consistent with the argument made above about the choice for NWS being progress or rollback, not progress or status quo, Ibrahim Karawan argues that the alternatives for Israeli security planners are regional denuclearisation (including Israel) or proliferation. The latter would entail the further risks of heightened tension and increased instability. Karawan also points out that nuclear-weapons capability is of no use to Israel in deterring or managing the threat of terrorism. The same can be said of South Asia, where the threats to the security of all states are far more substantially rooted in internal socio-economic problems and fragile state structures than in external enemies.

Verification

Fifth, in order for everyone to have confidence in the credibility and effectiveness of a NWFZ, it should have a two-tier system for verifying the non-diversion of nuclear material from peaceful nuclear activities. Regionally, bureaucratic machinery should be established to facilitate on-site challenge and spot inspections. Internationally, a NWFZ should require submission to fullscope IAEA safeguards on all fissionable material in all peaceful nuclear activities within the territory of a party, under its jurisdiction or carried out under its control anywhere. With such a compliance and control system in force, applied to the complete nuclear fuel cycle for each party to ensure that any diversion of fissile material would be detected in good time, regional states as well as outsiders will have reasonable assurance that the NWFZ status is not being violated.

All four zones require IAEA fullscope safeguards. Tlatelolco, Bangkok and Pelindaba created organisations specifically for monitoring compliance with the regional NWFZ. The Agency for the Prohibition of Nuclear Weapons in Latin America and the Caribbean (OPANAL) holds regular sessions and can call special sessions if required. It has its own fulltime Secretary General and a five-member Council that must be able to function continuously. Under the original Article 16 of the Treaty of Tlatelolco, special inspections of suspicious activity could be arranged either by OPANAL or the IAEA. After an amendment in 1992, the right to conduct special inspections was vested exclusively in the IAEA. The implementation of the Treaty of Bangkok is to be overseen by a Commission for the Southeast Asian NWFZ (SEANWFZ) composed of all states parties, with an Executive Committee also comprising all parties (Articles 8 and 9). Pelindaba requires the establishment of a 12-member African Commission on Nuclear Energy (AFCONE) for ensuring compliance with zonal obligations (Article 12). AFCONE can request IAEA inspections accompanied by its own representatives (Annex 4, Article 4). SPNFZ has no standing verification machinery or officials of its own, only an ad hoc Consultative Committee with the power to appoint special inspection teams (Annexes 3 and 4).

Breaches of the zonal treaties *must* be reported to the OAS *and* the UN Security Council and General Assembly in the case of Tlatelolco (Article 21); they can be handled by the OAU *or* referred by the latter to the UN Security Council under Pelindaba (Annex 4, Article 4.g); are left entirely to the discretion of the South Pacific Forum in Rarotonga (Annex 4, Article 9); and *may* be referred by the SEANWFZ Commission to the IAEA and, if international peace and security is threatened, to the UN Security Council and General Assembly (Article 14). The Treaty of Bangkok is doubly distinctive. It requires the

Executive Committee to convene a special meeting of the Commission to decide on appropriate measures in the event of a breach of the non-use protocol by a NWS (Article 14.4); and it provides for the referral of disputes over the interpretation of the treaty to the International Court of Justice (ICJ) (Article 21).

The protracted negotiations on the CTBT threw up many problems, among them the political difficulty caused by the widening technological gap between the intelligence capabilities of the advanced industrial states and the developing countries. This remains a potential area of tension in the two-tier verification machinery of regional NWFZ as well. There is a qualitative discrepancy between the ability of developing countries and the US to detect possible violations of arms control agreements which can trigger international inspection. Countries like India have become suspicious that the United States has begun to transform disarmament instruments into non-proliferation modalities. The Americans exploit their technological edge to do this.

Another potential gap in a NWFZ regime is the lack of machinery for policing NWS compliance with the protocols. A control system can be established for verifying the behaviour of treaty parties, but is more problematical for monitoring the behaviour of nuclear powers within zonal limits. The IAEA system was greatly strengthened after the shock discovery of just how far advanced was Iraq's clandestine nuclear-weapons programme. But India, never having signed the NPT, reacts angrily to being bracketed with NPT rogue or cheat states and to the idea of being subject to intrusive, coercive and sovereignty-eroding international verification machinery.

The IAEA can be entrusted with the responsibility of verifying compliance of peaceful nuclear activities with non-weaponisation obligations. The prospects of credible NWFZ in Asia would brighten with the establishment of a counterpart to the European Atomic Energy Community (Euratom). 'Asiatom' could be given ownership of all fissile material (cf Article 86 of the Euratom Treaty) and, in partnership with the IAEA, enhance transparency and cooperative control to guarantee the peaceful uses of nuclear energy.

Peaceful Nuclear Development

Sixth, peaceful nuclear development should be permitted. The NPT was a bargain which facilitated the access of non-NWS to nuclear energy for peaceful purposes in return for a forswearing of nuclear weapons. In keeping with this bargain, a NWFZ cannot proscribe peaceful nuclear development. Yet Rarotonga was unequivocal in prohibiting the manufacture, acquisition, control or testing 'of any nuclear explosive device' (Articles 3 and 6), defined as 'any nuclear weapon or other explosive device capable of releasing nuclear energy, irrespective of the purpose for which it could be used' [Article 1(c)]. Zonal parties can be forbidden to transfer material or equipment, even for peaceful purposes, to states not subject to NPT and IAEA safeguards. That is, parties would be enjoined to ensure that any transfer of nuclear technology or material conformed to strict non-proliferation measures in order to provide assurance of exclusively peaceful use.

Geographic Scope

Seventh, the zone should have clearly defined and recognised boundaries. But how this can be achieved is not always obvious. The perimeter enclosing a zone can be a patchwork covering only the territories of member countries, or it can be a 'picture frame' incorporating all enclosed space within the zone. In the latter event, in the case of maritime zones the 'zone of application' of the treaty clauses becomes separate from the 'zone' as such, since they cannot extend to the high seas. For example, the major portion of SPNFZ comprises international waterways. Under customary international law codified in the 1982 UN Convention on the Law of the Seas (UNCLOS), all states have the right to enter and use such waterways. A group of states can agree among themselves to impose restrictions on their own activities, but not on that of others. (Although they can invite other states to sign relevant protocols containing similar restrictions.)

Zonal prohibitions should encompass the total land, territorial sea and airspace of states parties. The status of exclusive economic zones (EEZ), archipelagic waters and straits is more contentious. SEANWFZ obligations extend to the continental shelves, archipelagic waters and EEZ of states parties (Article 1a, 1b and 2.1), but without prejudice to the freedom of the high seas and rights of innocent passage and transit (Article 2.2). The problem arises in that coastal states enjoy full jurisdiction only over internal territorial waters; all states enjoy rights of 'innocent passage' in territorial seas and archipelagic waters.

Coastal states have no jurisdiction over the naval vessels or weapons of other states in EEZ or on the high seas.

Another problem arises with respect to territories inside the zone (such as colonies or dependencies) belonging to extra-regional countries. The clearest example in recent times of such a situation arose with respect to French Polynesia, the site of nuclear testing by France from 1966 to 1996.

A third problem area is the status of members who join a regional organisation after a NWFZ is already in place. Typically, a zone extends to the total membership of the regional organisation that has been the formal forum for discussions and negotiations leading to the establishment of the NWFZ. In the case of SPNFZ, the treaty is open for signature by any member of the SPF [Article 12(1)]. As noted above, the FSM, Marshall Islands and Palau became members of the SPF after the signing of the Treaty of Rarotonga in 1985; not one has signed the Treaty of Rarotonga. All three have a complex set of arrangements defining their constitutional relationships with the United States under compacts of free association which vest responsibility for the defence and security of the three territories in the US.

A fourth and related problem concerns accession to the regional organisation and zone by a new member whose territorial boundaries extend beyond the existing geographical scope of the NWFZ.

The fifth and final difficulty arises with respect to territory in dispute between two or more countries. In the case of Tlatelolco, Argentina claims sovereignty over the Islas Malvinas/Falkland Islands which are physically under British control. In the case of Pelindaba, the British dependency of Chagos Archipelago/Diego Garcia is claimed by Mauritius and as such included within the African zone, but without prejudice to the question of sovereignty (Annex 1). The settlement of the territorial disputes, it is assumed, are separate from and independent of the NWFZ and do not affect the management of the latter. Argentina and Britain are signatories to the treaty and protocols of Tlatelolco; the Treaty of Pelindaba does not invite Britain to sign Protocol III on dependencies. In a South Asian NWFZ which did not include China, what would be the status of territory claimed by India but occupied by China? Tlatelolco and Pelindaba provide useful precedents for how the difficulty might be resolved or shelved without affecting the integrity of the regional NWFZ.

Between them, the established zones offer models for continental as well as maritime strategic environments. The zonal prohibitions under the treaties of Tlatelolco and Bangkok extend to maritime areas adjoining the territorial waters of member states. The South Pacific zone adopted a 'picture frame' rather than an 'incomplete patchwork' approach. It drew the outer boundaries of the zone and included the total enclosed space as the nuclear-free zone. But in fact the denuclearisation provisions do not apply beyond territorial waters; only the antidumping clauses do. SPNFZ also included a provision whereby, if a new member with territory outside the existing zone signed the treaty, then the zonal boundary 'shall be deemed to be amended' to include the territory of the new member within the SPNFZ boundary [Article 12(3)]. The picture frame approach may not be relevant to the Middle East and Northeast Asia. But it could be relevant to South Asia, bearing in mind that India has island possessions to the east (the Andaman and Nicobar group) and west (the Lakshadweep group). If however a picture frame approach was to be adopted for South Asia, then India might well try to push the frame outwards to incorporate Diego Garcia within the zonal boundary. This would then set up a clash of interests with the United States.

Freedom of the Seas

Eighth, in defining the territory of the zone, members must respect the freedom of the high seas and straits used for international navigation, and of international airspace. A holistic picture frame zone immediately raises the spectre of infringement of well-established rules of international law with regard to naval navigation. However, unlike 'innocent passage' which is accepted by all four zonal regimes, 'hostile passage' – transit of vehicles carrying prohibited weapons in an active mode through the NWFZ for use against targets beyond it – is unlikely to be acceptable to any of the four zones.

As confidence-building more than arms control measures, NWFZ strengthen the non-proliferation norm epitomised in the NPT. The most significant component of a normative world order is international law. Parts of the legal order may well be flawed, parts archaic and parts ineffectual. The remedy is to modify, codify and develop legal principles and enforcement mechanisms, not to violate them. Imposing restrictions on established maritime rights would not be proper because ultimately it would be damaging to the goal of creating a civilised world ruled by law and reason. A NWFZ must therefore function within the existing laws of the sea.

NWS Support

Finally, NWFZ should have the support of the NWS. The existing zones seek to integrate the NWS through protocols to the treaty. This is not always successful. China and Russia endorsed the South Pacific zone fairly promptly; France, Britain and the US did so only a decade later, after the Cold War had ended and French nuclear testing in the Pacific had ceased. This despite the fact that SPNFZ negotiators had engaged in early and frequent consultations with the US in drafting the treaty in such a way that it did not impede any existing US activity. With the Soviet profile barely visible in the South Pacific and proliferation not a threat in the region, Washington did not see any of its goals being advanced by SPNFZ. Conversely, the zone did have a negative impact on NATO ally France. It could also have set a precedent for the spread of the anti-nuclear 'allergy' to other regions, and the cumulative impact of NWFZ could create obstacles to the free movement of US nuclear forces around the globe.

The United States signed Protocol I of the Treaty of Tlatelolco, applying the denuclearisation provisions to its territories within the zone, under the Carter Administration in 1977, and ratified it under the Reagan Administration in 1981. Washington excluded Guantanamo Base in Cuba from its coverage until such time as Cuba itself joined the treaty. (Cuba signed Tlatelolco in 1995 but has not yet ratified.) Protocol II, containing the negative security assurances on neither using nor threatening zonal members with nuclear weapons, was signed by the US in 1968 and ratified in 1971. This was the first example of the US entering into an obligation restricting the use of its nuclear weapons.[13] Washington concluded that the treaty marked a significant contribution to its security interests by prohibiting the type of nuclear-weapons deployment that had provoked the Cuban missile crisis in 1962, instituting regional compliance machinery, requiring IAEA safeguards by member states and promoting the cause of a universal non-proliferation treaty. Nevertheless Washington attached a unilateral interpretation setting conditions to the protocol, namely US obligations would cease in the event of an attack by a party with the assistance of a NWS.[14] This was to set the pattern for conditions attached by almost all the NWS to the negative security assurances of almost all the NWFZ. A second set of reservations sometimes noted by the NWS, for example China and the UK with respect to SPNFZ, concerns material breach of the zonal treaties by members. Finally, none of the NWS has signed the SEANWFZ protocols because of the infringements on rights of innocent passage and freedom of the seas.

The problem with zonal arrangements for South Asia and Northeast Asia will be that NWS are major regional actors: China *vis-à-vis* South Asia, China and Russia in Northeast Asia. Another problem with regard to the NWS arises in the context of what Jan Prawitz and James F. Leonard call the 'thinning out' of nuclear weapons and facilities in areas adjacent to a NWFZ: 'Thinning-out' arrangements imply 'the withdrawal of weapons that are targeted against the zone or that have short ranges and are deployed very close to the zone, thus making them usable primarily against the zone'.[15] Non-use commitments would be less credible without the partial or total withdrawal of such weapons. This will be relevant to a SANWFZ with respect to the deployment of Chinese nuclear weapons in Tibet whose primary targets are located in India. Thinning out arrangements will be central to a NEANWFZ, since virtually the entire perimeter of the zone will be ringed by the strong military presence of three NWS (China, Russia and the US). Only the relocation of such weapons at distances well removed from zonal targets will give credibility to non-use pledges in the zonal treaty protocols. On 27 September and 5 October 1991 respectively, Washington and Moscow issued matching but unilateral declarations withdrawing all substrategic nuclear weapons from their land theatres of deployment and naval vessels. The weapons would either be dismantled or stored in central storage facilities in home countries.[16] Codifying the unilateral declarations into binding treaties among all five NWS would entrench them and give ballast to the thinning out of nuclear weapons around NWFZ.

The Utility and Limitations of NWFZ

NWFZ are, above all, about creating norms which delegitimise nuclearism. The traditional – mostly US – argument against NWFZ was that they encouraged the 'nuclear allergy' and in so doing undermined deterrence. In the post-Cold War era this argument is no longer relevant. Instead, anti-proliferation goals are now accorded higher priority. NWFZ can play a modest role in the global campaign against nuclear proliferation precisely by heightening the nuclear allergy. The disarmament process could of course be reversed. Relations between any two or all three of Russia, China and the US could deteriorate to the point of a new cold war. Treaties already negotiated and signed could unravel through non-ratification or breakouts. The Conference on Disarmament could suffer a quiet death. The testing of nuclear weapons could be resumed by one of the five NWS or one of the three threshold NWS. By maintaining the momentum for the continued stigmatisation of this weapon of mass destruction, NWFZ sustain the structure of normative restraints on the acquisition, multiplication, deployment and use of nuclear weapons.

Critics and supporters alike agree that, for reasons of international security, NWFZ contribute to the marginalisation of nuclear weapons as tools of national security. They institutionalise non-proliferation norms, consolidate non-proliferation successes and maintain the momentum to denuclearisation ahead of the willingness of the NWS to renounce their own nuclear arsenals.[17] In his discussion of the idea of a hemispheric NWFZ, Terence O'Brien notes that NWFZ are integral components of the mosaic of international action on denuclearisation and delegitimisation of the entire edifice of nuclear weapons (possession, testing, deployment, doctrines and strategies).

The search for a NWFZ for the Middle East, South Asia and Northeast Asia can be justified on grounds of the risks which attend the rivalry between the nuclear powers, the proliferation propensity of regional actors, and the dynamics of interaction between local and international actors. It is a sobering fact that all three threshold NWS are in the Middle East and South Asia, and three of the five declared NWS are engaged in a competitive rivalry in Northeast Asia (China, Russia and the United States).

The Middle East has been a cauldron of regional conflict for the entire period since World War II. The axis of the regional conflict has often intersected with that of global rivalry. The 1990–1 Gulf War was the most substantial deployment and use of military force since 1945. The region has been the setting for the acquisition and use of weapons of mass destruction: Israel is a threshold NWS, Iraq is known to have been pursuing a clandestine but well-advanced programme of nuclear-weapons acquisition, and chemical weapons were used during the Iran-Iraq war (1980-8).

The world interest is engaged in South Asia because of the numbers of people involved – some one-fifth of humanity – and because of the risks of a nuclear conflict. India and Pakistan have a rivalry as intense and long as the Israeli-Palestinian conflict. It has led to three wars in the past and could escalate to a nuclear cataclysm in the future. By the mid-1990s relations between India and Pakistan had deteriorated to the most dangerous level since 1971. India's strategic environment is unique in that it has major border conflicts with a NWS on one side and a threshold NWS on another.

The North Pacific remains a potentially unstable zone of confrontation. History does not inspire confidence that major-power interactions will remain forever harmonious and free of a clash of interests. The Korean peninsula is located in a strategic zone, subject to the pulls and pressures of relations between China, Japan, Russia and the United States. The *unification* of the peninsula may be a purely internal decision for the people of Korea and a product of negotiations between the two parallel sets of authorities north and south of the demilitarised zone (DMZ). The *stability* of the peninsula will be a function of the interaction between local dynamics and major-power relations. This gives rise to the question of how Korea might be removed from the zone of strategic confrontation. The great powers could seek to establish a de facto concert to stabilise the peninsula; or they could seek to promote neutrality or impose neutralisation on the Koreans as a condition of unification; or they could try to develop subregional and multilateral forums for security dialogues. In their papers, Bon-Hak Koo and Naoko Sajima try to evaluate another alternative, namely the establishment of a NEANWFZ.

Success or failure in efforts to establish NWFZ depend in part upon the right mix of structural, locational and perceptual variables, and timing. The NPT embodies the global non-proliferation (but not disarmament) agenda. The inherent imbalance of obligations between the NWS and non-NWS in the NPT was imposed by the former.[18] A NWFZ codifies the relevant regional anti-nuclear norm whose goals are simultaneously non-proliferation (Africa, Southeast Asia, the South Pacific and Latin America) and disarmament (the Middle East, South Asia and the Korean Peninsula). This list might suggest that a

NWFZ is easier to establish when it functions primarily as a non-proliferation rather than a disarmament instrument. From the perspective of the NWS, NWFZ are non-proliferation measures only, with no relevance for nuclear disarmament, nuclear-weapons deployment or strategic doctrines. From a regional perspective, NWFZ express in-theatre efforts to disengage from the nuclear weapons, deployment policies and strategic doctrines of the NWS. Sometimes a NWFZ may prove its value as an alternative to the NPT in achieving non-proliferation. For example, Brazil's non-proliferation status was codified within the Tlatelolco arrangements before it signed the NPT. In other contexts a regional NWFZ can offer additional benefits in helping to reduce the risks of nuclear conflict within a nuclear-charged local rivalry, as between India and Pakistan.

Serrano makes the interesting argument that the Treaty of Tlatelolco helped to embed and institutionalise the non-proliferation norm in Latin America, and thereby raised the cost of violating the regional-cum-global norm. That is, regional NWFZ can assist in ensuring higher levels of compliance with the non-proliferation regime. In addition, and just as importantly, Serrano argues that compliance with the non-proliferation norm has in turn contributed to the redefinition of national security interests by the major Latin American players. Argentine and Brazilian nuclear aspirations, she writes, were 'socialised' and successfully contained within the framework of the Latin American NWFZ. The institutional components of the regional NWFZ arrangements help to absorb nuclear strains and stresses and to undermine the strategic and political utility of nuclear weapons.

The authors of this book are split on the relationship between the process and substance of negotiating the modalities of a NWFZ in each of the contested zones. Who should initiate and organise the discussions – the principal rivals in the region or the relevant regional organisation? How can Israel enter into talks with countries that refuse to sign peace agreements with it? How can India and Pakistan engage in meaningful talks on nuclear issues when neither acknowledges the possession of nuclear weapons? As these questions indicate, there is a symbiotic relationship between process and substance.

Some commentators argue that NWFZ arrangements can only come after a general improvement in the security atmosphere in presently volatile and conflict-riven regions. Nations do not distrust each other because they are armed; they are armed because they distrust each other. Therefore, as with the relationship between arms control and conflict, a NWFZ in regions of high conflict intensity may have to follow rather than cause the end of conflicts. Dipankar Banerjee and Gerald Steinberg make this point with regard to South Asia and the Middle East, arguing further that premature insistence on a regional NWFZ could heighten regional tensions and instability. Samina Yasmeen and Ibrahim Karawan, on the other hand, insist that NWFZ can themselves comprise CBM on the road to peace. Bon-Hak Koo goes one step farther, arguing that the confidence built among regional states through a NWFZ can spill over into other areas of regional interactions. For all proponents of NWFZ, the difficulties raised by countries from within potential zones heighten the suspicions of others in the region and the world about their nuclear intentions.

There is a two-stage paradox of trust with regard to NWFZ. The more intense the suspicions and hostility between regional rivals, and the greater the likelihood that one or more of them are engaged in nuclear-weapons programmes, the greater is the need for a regional NWFZ as a means of lowering tensions and building trust. Bon-Hak Koo observes that peace and security cannot be consolidated in Northeast Asia without the prior resolution of nuclear issues. This is so because of the uniquely horrific nature and scale of the destructive effects of nuclear weapons. But negotiations, perhaps even pre-negotiations, towards a NWFZ will prove stillborn unless there is a minimum level of trust among the regional countries. Once this minimum condition is satisfied, however, then the very experience of working together in negotiating a zonal arrangement, and then working together once the zone is operational, generates habits of cooperation and sustains mutual confidence which are necessary conditions for resolving other regional security issues. This is a variant of the familiar functionalist spillover argument from the old integration theories.

In other words, the vicious cycle of fear, mistrust and hostility sustaining open or ambiguous nuclear-weapons programmes and postures can be replaced by the virtuous cycle of unequivocal non-nuclear status sustaining mutual confidence and cooperation.

NWFZ as CBM

Some of the criticisms of NWFZ arise from a confusion between arms control agreements and confidence-building measures. Unlike the

NPT, NWFZ are regional CBM, not simply in the obvious sense of being a legal mechanism for member states to assure each other of their peaceful intentions, but also because the very process of creating a NWFZ necessitates mutual regional cooperation. A NWFZ may be defective if viewed as an arms control agreement; it can be valuable as a CBM which expands the area of peace. It may not eliminate the possibility of nuclear-weapons use in the region; it can promote security and raise the threshold of nuclear initiation in the region by reducing instabilities, and diminishing uncertainties about military arrangements by facilitating exchanges of information on nuclear-related military activity. A NWFZ is primarily a means of influencing the nature of peacetime relations between the NWS. Non-nuclear NPT parties are legally committed to their non-nuclear status. A NWFZ adds no further legal obstacle to their acquisitions of nuclear weapons; it does construct a legal barrier to the introduction of the nuclear weapons of other states into the region. Most importantly, it takes away nuclear weapons from any future security architecture being drafted for the region.

NWFZ do not prohibit many activities and facilities of great concern to anti-nuclear activists: transit of nuclear warships through international waters within the zone, port visits by nuclear warships for rest and recreation, delivery systems, installations that may be integral components of the worldwide footprints of nuclear weapons. Attempts to ban transit of nuclear-armed ships through zonal high seas, by being impermissible, unverifiable and unenforceable, would merely generate international scepticism towards the zone as a whole. Any plans to ban the entry of nuclear weapons aboard visiting warships would also have raised difficult technical and political questions of verification, since most NWS followed the policy of 'neither confirming nor denying' the presence of nuclear weapons on their ships. In any case, this question has now been rendered academic. Because of steps taken by the NWS in the 1990s, nuclear weapons have been removed from most ships.[19] Since July 1992 the US formula of 'neither confirming nor denying' has been replaced by 'It is general US policy not to deploy nuclear weapons on board surface ships, attack submarines and naval aircraft. However, we do not discuss the presence or absence of nuclear weapons on board specific ships, submarines or aircraft'.[20]

Should the prohibition against stationing extend to delivery vehicles as well as nuclear warheads? In the case of Rarotonga, treaty drafters believed that the dual-use nature of delivery systems would have presented difficulties, including with respect to verifiability, in attempts to include them within banned devices. What of other installations that are integral components of nuclear-weapons systems, such as the so-called joint Australian-US facilities in Australia, concerned with military communications, navigation, and satellite tracking and control, which are integrated into the global US nuclear infrastructure? During the Cold War they collected vital military intelligence, spied on Soviet missile sites, detected nuclear explosions, helped verify arms limitation agreements, and were meant to provide the Americans with early warning of any Soviet attack. Not including such installations within the scope of prohibited items will inevitably dilute the effect and credibility of a NWFZ. However, efforts to include them may abort negotiations on the establishment of the zone. As a compromise, restrictions might be placed perhaps on upgrading, expanding or multiplying such facilities.

A NWFZ could go beyond a CBM and have a clear arms control and disarmament significance if it led to the destruction or retraction of nuclear weapons already deployed on territory inside the zone. The first might occur if threshold NWS like Israel, or Pakistan and India, agreed to the establishment of NWFZ in the Middle East and South Asia. Alternatively, the declaration of a NWFZ in Northeast Asia might require the removal and relocation of weapons deployed or stationed in the region by China, Russia or the United States. So far at least neither of this has happened. One reason might be that it comes into conflict with the principle of undiminished security for everyone – zonal states as well as external powers with security interests at stake. For threshold states this goes back to the 'chicken and egg' vicious cycle of the linkage between non-proliferation and disarmament.

Conclusion

It would be prudent to recognise the very real difficulties on the road to establishing any more NWFZ. In the Middle East and Northeast Asia, there is no existing sub-regional organisation to initiate and guide negotiations, no sub-regional dialogue process that can form the backdrop to a NWFZ negotiation. The Israeli, Pakistani, Indian and North Korean nuclear status must somehow be resolved before any meaningful discussion can begin on NWFZ. There is the politically sensitive issue of how China and Taiwan might be integrated into a regional

NWFZ. Nor is the overall political environment very propitious for the conclusion of a NWFZ treaty in any of the three regions.

The seven regional case studies presented here suggest then that a NWFZ is more likely to be established as a CBM among states that have already forsworn the nuclear option. It is less likely to be established as an arms control or disarmament measure to constrain the future potential of states that retain the nuclear option in their national security calculus. That is, it can entrench a non-nuclear status and make future nuclear breakout less likely; but it cannot circumvent determined opposition to the NPT and what it stands for.

The central purpose and utility of NWFZ can be demonstrated with an analogy. In recent years, the movement to create an expanding circle of smoke-free zones has become quite powerful in many countries. Such zones would be meaningless in practice if they applied only to non-smokers. On the other hand, smokers are required neither to give up on their addiction totally and in all places, nor to hand over their packets of cigarettes to gatekeepers when entering a smoke-free zone. The zone is fully effective if smokers refrain from lighting up while they are inside the zone. Similarly, in itself a NWFZ is an agreement by non-NWS to sanctify their status within a regional treaty-based zone. But its core provisions should have the support of the NWS with respect to their activities within the zone.

Until such time as a reliable system of international security is in place, a NWFZ is a useful collateral substitute for global arms control. But it is a policy neither of global disarmament nor of national defence. States will be attracted to one only when convinced that their vital security interests will be enhanced and not jeopardised by participation. Zones have been established in Latin America, the South Pacific, Southeast Asia and Africa because countries of these regions believe that their security environment can be stabilised through NWFZ. Conversely, zones have proven difficult to negotiate for other regions because states there remain sceptical of substantial security benefits.

Notes

1. Jozef Goldblat, 'Nuclear-Weapon-Free Zones: A History and Assessment', *Nonproliferation Review* 4 (Spring–Summer 1997), p. 18.
2. *Towards a Nuclear-Weapon-Free Zone in the Middle East* (New York: United Nations, 1990), Document A/45/435.
3. While Rarotonga prohibits the dumping of wastes at sea, Pelindaba prohibits it anywhere in the zone (Article 7 of each treaty).
4. 1995 NPTREC document NPT/CONF.1995/32/DEC.2.
5. Jayantha Dhanapala, 'The Role of NWFZ and the NPT', Address delivered at the International Conference on Central Asia Nuclear-Weapon-Free Zone, Tashkent, 15–16 September 1997.
6. Tariq Rauf, 'Proliferation of Nuclear, Chemical and Biological Weapons after the Cold War', paper delivered at the ARF Track Two Seminar on Nonproliferation, Jakarta, 6–7 December 1996.
7. *Comprehensive Study of the Question of Nuclear-Weapon-Free Zones in All of its Aspects* (New York: United Nations, Special Report of the Conference of the Committee on Disarmament, 1976), Document A/10027/Add.1; and *Study on the Question of Nuclear-Weapon-Free Zones*. The latter was never finalised, and officially may not exist. But it forms an annex to a letter of 9 February 1985 from the chairman of the Group of Experts, Klaus Törnudd of Finland, to the Secretary-General of the United Nations.
8. See S. Neil McFarlane and Thomas G. Weiss, 'Regional Organisations and Regional Security', *Security Studies* 2 (Autumn 1992), pp. 7, 11, 31.
9. Barry Buzan, *People, States and Fear: An Agenda for International Security Studies in the Post-Cold War Era* (Boulder: Lynne Rienner, 2nd ed. 1991), p. 190.
10. Mohammed Ayoob, *The Third World Security Predicament: State Making, Regional Conflict, and the International System* (Boulder: Lynne Rienner, 1995), p. 156.
11. Taiwan's position is anomalous. It has signed the NPT but is often not treated as a state party to the treaty since it is not considered by many to be a state. Taiwan's nuclear facilities are, however, under IAEA safeguards even though Taiwan is not a member of the IAEA.
12. For contrasting discussions of the New Zealand–US dispute, see Kevin Clements, *Back from the Brink: The Creation of a Nuclear-Free New Zealand* (Wellington: Port Nicholson Press, 1988); and Ramesh Thakur, 'Creation of the Nuclear-Free New Zealand Myth: Brinksmanship Without a Brink', *Asian Survey* 29 (October 1989), pp. 919–39.
13. *Arms Control and Disarmament Agreements* (Washington DC: US Arms Control and Disarmament Agency, 1982), p. 63.
14. Proclamation by President Richard Nixon on Ratification of Protocol II of the Treaty of Tlatelolco, 11 June 1971; ibid., p. 78.

15. Jan Prawitz and James F. Leonard, *A Zone Free of Weapons of Mass Destruction in the Middle East* (Geneva: UN Institute for Disarmament Research, 1996), p. 49.
16. For the texts of the declarations, see *SIPRI Yearbook 1992* (Oxford: Oxford University Press for the Stockholm International Peace Research Institute, 1992), pp. 85–8.
17. Zachary S. Davis, 'The Spread of Nuclear-Weapon-Free Zones: Building a New Nuclear Bargain', *Arms Control Today* 26 (February 1996), pp. 16, 18.
18. The NPT was a double bargain. In return for intrusive end-use control over imported nuclear-related technology and material, non-NWS were granted access to nuclear technology, components and material on a 'most favoured nation' basis. The second bargain was in Article 6 of the NPT, whereby most states renounced the nuclear option in return for nuclear disarmament by the NWS. The problem was that the non-nuclear-weapon status was immediate, legally binding and internationally verifiable and enforceable. But there were no intrusive safeguards for the NWS in their roles as suppliers of critical technology and components. More importantly, their commitment to disarm was neither time-tabled, precise, binding nor honoured. The existence of weapons-proliferating NWS within the NPT undermined the non-proliferation norm and seemingly institutionalised international nuclear 'apartheid'.
19. On 27 September and 5 October 1991, repsectively, Presidents George Bush and Mikhail Gorbachev declared that all nuclear weapons would be withdrawn from surface ships and submarines; the policy would hold so long as peace held. Britain and France followed suit with similar declarations. At present only ballistic missiles are based on strategic submarines, and the latter do not make a habit of calling at foreign ports.
20. Quoted in Prawitz and Leonard, *A Zone Free of Weapons of Mass Destruction in the Middle East*, p. 54, n135.

PART TWO
The Four Established Zones

2
Latin America – The Treaty of Tlatelolco

Monica Serrano

Thirty years on from the Tlatelolco summit, which inaugurated the Latin American Nuclear-Weapon-Free Zone (NWFZ), the framework there agreed not only remains in place, but also in vigorous health. Indeed, over three decades the Latin American NWFZ has shown a remarkable capacity to adjust. There is no better example of this than the successful containment and subsequent surrender of Argentina's and Brazil's nuclear aspirations. The task of this paper is therefore to account for a success story.

The signature of the Treaty of Tlatelolco in 1967 was the result of a complicated process extending over a four-year period. Although the process of negotiations revealed the existence of contentious issues which were reflected in the final text, there is little doubt that the Latin American NWFZ established under this treaty was the result of imaginative 'entrepreneurship'. This ingredient enabled regional states to accommodate their interests with a view to upholding the non-proliferation norm. Leadership was not only provided by the coalition of those states, like Costa Rica, Mexico and for a short interval Brazil, genuinely convinced of the advantages attached to non-nuclear postures, but was greatly assisted by the discreet but firm support of the United States.[1] Indeed, the presence of what could be characterised as a creative leadership made possible the active participation of the coalition of those states more inclined to undertaking the nuclear path, namely, Brazil and Argentina.[2]

Once the participation of these states was ensured, negotiations proceeded towards the creation of mutually acceptable institutional arrangements on which a NWFZ or a regional non-proliferation regime could be established. A multilateral regime was then created. Since 1967 this regime has coordinated relations among Latin American states on the basis of the principles embodied in the non-proliferation norm. Not only was the bargaining process facilitated by the setting up of COPREDAL (*Comisión Preparatoria para la Denuclearización de América Latina* – Preparatory Commission for the Denuclearisation of Latin America), an organisation responsible for negotiations, but in order to help enforcement of the treaty, regional states resolved that an organisation in charge of its implementation would be necessary.

The institutional expressions bequeathed by COPREDAL were a multilateral regime, embodied in the Treaty of Tlatelolco, and the presence of a more tangible and visible multilateral organisation, OPANAL (Agency for the Prohibition of Nuclear Weapons in Latin America and the Caribbean). OPANAL became part of a Latin American tradition in multilateralism, a tradition which has been encouraged by a unique situation in which regional states have shared a common history and culture. The recurrence of multilateral institutions in Latin America has been explained on the basis of this historical and cultural tradition which occasionally has been geared towards limiting the US power and at times has also embodied collective responses to US neglect.[3] What is clear is that a multilateral non-proliferation scheme enabled regional states both to extract negative security guarantees from nuclear powers – including the first US commitment in this direction – and to secure the right to peaceful nuclear development.[4]

The creation of the Latin American NWFZ encompassed a number of instruments ranging from a preliminary session which confined the scope of negotiations, to the creation of COPREDAL, the negotiations and signature of the Treaty of Tlatelolco, the setting up of OPANAL, and more recently the Argentina-Brazil Accounting and Control Commission (ABACC). These mechanisms provided Latin American states with an institutional setting to help guarantee the absence of nuclear weapons from the region as well as full observation of non-proliferation commitments.

While all agencies have been devoted to fulfilling the same goal, namely ensuring compliance with non-proliferation in the region, not only have they presented distinctive features; they have also performed different roles. This paper examines the contribution of these different agencies to the satisfactory performance of the Latin American NWFZ.

The Creation of the Latin American NWFZ

The creation of the Latin American NWFZ involved intense bargaining and a number of compromises among the Latin American states leading to the signature of the Treaty of Tlatelolco in 1967. The negotiation of this treaty was facilitated by the creation of an international organisation responsible for negotiations, COPREDAL. Although the negotiation of this treaty was a long and complicated process, COPREDAL provided an umbrella under which negotiations took place and a preliminary consensus was built as a basis for subsequent and more specific regulation. The decision to set up a commission devoted to the writing of a first draft treaty was taken in November 1964 during a preliminary meeting held among fourteen Latin American delegations in Mexico City. The issues discussed during this meeting included:

- The advantages and viability of a NWFZ in the region;
- The benefits of setting up a commission;
- The geographical definition of the envisaged NWFZ; and
- The impact of China's nuclear explosion and the terms of expected nuclear powers' guarantees.

Not only did the parties focus on specific questions such as geographical limits and possible means of verification, but the newly created commission was also assigned relatively precise responsibilities. These included the definition of geographical limits, the formulation of a system of control and verification, and the pursuit of diplomatic contacts to ensure both the cooperation of all regional actors and the commitment of nuclear powers. As would become clear, the decision to set up this commission was crucial both in assuring Brazil's participation in the negotiations as well as in framing the role to be played by nuclear powers and states with territorial responsibilities within the region. Earlier Brazilian enthusiastic support disappeared after the 1964 military coup and the ensuing shift of Brazilian views concerning nuclear issues.[5] Shortly after Brazilian participation had been ensured Argentina, the country which had openly acknowledged its quest for nuclear energy development, followed suit. Both countries made clear their anxiety over any commitment that could set limits to their independent stand on nuclear energy issues.

COPREDAL's workings were organised in four rounds of negotiations starting in March 1965. During COPREDAL's first round the Caribbean dimension of the regime was sanctioned with the incorporation of Jamaica, Trinidad and Tobago. In addition, three alternative systems of control were discussed: a fixed number of annual inspections; inspections made through request by two-thirds of the parties; and annual obligatory inspections. It was agreed that such inspections had to be carried by unbiased international authorities such as the International Atomic Energy Agency (IAEA). Finally, the parties addressed the issue of disputed territories and concluded that negotiations with foreign powers responsible for those territories should not affect their political status, nor could they be interpreted as negatively affecting related Latin American interests.

COPREDAL's first period of sessions ended with the decision to set up three specialised groups in charge of establishing a geographical definition, studying enforcement mechanisms and securing the nuclear powers' guarantees.[6]

The second round of COPREDAL took place during the summer of 1965 and was mainly devoted to procedural questions and the discussion of a first draft. By this time the number of parties had considerably widened, including both active participants and observers. The interest shown by numerous delegations provided well-grounded evidence of the support that efforts aimed at non-proliferation would elicit.[7] Not only did the superpowers extend their support to the Latin American effort, but the first treaty draft discussed during these sessions was sketched under the supervision of William Epstein, Director of the Disarmament Division of the UN Secretariat. Between the second and third periods of sessions the US official position was announced. The United States offered to include the Guantanamo base and the zone of the Panama Canal as long as that did not affect in any way 'international transit rights'. Yet it made clear that Puerto Rico and the Virgin Islands could not be incorporated into the zone. By that time President Fidel Castro's return to a confrontational policy had not only increased Cuba's regional isolation but had also revealed that the island's participation would be one of the greatest challenges facing the new enterprise. The US move was followed by the decision of Great Britain to appoint a formal representative and to discuss with the governments and authorities of dependent territories their inclusion within the regional scheme. Similarly, the Soviet position reaffirmed its commitment to NWFZs as long as they were also supported by other nuclear powers and in such way distanced itself from Cuba.[8]

During COPREDAL's third round held in April 1966, a third treaty draft was negotiated and the division of the parties into two opposing factions became clear. The position led by Brazil, rather than seeing the difficult questions of Cuban participation, peaceful nuclear explosions (PNEs), and nuclear powers' guarantees as long-term problems, used them as a shield to defend particular interests. This position was aimed at averting the conclusion of a 'rigorous treaty' and if possible at delaying and obstructing the course of negotiations.[9] In contrast, the coalition headed by the Mexican delegation showed greater inclination to compromise national sovereignty in order to ensure the rapid conclusion of the treaty.

Notwithstanding this, the Brazilian delegation succeeded in advancing a third, 'Brazilian' treaty draft closer to the Argentine position which was also determined to encompass the long disputed Falklands/Malvinas Islands within the geographical definition of the NWFZ.[10]

The main issues discussed during COPREDAL's third period of sessions — ratifications, the obligations of nuclear powers, the relationship of the agreement to the Organisation of American States (OAS) and the transport of nuclear weapons — soon led to further disagreements. Firstly there was lack of agreement as to the total number of ratifications required to make the treaty fully binding and to initiate the workings of the organisation responsible for the implementation and enforcement of the agreement as envisaged by the treaty itself. Argentina and Brazil firmly demanded signature and ratification by all states parties.

Similarly the guarantees to be offered by the nuclear powers led to further differences. While one coalition considered such guarantees merely an 'extremely advisable condition', Brazil insisted that they were the non-negotiable requirement for the treaty to be made legally binding. Although at the time the superpowers' support could be realistically envisaged, a number of difficulties had yet to be faced. For a while the Soviet commitment would remain tied to Cuban participation and as would become evident the French participation would be long deferred.[11]

On balance the various responses given by nuclear and external powers offered hints of the wide and genuine sympathy generated by the Latin American initiative. Yet they also made clear that a number of obstacles had to be overcome before fully reliable commitments could be achieved. In the light of this, the 'optimistic' position headed by the Mexican delegation insisted on the need for patience and continued efforts to turn that sympathy into legally binding commitments.

Notwithstanding the differences, by the end of these sessions progress in the formulation of the agreement was clearly perceived. Nearly the totality of the treaty had already been endorsed by all delegations. The fourth and last period of sessions was preceded by statements reiterating US support, including references to the US willingness 'to offer collectively the nuclear defence that Latin American states would abjure individually'.

The British and US comments on the draft treaty tilted the balance of the two competing interpretations on PNEs in favour of the one propounded by Mexico. Both the American and British opinions insisted on the technical impossibility of distinguishing peaceful from non-peaceful nuclear explosions but in principle recognised the legitimate claim of developing countries to nuclear technology.[12]

In the light of the arguments put forward by both Brazil and Argentina in favour of PNEs it became clear that only by accepting the eventual distinction between peaceful and military nuclear explosions, dependent upon technological developments, would the Latin American countries accept a treaty and the approval of a final text.[13] Yet the US did not cease attempts to advance its own view. While publicly criticising the failure to ban PNEs, it also acknowledged that this was the best possible compromise that could have been expected. Explicit recognition was mainly manifested in relation to COPREDAL's decision to adopt IAEA safeguards. The Soviet view on PNEs was similar to the Anglo-American, but prevailing doubts about Cuban participation prescribed a cautious posture.[14]

The difficult issue of the transport of nuclear weapons was also addressed during the last period of sessions in February 1967. Despite Argentina's reiteration of the need for the total prohibition of both transit and transport, a 'softer' line was adopted. Given the lack of reference throughout COPREDAL's sessions to the contemporary debate over nuclear deterrence, the adoption of a compromise seemed to mark the recognition of the complexity of that issue and of the limited prospects for effective regulation.[15]

With respect to the geographical definition of the zone, it was finally agreed that it be based on the Panama declaration of 1939 and on Article 4 of the Rio Treaty.[16] Differences regarding the entry into force of the agreement were partially resolved by the adoption of the Chilean proposal, based on the system used within the OAS and the Rio Treaty. In both cases full enforcement of the treaty had taken place when two-thirds of the parties had signed and ratified the agreements. COPREDAL's fourth period of sessions ended with the adoption of resolutions to open the treaty to signature immediately and take the final version of the treaty to the UN General Assembly, the Eigtheen Nations Disarmament Committee and the IAEA Director General.

The numerous problems of a procedural character arising throughout the negotiation of the treaty were in fact expressions of a deeper disagreement, but it was gradually recognised that only with compromise could a final treaty be achieved. Both the transport formula and the final, though ambiguous, acceptance of PNEs within the body of the treaty represented a compromise between the two opposing coalitions. The Mexican delegation came to accept this compromise as a second best. The rationale behind this posture seems to be that although the right of PNEs would be recognised in principle, pressure would be exerted systematically through continued reiteration of their unfeasibility. In the meantime nuclear proliferation would be prevented through the workings of the system of control and verification to be established by the treaty. Finally, despite Argentine and Brazilian ambiguity, it was probably expected that as soon as they became parties to the agreement, international pressure on their respective nuclear programmes would considerably increase.

The negotiation of the Treaty of Tlatelolco was a genuine example of 'modern treaty making'.[17] Tlatelolco's negotiation, as its subsequent implementation, constituted a creative endeavour which helped Latin American states to assess continuously the benefits and costs of non-proliferation commitments. In this way Latin American states, and in particular Argentina and Brazil, simultaneously explored and reconsidered their nuclear interests.[18] Whilst at the time the compromises underpinning this agreement rightly precluded some observers from seeing it as an 'optimum' outcome, it could be argued that it represented a relatively successful bargaining process owing to the capacity of the parties to agree on a minimum criterion of fairness.[19]

Those arguments which emphasised how the compromise features of Tlatelolco weakened the agreement were undoubtedly strong. Nonetheless, one could say with some certainty that the treaty adopted in 1967 strengthened the position of those favouring non-proliferation throughout the region and, most importantly, that it raised significantly the costs of violating what was becoming a norm. Indeed by becoming part to the Tlatelolco Treaty Latin American states were already altering their mutual expectations in accordance with the treaty's terms. Notwithstanding this, it was also clear that institutionalising the regional effort through the creation of a distinct organisation could significantly assist the task of ensuring higher levels of compliance. The creation of OPANAL would certainly contribute to strengthening the legitimacy of the non-proliferation norm.[20]

A number of articles included in the Treaty of Tlatelolco provided a relatively organised structure to administer the regime. As mentioned earlier, not only were institutional arrangements used in the bargaining process, but these were also considered with view to guaranteeing enforcement of the agreement. To a considerable extent the incentives to establish a regional organisation responsible for the implementation of the treaty, derived both from the nature of the stakes involved as well as from the compromises that came to underpin the regime. The compromise formulas that had characterised the agreement made it necessary to guarantee minimum standards of compliance. The need for surveillance was rooted not in military realities but rather in the recognition of the need to supply the regime with sufficient mechanisms to deal with eventual evasions. It was therefore concluded that the control of nuclear proliferation within the region required the setting up of an organisation to monitor compliance with the non-proliferation norm.

Both reliance on COPREDAL and the decision to set up an agency for collective control and verification was partially facilitated by the longstanding experience Latin American countries possessed in multilateralism. The Latin American NWFZ was soon characterised by a relatively formal articulation and the presence of distinct organisations. In the first place, the decision to set up a specialised organisation responsible for the treaty's implementation hinted at the achievement of a limited agreement whereby an institutional form would multilaterally oversee state conduct in the nuclear field. Far from being static, this regime has evolved and changed over the course of three decades. The direction and scope of such change has, to a considerable extent, been influenced by the presence of OPANAL and more recently of ABACC.

The Implementation of the NWFZ in Latin America

OPANAL responsibilities originated with the implementation of the Tlatelolco Treaty and subsequently expanded as the conditions required to ensure the effective operation of the regional non-proliferation regime became more complex. Clearly, a comprehensive evaluation of OPANAL's role should address its capacity to continue securing the effective operation of the NWFZ.

Undoubtedly OPANAL's major contribution has been reflected in the overall progress made towards full implementation of Tlatelolco. Whilst it would be wrong to suggest that no obstacles have hindered the implementation of this regime, it would be equally erroneous to under-estimate those steps indicating clear progress in the direction of its original goals. OPANAL's efforts have been a crucial factor in this process. The agency was created by a group of nine articles which also specify its responsibilities in the implementation and enforcement of the agreement. Article 28 of Treaty of Tlatelolco not only embodied a 'conditional' regulation for the treaty's entry into force (as opposed to the 'general rule' which applied upon ratification) but stipulated the conditions required for the creation of this organisation. These conditions were finally met in 1968 with the signature of Barbados. Based in Mexico City, OPANAL started working in 1969. It was created as an independent international organisation aimed at ensuring the fulfilment of the obligations embodied in the Tlatelolco Treaty. Article 7 describes its main characteristics and responsibilities, while its main agencies – a General Conference, a Council, a Secretariat and two Commissions in charge of legal, political, technical and administrative affairs – are established by Article 8.[21]

The structure, characteristics, organisation and procedures of the Council (consisting of 5 parties elected by the General Conference on the basis of balanced geographical representation) are also defined in Article 9. The Council's major responsibility is to ensure effective control and verification. Its resolutions have mostly been related to the completion of agreements with the IAEA (Article 13), the production of biannual reports of the parties (Article 14) as well as the signature and ratification of Protocol I.[22]

Article 11 established a Secretariat including the General Secretary and personnel under his/her responsibility. The General Secretary is in charge of the proper operation of the system of control and those tasks assigned to him by the General Conference. If compared with other international instruments of a similar nature, including those of the Non-Proliferation Treaty (NPT), the system of control contemplated by Tlatelolco was particularly comprehensive and effective. However, in practice it was seldom activated and it mostly relied on the IAEA system of safeguards.[23]

Articles 16 and 20 provide a number of mechanisms to prevent violations of the agreement. These range from requests for special inspection, warnings and notification to the UN Security Council and General Assembly, to the IAEA's suspension of all technical and material assistance. In addition, peaceful settlement mechanisms were contemplated in Article 24 which states that unless the parties agree on an alternative to peaceful settlement, any question or dispute concerning the interpretation or application of the treaty shall be referred to the International Court of Justice (ICJ).

Eight years after the treaty had been concluded it had come into force for 17 of the 22 parties for whom it was originally opened for signature. This meant that those 17 states had not only signed and ratified it, but had also waived the requirements attached to Article 28 so that the treaty had entered into force for them all. Progress was particularly clear in the implementation of Protocols I and II. The Chinese and French adherence to Protocol II was rightly considered as a significant achievement given their mutual opposition, at the time, to both the Partial Test Ban Treaty and the NPT. Having the US, Great Britain, China and France as parties to this protocol increased the likelihood of Soviet participation which materialised in 1979. Although full implementation of Protocol I was halted until the recent French ratification, at the time the rapid adherence of all states with territorial responsibilities within the region was correctly perceived as a major achievement.

Although different obstacles blocked Cuba's participation for years, Cuba finally signed the agreement in March 1995 and its ratification will bring to a completion the ratification process. In fact a number of steps had long before made clear the island's increasing interest in the regional regime. On the one hand, the traditional conditions stated by the Cuban government were progressively and drastically modified (from demanding US withdrawal from Guantanamo and the incorporation of the Virgin Islands and Puerto Rico, to the prior enforcement of the agreement by all Latin American states) and on the other, since the 12th General Conference Cuba has participated in OPANAL sessions as an observer.

These changes, together with a number of measures implemented during the period of Stempel Paris as OPANAL's General Secretary, contributed to bringing the Tlatelolco system closer than ever to its full implementation. The amendment of Article 25 carried out in 1991 made possible the incorporation of both Guyana and Belize, a move that was followed by the decision of St Vincent and the Grenadines and St Lucia to join the agreement.[24] Although for years Brazil and Chile failed to waive the requirements attached to Article 28, the amendments made in 1992 to Articles 14, 15, 16, 19 and 20 removed all obstacles to their full adherence to Tlatelolco.[25] The long-expected ratification of Argentina finally materialised on 18 January 1994. Brazil followed suit by the end of May of that same year. The decision of both parties to roll back the nuclear option was further reinforced with their moves to reaffirm other non-proliferation commitments.[26] These included their incorporation in the Nuclear Suppliers Group and Argentina's ratification of the NPT in February 1995.[27]

While it is true that the disintegration of the USSR raised new challenges to the system established by the protocols, wider efforts to incorporate the former Soviet states to the NPT proved highly beneficial to Tlatelolco.

OPANAL's collaboration with the IAEA is regulated by Articles 12 and 13 of the Treaty of Tlatelolco which define the scope for verification encompassing inspection of devices, services and facilities intended for peaceful use of nuclear energy, so as to ensure that none of the activities prohibited in Article 1 is carried out.[28] Article 13 made IAEA safeguards agreements the cornerstone of the treaty's general control system and this has been reinforced by the amendments made to Article 16 which have transferred to the global agency total control over the conduct of special inspections, eliminating the previous notion of 'challenge inspection'.

The conclusion of safeguards agreements between the IAEA and the newly created ABACC in December 1991 led OPANAL to underline the need to incorporate special inspections within the framework previously established by the agreement signed between this organisation and the IAEA. An agreement between OPANAL and ABACC for cooperation on nuclear non-proliferation within Latin America and the Caribbean was signed in May 1993. This agreement established regular consultations, harmonisation of activities, participation in their respective General Conferences, exchange of information and publications, as well as mutual technical and scientific support.

There is little doubt that the framework established by the Treaty of Tlatelolco played a crucial role in the process through which Latin American states and more specifically those which had previously embraced nuclear aspirations, came to discover and redefine their conceptions of national interests. Clearly the regional consensus favouring non-proliferation worked as an international pressure that neither Argentina nor Brazil could easily neglect.

Notwithstanding the deficiencies of Tlatelolco's system of verification, it offered a flexible environment which allowed both Argentina and Brazil to endorse, even if partially, the non-proliferation norm. Among the various factors underlying Argentine and Brazilian limited commitment to Tlatelolco the system of control was of particular importance. The standardisation of the system of safeguards with that of the NPT represented for decades one of the main obstacles to Tlatelolco's full implementation. Notwithstanding the perception of this system by Argentina and Brazil as a threat to nuclear energy development, they continued to emphasise their preference for Tlatelolco over the NPT. This could be partly explained by the fact that nuclear development in these countries has not solely responded to national security considerations, but also to strong interests in energy and technological development.[29]

The forum provided by OPANAL, and more broadly Tlatelolco, proved particularly useful in dealing with the potential nuclear rivalry between Argentina and Brazil. These institutions revealed their capacity to absorb nuclear developments with remarkable stability and, equally important, helped to reinforce the legitimacy of the non-proliferation norm by downplaying the political and strategic utility of nuclear weapons. The reversal of the right to PNEs clearly illustrates these mechanisms at work: while they were in principle allowed through a compromise, to the extent that the distinction between peaceful and non-peaceful nuclear explosions proved unfeasible Argentina and Brazil finally renounced them.

The Argentine-Brazilian Nuclear *Rapprochement*

Although the Argentine-Brazilian nuclear *rapprochement* – initiated under military rule with the signature in 1980 of four agreements on the peaceful uses of nuclear energy and on nuclear research and development – was a positive step that reinforced the vitality of nonnuclearism, concerns about its long-term prospects remained. The need to institutionalise this process and to guarantee Argentine and Brazilian compliance with the non-proliferation norm was widely recognised at the domestic, regional and international levels.[30]

Whilst it is true that the Argentine-Brazilian nuclear *rapprochement* was inaugurated by and received the blessing of the military governments in both countries, this cannot disguise the fact that the transition to democracy in Brazil and Argentina in the mid 1980s added an extra incentive to monitor nuclear activities. In an important sense, the institutionalisation of their nuclear *rapprochment* and the creation of bilateral inspection mechanisms would help civilian authorities in their efforts to secure control over nuclear activities and to reduce the military's influence and prerogatives.[31] Both the disclosure of the Brazilian 'parallel programme' eight years after the nuclear *rapprochement* had been started, and the continuation of important military programmes in the field of missile technology and nuclear submarines, left no doubt about the benefits of incorporating such *rapprochement* into a more durable pattern of common security.[32] In consequence an emerging consensus increasingly acknowledged that the ongoing process of confidence-building measures had to be underpinned by more formal control and verification mechanisms.[33]

The need to gear the Argentine-Brazilian nuclear *rapprochement* to institutional channels, which could further contribute to the consolidation of their non-proliferation obligations, was widely supported. Proposals to provide the Argentine and Brazilian nuclear activities with reliable safeguards, and in such way to reassure regional states about the peaceful character of their nuclear programmes, were considered as a necessary step not only in the stabilisation of their bilateral relation but also in the effective implementation of the regional regime. Not surprisingly, the Argentine-Brazilian nuclear *rapprochement* raised expectations about their full incorporation into the Tlatelolco system. In the early 1990s the framework of the Latin American NWFZ was again adjusted to meet the new realities as the task of monitoring of Argentina-Brazil was assigned to a new organisation which will further expand the NWFZ's institutional framework. The increasing relevance that control and verification tasks acquired since the Iraq war soon reached Latin America and influenced the decision to set up a new agency, ABACC, in 1992.

ABACC

Pressures to institutionalise the Argentine-Brazilian *rapprochement* increased after the Iraq war. Indeed the limits to acceptable compliance underlying the non-proliferation norm were further narrowed following the events in Iraq. Although on earlier occasions Argentina and Brazil had been urged to join the Treaty of Tlatelolco, in the 1990s pressures to adhere fully to the non-proliferation norm greatly increased.

The capacity achieved by both countries over the 1980s to enrich uranium had already offered sufficient evidence as to the need of some institutional adaptation of the regional non-proliferation regime. The conditions which permitted the effective implementation of this regime dramatically changed in the course of one decade not only as a result of the complex dynamics of the nuclear energy market, but also of the ambiguous posture which, similar to other threshold nuclear-weapons states, increasingly characterised the behaviour of Argentina and Brazil. Indeed, not only did nuclear programmes accelerate in the Southern Cone, but also the development of weapons systems in the field of missile technology.[34] In Latin America, as in many other areas of the world, the margins of acceptable levels of compliance with the non-proliferation norm narrowed significantly after the Iraq war. Although ensuring a minimum of Argentine and Brazilian compliance had for decades been regarded as a priority, under the new circumstances this was perceived as a *sine qua non* for the regime's preservation.

However there is a danger of overstating the weight of direct external pressure leading Argentina and Brazil to roll back their military nuclear aspirations. Equally important was the unfavourable

Latin America – The Treaty of Tlatelolco 49

international scenario which most Latin American countries faced throughout the 1980s. Indeed the prevailing conditions in the international economy foreshadowing the need for closer integration with the US could shed light on the utility of the political symbolism of changing nuclear policy.[35] The external setting after the end of the Cold War and the lessons from Iraq enhanced the symbolic potential of all those policies which could help these countries to reassert their western self-perception and in such way to avoid their identification with potential regional threats and destabilising forces. Also important was the impact of policies of denial on Argentine and Brazilian access to sophisticated technologies, which were not any longer restricted to the nuclear industry (such as high-speed computers), in accelerating the process leading to the setting up of ABACC.[36]

The creation of ABACC was clearly a response to the combination of all these elements, including the perceived advantages in supplementing the advances achieved in confidence-building between the Argentine and Brazilian nuclear programmes, with more formal surveillance mechanisms. Building on a decade of increasing economic and security cooperation symbolised by the Argentine-Brazilian nuclear *rapprochement,* the decision to create ABACC was taken in July 1991. Its main task is the implementation of the Argentine-Brazilian Common System of Accounting and Control on that material which has not been covered by the IAEA system of safeguards.[37] The provisions for its creation were included in the agreement signed in July 1991 in Guadalajara between Argentina and Brazil for the exclusively peaceful use of nuclear energy. This was the first of a number of steps which had been envisaged by the joint declaration on common nuclear policy signed at Foz de Iguacu in 1990. Negotiations with the IAEA on an acceptable regime for common safeguards based on their bilateral accounting system started in March 1991 and led to the signature of safeguards agreements in Vienna nine months later. The Guadalajara agreement granted full access to their respective nuclear facilities and set up an agency for independent control but linked to the IAEA. Formal links were established between ABACC and OPANAL through an agreement endorsed by its General Conference during its 13th period of sessions in May 1993.

ABACC was officially established in December 1992 with its headquarters in Rio de Janeiro. This agency has assumed total responsibility over the administration and implementation of the Common

System of Accounting and Control. ABACC's activities have brought together the efforts of its own personnel, of staff attached to nuclear facilities and the high-level authorities of both countries. These teams work together on technical support, workshops and training of personnel and inspectors.[38]

The new agency has been integrated by a Commission of four members elected by the two countries on an equal basis and a Secretariat. The Secretariat includes a General Secretary. The posts of General Secretary and Assistant Secretary alternate annually on the basis of nationality. In addition, the Secretariat encompasses three specialised groups, one of high-level officials, a second group of administrative assistants and around 50 inspectors selected by the parties on an equal basis. The structure of ABACC is therefore divided into a technical unit and an administrative and financial office.

The safeguards agreements negotiated among Argentina, Brazil, the IAEA and ABACC set the basis for close cooperation between the two organisations.[39] The quadripartite agreements require the parties to place all nuclear material under the IAEA system of safeguards. Although in principle ABACC implements the safeguards, the IAEA through additional safeguards can as well verify the figures issued by the Common System of Accounting and Control. Moreover, joint inspections have been carried out since June 1994. In case of controversy a dispute settlement mechanism would be integrated by five members belonging to both ABACC and the IAEA. Safeguards procedures include material records and IAEA's inspections – ad hoc, ordinary and special inspections.

In the light of this it becomes clear how the first two years were devoted mostly to the organisation of the agency itself, while the Common System of Accounting and Control of Nuclear Materials was designed and organised in 1993. By 1994, when the tripartite agreements entered into force, this scheme was already consolidated.[40]

Concluding Remarks

The negotiation, creation and subsequent implementation of the Latin American NWFZ has played a key role in the emergence of a consensus favouring non-proliferation in the region. Moreover, and in contrast with other regions of the world, over three decades this framework has stood the test of nuclear aspirations. As this paper has tried to show this can only be explained in terms of the long process by which regional states overcame disagreement about substantive issues, reached a number of compromises and ultimately managed to accommodate their nuclear interests.[41]

During the period, not only did the Latin American NWFZ show a remarkable flexibility, but also a capacity to adjust and meet new challenges. The creation of a number of agencies and mechanisms was particularly helpful to the task of regional non-proliferation. Observers may disagree about how much weight to give to these institutions and about their actual contribution. Yet, and even if sceptics question the verification authority granted to regional agencies, it is worth remembering that this framework proved to be effective in securing nuclear stability in Latin America. It was a compromise between those ready to endorse non-proliferation and those sheltering peaceful or non-peaceful nuclear aspirations. Tlatelolco proved to be particularly useful for member states, both in their attempts to regulate and control the development of nuclear energy within the region, as well as in their efforts to contain pressures in favour of nuclear militarisation.

Yet, and while it could be argued that the Argentine and Brazilian limited participation in the NWFZ was aimed at appeasing other Latin American states and the US, their decision not to adhere fully to the Tlatelolco Treaty not only revealed their interest in nuclear energy development, but also some degree of caution with regard to open transgressions. Clear deviations from international non-proliferation obligations would have certainly put Argentina and Brazil in an uncomfortable position. Rather than taking on obligations that they feared would subsequently be disregarded, these countries opted instead for partial commitments.[42]

As the 1990s progressed the need to adapt regional institutions and strengthen verification mechanisms became apparent. The creation of ABACC in 1991 clearly responded to this demand. Although the ambiguity long endorsed by Brazil and Argentina did not directly threaten the NWFZ, it certainly delayed its full implementation and by the mid-1980s raised doubts about its ultimate viability.

The creation of ABACC and the signature of the safeguard agreements with the IAEA paved the way to the full incorporation of these states into both Tlatelolco and the NPT. Yet, and while these are undoubtedly positive steps, I would still argue that the bilateralism that came to dominate the Argentine-Brazilian nuclear *rapprochement* could affect the vitality of Latin American nuclear multilateralism.[43]

The record of non-proliferation in Latin America contrasts sharply with that of many other regions. In this experience, the multilateral framework provided by the NWFZ was a key factor. Indeed it could be argued that the Argentine and Brazilian nuclear aspirations were 'socialised' and successfully contained within the multilateral framework of the Latin American NWFZ. This regime not only introduced the non-proliferation norm to the region, but over the course of nearly four decades has vested it with a moral quality of its own.

Notes

1. The history of the negotiations leading to the signature of the Tlatelolco Treaty makes clear not only the US interest but also the extent of superpower cooperation with respect to non-proliferation in the region. See Monica Serrano, *Common Security in Latin America: The 1967 Treaty of Tlatelolco* (London: Institute of Latin American Studies, 1992).
2. The process was also prompted by the Cuban missile crisis which served as a catalyst to the search for agreement among Latin American states. This 'external shock' not only made clear the stakes involved but also highlighted the advantages of denuclearisation, providing in turn the impetus to institutional arrangements. Oran R. Young, 'The Politics of International Regime Formation: Managing Natural Resources and the Environment', *International Organization* 43 (Summer 1989), pp. 368–72.
3. Throughout the 1980s, and despite US indifference and even undermining of multilateralism in the region, efforts such as Contadora, Esquipulas, the Cartagena and the Rio Group showed the capacity of Latin American countries to establish multilateral frameworks for negotiation. In contrast, and despite the need for greater cooperation to cope effectively with environmental, drug trafficking and migration problems, the Inter-American system dwindled in the 1980s. Notwithstanding this, by the end of the decade the Organisation of American States (OAS) showed new signs of vitality. Richard J. Bloomfield and Abraham Lowenthal, 'Inter-American Institutions in a Time of Change', *International Journal* 45 (Autumn 1990).
4. By becoming a party to Protocol II of the Treaty of Tlatelolco the US entered, for the first time, into an obligation that restricted its use of nuclear weapons. Although several of the parties to this protocol submitted 'understandings', not only did the language of the protocol remained unchanged, but these have not been rejected by regional parties. For a recent analysis of security guarantees, see 'Security Assurances to Non-Nuclear-Weapon States: Possible

Options for Change', Issue Review, Programme for Promoting Nuclear Non-Proliferation, No.7, September 1996.
5. A number of factors led to a reassessment of nuclear issues which emphasised the use of nuclear energy to meet Brazilian energy needs and its potential to fulfil eventual national security requirements. Such reassessment took place within a context dominated by the military. During this decade nuclear energy came to be seen as one of the main pillars of economic and scientific development. Humberto de Alencar Castello Branco, *Mensagem ao Congresso Nacional*, 1965–8.
6. The first, based at the UN was integrated by Argentina, Costa Rica, Chile, Ecuador, Panama and Uruguay and was devoted to the geographical definition. A second group integrated by El Salvador, Honduras, Mexico, Paraguay and Peru was commissioned to study and recommend verification, inspection and control mechanisms. A third group, consisting of Bolivia, Brazil, Colombia, Nicaragua, Dominican Republic and Venezuela was made responsible for securing the nuclear powers' guarantees.
7. The composition of the conference during COPREDAL's second round was the following: Argentina, Bolivia, Brazil, Colombia, Costa Rica, the Dominican Republic, Ecuador, El Salvador, Guatemala, Haiti, Honduras, Mexico, Nicaragua, Panama, Paraguay, Peru, Uruguay and Venezuela. Those participating as observers were: Canada, Denmark, the US, the USSR, the UK, Italy, Japan, Norway, the Netherlands, Sweden and Yugoslavia. COPREDAL/CN/1.
8. By then differences with Cuba were clear. The pursuit of a more pragmatic policy within the region became evident not only with regard to ideological commitments and the role of communist parties in peaceful change, but also in the field of arms control. See Nicola Miller, *The Soviet Union and Latin America* (Cambridge: Cambridge University Press, 1993).
9. A number of complicated proposals such as the elimination of the need for previous authorisation of PNEs stipulated by Article 13, and the request that the additional protocols embodying the commitment of nuclear powers and of states with territorial responsibilities were signed and ratified before the agreement entered into force, underlined Brazil's ambivalent intentions.
10. Thanks to the support of Argentina, Venezuela, Guatemala, Brazil and Uruguay a similar mechanism to the one used by the Inter-American Conference on the admission of 'political entities' subject to territorial disputes was approved. Until recently Article 25 blocked the adherence of both Belize and Guyana. COPREDAL/AR/37.
11. Although the French government notified the Commission that it had no intention of carrying out nuclear experiments within the territories of its American departments, it continued to refer to constitutional constraints barring it from formal commitments to the agreement. COPREDAL/AR/23.
12. Not only was the US position on this question promptly transmitted to Mexico, but also its request to have a number of articles modified.

13. Both countries had shown interest in developing independent nuclear programmes since the 1950s, yet only Argentina consistently pursued this goal. Although Brazil abandoned for some time this objective, the reluctance shown by this country at COPREDAL foreshadowed a longer term posture.
14. Serrano, *Common Security*.
15. The compromise that was adopted was based on the following argument. If the transporter was one of the parties, then transportation had already been included in the general prohibitions of Article 1. But if the transporter was a non-party state, the action would not be transport but transit. Since the treaty made no reference to transit of nuclear weapons, the principles and law of international law should apply. This interpretation granted the territorial state the sovereign right to permit or deny such transit. COPREDAL/AR/40.
16. The zone of application would then extend south of parallel 30° North (with the exception of the territory and territorial seas of the United States).
17. On the characteristics of modern treaty making see Abram Chayes and A. H. Chayes, 'On Compliance', *International Organization* 47 (Spring 1993).
18. Undoubtedly, active participation in COPREDAL's sessions enabled both Argentina and Brazil to jointly develop an ambiguous posture towards their non-proliferation commitments. Their participation set the basis for a gradual cooperation evolving from this common resistance to nonproliferation to the more recent nuclear *rapprochement*. For a more detailed account of the process leading Argentina and Brazil to roll back from the nuclear option see Monica Serrano, 'Brazil and Argentina' in Robert S. Litwak and Mitchell Reiss, eds., *Nuclear Proliferation after the Cold War* (Washington DC/Baltimore: Woodrow Wilson Press and Johns Hopkins University Press, 1994).
19. According to Young, successful bargaining outcomes do not depend solely on allocative efficiency but rather on standards of equity and fairness. Young, 'Politics of International Regime Formation', pp. 368–9.
20. The adoption of a treaty, like the enactment of any other law, established an authoritative rule system. Compliance is the normal organisational presumption; Chayes and Chayes, 'On Compliance', p. 179.
21. OPANAL's General Conference is integrated by all contracting parties, meets every two years, elects the General Secretary and the parties to the Council, approves its budget and sets the members' quotas. OPANAL, S/inf.510.
22. Over the past two years the Council was integrated by Bolivia, Ecuador, Jamaica, Uruguay and Venezuela. The main tasks included in its agenda were: implementation of Articles 13 and 14, as well as the supervision of the members' biannual reports. It continued to serve as a link between the IAEA and member states, encouraging the latter to conclude safeguards agreements. Important delays in negotiations were highlighted, including those with Antigua and Barbuda, Bahama, Barbados, Grenada and the French obligations under Protocol I. During its 5th Extraordinary session in 1990 it was agreed that Article 7 should be amended to include the Caribbean in the treaty's title. OPANAL, CG/390, 1 April 1993.

23. Article 13 requires each party to negotiate safeguards agreements with the IAEA within 180 days of the date of deposit of its respective ratification.
24. OPANAL, CG/389 Corr.
25. In March 1992 the Argentine, Brazilian and Chilean ambassadors submitted a revised version of the Treaty of Tlatelolco to the consideration of the Mexican Ministry of Foreign Affairs. The main modifications were aimed at greater confidentiality and included the elimination of a clause in Article 14 previously committing the parties to deliver their reports to the OAS. Biannual reports should be sent both to OPANAL and the IAEA and their circulation will be scrupulously restricted. The changes made to Article 15 confine the conduct of special reports to extraordinary events or circumstances. Undoubtedly Article 16 was the most extensively modified, the General Secretary's obligation to communicate to his/her UN counterpart and the Security Council the results of special inspections was eliminated, and the IAEA emerged as the main and only agency capable of conducting special inspections. OPANAL, CG/PV/E/73 and CG/385 and Secretaría de Relaciones Exteriores, DGORA, 28 June 1993.
26. For an account of this process and the Argentine-Brazilian nuclear *rapprochement* see Serrano, 'Brazil and Argentina'.
27. Not only has Brazil been slower in this respect, but its ratification of the NPT is not yet anticipated. According to some authors, this is due to 'parochial motives' linked to Brazil's traditional quest for technological independence rather than to military or strategic considerations. See Mitchell Reiss, *Bridled Ambition: Why Countries Constrain Their Nuclear Capabilities* (Washington DC: Woodrow Wilson Center Press, 1995), p. 66 and *Argentina Nuclear* 56 (May 1996).
28. Although the reports carried out during these years did not lead to major controversies, this was to a considerable extent due to the failure of Brazil and Argentina to fully adhere to Tlatelolco. As a result, the nuclear programmes of these countries were not subject to verification procedures.
29. Estimates of the share of nuclear energy in the total electricity generation in both Argentina and Brazil vary around 14 per cent and 0.7 per cent respectively. The contribution of revenues from nuclear exports at a time of badly needed foreign exchange has been also emphasised and Argentina's exports include three power plants and heavy water. Yet, while the peaceful applications of nuclear energy have been evident and have also contributed to the Argentine–Brazilian nuclear *rapprochement,* as Spector has observed, the ambitious incursion of both countries into the nuclear field could hardly be justified just in terms of obtaining 'research reactor fuel or improved maritime capabilities'. See 'Tránsito a un régimen de salvaguardas comprehensivas', *Argentina Nuclear,* No. 53, septiembre-octubre 1995; Virginia Gamba-Stonehouse, 'Argentina and Brazil', in Regina Cowen Karp, *Security with Nuclear Weapons?* (Oxford: Oxford University Press in association with SIPRI, 1991); Sara Tanis and Bennett Ramberg, 'Argentina', in William C.

Potter, ed., *International Trade and Non-Proliferation: The Challenge of Emerging Suppliers* (Lexington MA: Lexington Books, 1990), p. 102; Ethel Solingen, 'Brazil, Technology Countertrade, and Nuclear Exports' in Potter, ed., *International Nuclear Trade,* pp. 118–20 and 134; Ethel Solingen, 'Brazil', in Raju G. C. Thomas and Benett Ramberg, eds., *Energy and Security in the Industrializing World* (Lexington: University Press of Kentucky, 1990); Leonard S. Spector, 'Nuclear Proliferation in the 1990s: The Storm after the Lull', in Aspen Strategy Group Report, *New Threats: Responding to the Proliferation of Nuclear, Chemical and Delivery Capabilities in the Third World* (Lanham: University Press of America, 1990).

30. Following the arrival of Figuereido, Brazil and Argentina reached an agreement which not only put an end to the dispute over the Parana River but, most importantly, paved the way to wider cooperation in the energy sector; Serrano, 'Brazil and Argentina'.

31. The literature on transitions to democracy is now overwhelming. On the role of the military institution in the new democratic context see, among others, Paul E. Sigmund, 'Approaches to the Study of the Military in Latin America', *Comparative Politics* 29 (October 1993); Deborah L. Norden, 'Redefining Political-Military Relations in Latin America: Issues of the New Democratic Era', *Armed Forces and Society* (Spring 1996); David Pión-Berlín, *Through Corridors of Power: Institutions and Civil–Military Relations In Latin America* (in press); and Wendy Hunter, *Politicians on the Advance: Eroding Military Influence in Brazil* (in press).

32. Numerous factors seem to be at play behind the decision of states to adopt non-nuclear postures. A state may in fact consider its security enhanced by reassuring its neighbours about its safe use of nuclear material and would in turn invite its neighbours to attest that no diversion has taken place. Feinberg recommends the adoption of an open skies type agreement to deal with the risk of clandestine activities. Anthony Feinberg, *Strengthening the IAEA Safeguards: Lessons from Iraq* (Palo Alto: Stanford University, Center for International Security and Arms Control, 1993), p. 45.

33. Although the 1985 Foz de Iguacu declaration considered mechanisms to verify the peaceful use of nuclear energy, these were later abandoned in favour of 'mutual trust' agreements. Although at first preference for more informal confidence-building measures was apparent in both countries, the need to provide the Argentine-Brazilian nuclear *rapprochement* with control and surveillance mechanisms was continuously emphasised by experts such as Leventhal, Tanzer and Leonard Spector. See Spector, 'Nuclear Proliferation in the 1990s', p. 37 and the various contributions in Paul L. Leventhal and Sharon Tanzer, eds., *Averting a Latin American Nuclear Arms Race: New Prospects and Challenges for Argentine-Brazilian Nuclear Cooperation* (Basingstoke: Macmillan in association with the Nuclear Control Institute, 1992).

34. For a brief account of weapons programmes related to the nuclear industry see Serrano, *Common Security in Latin America*. Although some observers have

attributed an important role to the Missile Technology Control Regime (MTCR) in slowing the Argentine (Condor) and Brazilian missile programmes, the decisions of the Argentine and Brazilian governments have also been influenced by expectations of economic concessions from the US at a time of deep economic difficulties. John R. Harvey and Uzi Rubin, 'Controlling Ballistic Missiles', *Arms Control Today* 22 (March 1992); Thomas W. Graham, 'Winning the Non-Proliferation Battle', *Arms Control Today* 21 (September 1991); 'Brazil Chafes at Missile Curbs', *Space News*, 17 October 1991; Scott D. Tollefson, 'Argentina and the Missile Technology Control Regime: A Reassessment', paper presented at the 34th Annual Meeting of the International Studies Association, Acapulco, Mexico, March 1993.

35. Other dramatic gestures include the decision to leave the group of nonaligned countries, the cancellation of the Condor missile project, Argentina's application to become a permanent member of the MTCR, as well as its manifest willingness to cooperate in UN peacekeeping operations. Not only has Argentina been an enthusiastic participant in peacekeeping operations, but its efforts to assert its Western, Second World identity materialised as Buenos Aires became host of the plenary meeting of the Nuclear Suppliers Group in April 1995, the first to take place in the southern hemisphere. Brazil joined the group on that occasion. Interview with Minister Enrique de la Torre, head of the Directorate of International Security, Nuclear and Space Affairs of the Ministry of Foreign Affairs, and chairman of the April meeting. *Argentina Nuclear* 56 (May 1996).

36. Increased cooperation among the leading industrialised countries in nonproliferation efforts narrowed the margin of manoeuver of both Argentina and Brazil. This was clearly the case with the shift in Germany's nuclear policy towards fullscope safeguards in 1990 and the renegotiation of all previous nuclear agreements by 1995. This shift deprived Brazil of an important source of technology transfer for its nuclear programme. See Reiss, *Bridled Ambitions*, p. 63.

37. Following the 1985 Foz de Iguacu declaration, the Permanent Argentine–Brazilian Committee on Nuclear Policy was set up in 1988 which started discussing proposals for the creation of national safeguards systems and models of safeguards agreements with the IAEA. However, the apparent inclination in favour of informal confidence-building as opposed to verification may have delayed the adoption of these measures. The creation of the Common System of Accounting and Control of Nuclear Material was officially announced in the 1990 nuclear policy declaration of Iguacu. This declaration committed both Argentina and Brazil to set up a bilateral agency for accounting and control, to take the necessary steps to full adherence to Tlatelolco, exchange lists of nuclear inventories and mutual inspections, renounce peaceful nuclear explosions and, most importantly, start negotiations with the IAEA to agree on a an acceptable joint safeguards regime.

38. *ABAAC News*, January–April 1993.

39. ABBAC's safeguard system operates as follows: national authorities send to ABAAC an initial inventory of nuclear material and the characteristics and design of nuclear facilities. The inspectors carry out cross-checkings to test the validity of initial inventories. ABAAC submits reports to the national authorities and is in charge of elaborating inspection manuals to proceed to verification. Verification started in March 1993. *ABAAC News*, January–April 1993.
40. By this time the agency had become eligible for support from the Non-proliferation and Disarmament Fund of the US Department. Moreover, within the framework of the agreements reached with the US Department of Energy, ABACC inspectors now receive special training on uranium enrichment in the US. See ABACC, *Informe Anual*, 1995.
41. Compromises included: entry into force of the agreement, peaceful nuclear explosions and verification procedures. Since the late 1960s when Tlatelolco adopted the NPT system of safeguards, Argentina and Brazil systematically insisted on the need to provide the regional scheme with autonomous and non-discriminatory verification means. This demand was finally satisfied by the creation of ABACC.
42. While it is true that functional benefits have underpinned the participation of threshold nuclear-weapons states in the non-proliferation regime, they only account for part of the picture. The rest is often better grasped by socially constructed feelings of obligation. For an account of the interaction of these factors in non-proliferation, see Serrano, *Common Security in Latin America.*
43. Drawing on the Latin American experience some commentators claim that nuclear cooperation is best served by supportive bilateral frameworks. However, I would argue that the multilateral framework provided by Tlatelolco was in fact the catalyst of the Argentine-Brazilian nuclear *rapprochement*. Moreover, the bilateralism embodied in ABACC (which currrently aspires to expand its responsibilities to cover other Latin American countries including Chile, Uruguay and Paraguay) could adversely affect the vitality of the Latin American nuclear multilateralism as embodied in Tlatelolco. See Reiss, *Bridled Ambition.*

3
The South Pacific – The Treaty of Rarotonga

Michael Hamel-Green

'You can't climb a ladder by starting at the top', David Lange, then Chair of the South Pacific Forum (SPF), told a press conference at the 1985 signing of the South Pacific Nuclear Free Zone (SPNFZ) Treaty in the Cook Islands capital, Rarotonga.[1] At a time of increasing regional and popular frustration at a range of nuclear-weapons state (NWS) incursions into the South Pacific, including French testing at Moruroa, US nuclear-armed ship visits, and threats of nuclear waste-dumping, Lange's comment offered the hope that, modest and limited as the new treaty was, it would nevertheless lead to more promising arms control measures, regionally and globally.

Modest it certainly was, for while the treaty clearly and unequivocally banned the acquisition and stationing of nuclear weapons in member countries' land territories, and the testing of nuclear weapons anywhere in the zone, it continued to permit nuclear-weapons transit, nuclear-weapons-related communications, command, control and intelligence bases, and nuclear-capable delivery systems within the region. Furthermore, the non-use guarantees sought from the NWS were significantly weaker than those of the earlier 1967 Tlatelolco Treaty: while they involved the usual undertaking not to use or threaten to use nuclear weapons against zonal states, they imposed no constraint on NWS use or threat of use of nuclear weapons from within the zone (that is, against non-zonal states outside the zone).

Since the signing of the Rarotonga Treaty, there have been dramatic changes in the global political environment, including the end of the Cold War; the growing importance of regional forums and organisations; heightened international awareness of the dangers of nuclear-weapons proliferation, particularly in the context of regional conflicts; significant advances in arms control such as the US-Russian agreements on major strategic arms reductions and limitations on tactical nuclear-weapons deployment; indefinite extension of the Nuclear Non-Proliferation Treaty (NPT); and the conclusion of the Comprehensive Test Ban Treaty (CTBT). In this context, it is worth reappraising the key features, role and contribution of Rarotonga not only in relation to its original intentions, but also to its relevance and utility in the new regional and global environment, and to identifying what future zonal modifications or regional arms control initiatives might be warranted.

The Rarotonga Treaty was negotiated in the midst of some controversy. Regional peace movements and non-government organisations (NGOs) in Australia, New Zealand and the Pacific, and some Pacific Island governments (such as Papua New Guinea, Solomon Islands and Vanuatu) did not think the treaty went nearly far enough in controlling nuclear-weapons intrusions, particularly in the form of ship visits and missile testing.[2] On the other hand, there were others, especially the conservative opposition parties in Australia and the more conservative island governments, such as Tonga, who were concerned that the treaty went too far in outlawing nuclear-weapons stationing – an option that some wanted to keep open as part of a nuclear deterrent umbrella that might help protect the region against a Soviet threat.

Further, despite efforts by Australia which chaired the negotiations, to ensure that the treaty did not prohibit any actual or planned American nuclear activities in the region, the treaty failed to secure initial support and protocol signatures from the Western nuclear powers. This was predictable enough in the case of France, since its 1966–96 Polynesian nuclear test programme was a major target of the treaty provisions, boundaries and protocols. It was more surprising in the case of America and Britain, particularly as Australian diplomats had crafted the zone to accommodate Western concerns about transit and port calls. But US and British officials, it transpired, were worried about the precedent that Rarotonga might set in other regions where NATO allies might wish to deploy, or already be deploying, nuclear weapons, as well as about offending their NATO partner France.

The South Pacific – The Treaty of Rarotonga

Over a decade later, many of these original concerns have been lessened or transmuted by changes in the regional and global environment. The treaty now has universal support, both amongst the original group of SPF states,[3] and amongst all five nuclear-weapons powers. Following the French decision to end nuclear testing in the region in early 1996 and lessened US anxiety about the effect of the zone on other regions, the three Western nuclear states signed the treaty protocols on 25 March 1996.[4] At the same time, the two holdout Pacific island states, Tonga and Vanuatu, have also signed the treaty.[5] For anti-nuclear movements in the region, some of the original concerns about the loopholes in the treaty, particularly in regard to nuclear-weapons transit and hosting of nuclear bases, have been eased by the US decision to cease deploying tactical nuclear weapons on its surface vessels and a presumed end to Russian and Chinese targeting of US bases in the region following the cessation of the Cold War.

Key Features of the Zone

In its original 1975 comprehensive study and a subsequent General Assembly resolution defining nuclear-weapon-free zones (NWFZ), the United Nations identified a number of key features or criteria for assessing NWFZ proposals and arrangements.[6] These included, inter alia, the need for any zonal initiative to come from within the region; the need for a legally-binding multilateral treaty of unlimited duration guaranteeing the absence of nuclear weapons from the designated area; the need for inclusion of all militarily significant states within the region; the need for an effective verification and compliance system; the need for clearly specified boundaries; and the need for NWS to respect and fully guarantee the zonal members against the use or threat of use of nuclear weapons. While the UN study was not so unanimous about the relation of NWFZ to existing security arrangements, the Western states, particularly the US, insisted that such zones should not interfere with existing alliances and security arrangements. Similarly, in the case of maritime rights of transit and freedom of navigation on the high seas, in international straits, and in international airspace, there was also disagreement among the UN experts, with the US and Western countries insisting that any zones must respect existing transit and freedom of navigation rights. The US subsequently codified its own set of seven NWFZ criteria that specifically included the maintenance of existing parties' rights to grant or deny 'transit privileges' and 'port calls' and no restrictions on freedom of navigation and innocent passage, as well as prohibitions on 'peaceful nuclear explosives'.[7]

Taking each criterion in turn, the Rarotonga Treaty can be seen to meet the minimum requirements of both UN and US formulations.

Regional Initiative

In terms of constituting a regional initiative, the Rarotonga Treaty represented a response to long-held regional aspirations. As early as 1962–3, Australian and New Zealand peace movements and Labour Parties (then in opposition) were advancing regional denuclearisation concepts, such as a southern hemisphere NWFZ.[8] In 1975, regional NGO groups and some regional governments – in particular New Zealand, Fiji and Papua New Guinea – pressed for the establishment of a South Pacific NWFZ and won majority support at the 1975 UN General Assembly for the idea, although the Western nuclear powers did not support it and Australia was lukewarm.[9] Finally, with the return of Labour governments in Australasia in the early 1980s, the Hawke government of Australia revived the concept and secured full support from the SPF for developing it.[10]

Legally Binding Multilateral Treaty

The Rarotonga Treaty meets the key legal criteria established by the UN – it is a multilateral treaty of indefinite duration, binding upon all regional parties within the designated boundaries, as well as upon the NWS required to sign its associated protocols. As far as the regional states are concerned, it has relatively strict withdrawal provisions, requiring 12 months' notice and then only in 'the event of a violation by any Party of a provision of this treaty essential to the achievements of the objectives of the treaty or of the spirit of the Treaty' (Article 13). These requirements are more rigorous than the Article 30 withdrawal conditions of the earlier Tlatelolco Treaty (three months' withdrawal on the less restrictive grounds of circumstances affecting the 'supreme interest' or 'peace and security' of a party). Somewhat inconsistently, however, Rarotonga's three protocols have less rigorous withdrawal provisions, permitting nuclear powers to withdraw on only 3 months' notice if any 'extraordinary events' have 'jeopardised' their 'supreme interests' (Protocol 1 Art.5, Protocol 2 Art.6, Protocol 3, Art.5).

The treaty is also extremely clear on designating the boundaries of the zones to which its provisions apply, setting out in Annex 1 the precise coordinates of the zone. These take in the whole South Pacific, reaching to the Antarctic Treaty boundary in the South, the Tlatelolco boundary to the east, the Equator to the North and a more irregular boundary to the west that follows the western territorial boundaries of Papua New Guinea and Australia before meeting up with Longitude 115^0E. However, it should be noted that not all, nor even most, of the treaties' provisions apply to zone areas beyond the land and territorial seas of the member states. Only the non-testing and non-dumping provisions relate to the exclusive economic zones and high seas areas within the zone; the remaining provisions are confined to member states' territories only.

Membership

The treaty can readily be seen to meet the requirement that all militarily significant states in the region be party to the zone. Australia and New Zealand are the only states with significant nuclear capabilities and military establishments, and, of course, these were the countries that actually initiated the zone. With the recent accession of Tonga and Vanuatu, treaty membership within the originally-designated zone is now complete, although issues remain about the possibility and desirability of membership by new Micronesian Forum members, such as the Federated States of Micronesia (FSM) and the Marshall Islands, whose territory currently lies outside the designated zone boundaries.

Existing Security Arrangements

The Hawke Labor government, as the initiator and chair of the negotiations that led to the conclusion of the Rarotonga Treaty, was particularly concerned to ensure that the treaty respected existing security arrangements to which Australia and New Zealand were party, namely the ANZUS Treaty with the United States. As a consequence, there is nothing in the treaty that can be construed as prohibiting any possible US military assistance to Australia and New Zealand. In fact, there is nothing in the treaty that would preclude the use of US nuclear weapons in defence of the region so long as such weapons were not targeted on any member country within the region. Reciprocally, there is nothing to prevent member countries participating alongside the United States in a nuclear conflict outside the region so long as they do not themselves possess or use nuclear weapons. Further, there is nothing in the treaty that would prevent member states from continuing to engage in joint military exercises with the nuclear-armed or nuclear-capable forces of NWS. From the viewpoint of those states, particularly the Western states, who insist that NWFZ should not disturb existing security arrangements, the Rarotonga Treaty would seem to pose few problems. The only possible problem that some alliance or deterrence advocates might have with the treaty is its preambular support to the broad principle of eliminating all nuclear weapons because of 'the terror which they hold for humankind and the threat they pose to life on earth'. Such a principle, of course, conflicts with the contention that nuclear weapons are a necessary and integral part of defence arrangements.

Transit and Port Call Rights

The issue of transit and port call rights in relation to NWFZ has been a subject of great contention, particularly during the Cold War era. The Western nuclear powers have always insisted on transit and port call rights for nuclear-armed vessels, but some specialists insist that unrestrictive granting of such rights inherently conflicts with the spirit and essential requirements of the NWFZ concept.[11] However, following the reciprocal American and Russian initiatives to cease deploying tactical nuclear weapons on surface vessels and aircraft, much of the heat has now gone out of this issue.

In the case of the Rarotonga Treaty, the Australian negotiators took every care to ensure that the treaty upheld the right of individual member states to permit port calls by nuclear-armed vessels as well as claimed rights of transit and innocent passage in both territorial waters and the high seas. It did this through Article 2(2) which affirms the rights of any state 'under international law with regard to freedom of the seas' and Article 5(2) which allows any member state to 'decide for itself' whether to permit port calls or transit in territorial waters. This formulation would seem consistent with US stated policy on the issue. Since the treaty was included, Australia has, in fact, continued to host visits by nuclear-capable US warships. It should be noted, on the other hand, that the treaty formulation also permits regional states to refuse such visits, as happened in the case of New Zealand.

Peaceful Nuclear Explosions

The issue of whether a NWFZ treaty should allow so-called 'peaceful nuclear explosions' has also been a contentious one, with some developing countries arguing that such explosions might be feasible, assuming sufficient monitoring. The Western nuclear states, and most non-proliferation experts, have argued, however, that there is no effective way to distinguish and control such explosions and that NWFZ treaties should specifically outlaw them. In this case, the Rarotonga Treaty did, indeed, set a valuable precedent by relying on an all-embracing definition of a nuclear weapon as 'any nuclear weapon or other explosive device capable of releasing nuclear energy, irrespective of the purpose for which it could be used' [Article 1(c)].

Verification and Control System

The Rarotonga Treaty would seem to meet the minimum requirements for instituting a verification and control system. Article 8 provides for reports and exchanges of information as detailed in Article 9; consultations as specified in Article 10 and Annex 4 (1); International Atomic Energy Agency (IAEA) safeguards on peaceful nuclear activities; and a formal complaints procedure as specified in Annex 4. In a context where there is a high degree of trust and little current indications of weaponising intentions, it may be contended that this is sufficient. However, the treaty's control system is less rigorous than that contained in either the earlier Tlatelolco or the later Pelindaba treaties. Tlatelolco, for example, created a specialist control and verification agency whereas Rarotonga relies on the SPF Secretariat and Forum Conferences. Further, Rarotonga relies on the SPF as the final court of appeal for complaints whereas the other three established NWFZ envisage last-resort referral to the UN General Assembly and Security Council. As illustrated in the Security Council's determined non-proliferation intervention in Iraq, the possibility of referral to the UN can only add to the effectiveness of any NWFZ control system. Compared to Tlatelolco and Pelindaba, the Rarotonga control system relies to a far greater degree on ad hoc rather than systematic and regularised verification procedures, places difficulties in the way of validating treaty violations, limits the final court of appeal to regional rather than international bodies, and is susceptible to political pressure in a context where potential Pacific Island complainants are highly dependent on Australian, New Zealand and US economic aid.

NWS Support

The Rarotonga Treaty would seem to be consistent with the desired minimum NWFZ criteria both of the UN and the Western nuclear powers, including the US. Yet, as already noted, it did not secure immediate recognition and support from all five nuclear powers. Russia and China gave it immediate support but the three Western nuclear powers were not to sign the treaty protocols until 25 March 1996, over a decade after the treaty was established. The willingness of South Pacific regional states to pursue the initiative despite Western NWS reluctance would seem to contradict the notion that NWFZ are being foisted onto non-nuclear states by the nuclear powers.

France's initial refusal to sign was unsurprising in view of its ongoing test programme in the region. The initial US and UK refusal to sign was less anticipated, particularly in view of Australia's close alliance relationship with the US and its crafting of the treaty to accommodate US strategic concerns. J. Stapleton Roy, Deputy Assistant Secretary for East Asian and Pacific Affairs in the Reagan Administration, explained the US position at the time as being motivated by concerns over the effect that US signature might have on encouraging zones elsewhere:

> The growing number of [NWFZ] proposals, if pursued and implemented, would undermine our worldwide security commitments. We could not, therefore, ignore the fact that our adherence to the South Pacific protocols would be used by others to argue for those proposed zones.[12]

The Bush Administration continued to withhold support, and it was not until the new Clinton Administration conducted reviews of both its general policy towards NWFZ (1993) and the Rarotonga Treaty (1994) that US policy began to change. According to Robert Bell, Senior Director for Defense Policy and Arms Control for the National Security Council, there were three reasons for previous US resistance to signing – an unwillingness to 'break ranks' with France; the impact on the US's own programme to retain 'the technical capability to resume atmospheric nuclear testing in the Marshall Islands'; and the possible 'contagious effect' of the SPNFZ on proposals to establish a similar zone in Europe, where the US was (and still is) deploying intermediate range nuclear weapons.[13]

Even though the Clinton Administration's internal 1993 and 1994 NWFZ reviews concluded that the US should support such zones so long as they were consistent with the seven NWFZ criteria (see above) and that America should sign the Rarotonga Treaty, US signature continued to be withheld in deference to France. Only with the end of French testing in February 1996 and the Administration's decision to support a CTBT were the key obstacles to US signature overcome.

While NWS support has finally been forthcoming, it should also be noted that this support is by no means unconditional. Four of the five nuclear powers have attached reservations, or 'interpretations' to their signature of the treaty protocols. In the case of the US, it listed five 'understandings and declarations' at the time of signature, including its understanding that the term 'inland waters' does not include ports and harbours; that nothing in the treaty affected rights of passage or freedom of the seas as reflected in the 1982 Law of the Sea Convention; that it would regard any involvement of a regional state in a NWS attack on the US as a breach of the treaty; and that US signature 'in no way affects the US position with regard to other nuclear-weapon-free zone treaties'.[14]

France has expressed 'reservations' that nothing in the Treaty 'shall impair the full exercise of the inherent right of self-defence provided for in Article 51 of the UN Charter'; and that it would not give assurances to any treaty member not party to the NPT.[15] Britain expressed a similar reservation to the US in relation to attacks on it by a member state in alliance with another nuclear power; and indicated that it would similarly not be bound by the treaty 'if any party ... is in material breach of its own non-proliferation obligations under the Treaty'.[16]

China, for its part, reserved the right to 'reconsider' its obligations 'if other nuclear-weapon states or the contracting parties to the treaty take any action in gross violation of the treaty'.[17] By contrast, the former Soviet Union under Mikhail Gorbachev was the only nuclear power to ratify the treaty unconditionally (having initially imposed some reservations but then withdrawing them in response to a complaint from the 1987 South Pacific Forum).[18]

The imposition of reservations, whether called reservations (as explictly labelled in the French statement) or reservations by another name (understandings, declarations) would seem to contradict the letter and/or spirit of the Treaty's Article 14, which specifies that the treaty 'shall not be subject to reservations'. In the case of France, the very generally worded reference to its right of 'self-defence' leaves open a theoretical loophole for a resumption of French testing in some future contingency where it regards itself as threatened, whether by conventional or nuclear weapons. In the case of China, its reservation would seem to give it a unilaterally-defined loophole if it were to deem US bases in Australia or US transit through the region as 'gross violations' of the treaty.

Despite the reservations, however, the signature of the Rarotonga Protocols by all five nuclear powers enhances the treaty's international standing and represents a significant expansion of legally binding NWS negative security guarantees to non-NWS.

Role and Contribution of the Treaty

To assess the role and contribution of the treaty in any depth, it is necessary to distinguish several areas in which it could be expected to have exerted an impact – regional arms control and security; global arms control and disarmament; the environment; and as a model and legal precedent for arms control elsewhere. Each area will be considered in turn before examining the wider prospects for the treaty and regional arms control in the South Pacific.

Regional Impact

Looking initially at the regional impact, the treaty represented the first significant arms control agreement amongst the SPF states. This in itself demonstrated the growing strength and maturity of regional organisations in the South Pacific, since the SPF had itself only come into being fifteen years before following the accession to independence of a number of island states. It also demonstrated a regional competence and capacity for negotiating relatively complex arms control agreements that could potentially be applied to other issues.

In the case of one of its key objectives – to end nuclear testing in the region – it provided a vehicle for diplomatic pressure on France to cease testing in the region, and on the US to recognise the treaty and side with Forum countries in isolating France. In the event, the US chose to show solidarity with France rather than sign the treaty. Nevertheless, it could be argued that the treaty provided an ongoing focus for expressing regional sentiment against French testing – the unsigned protocols, like empty seats on a speaker's platform, offered multiple diplomatic opportunities for politically embarassing the absentee states.

Further, once the tests were over, the treaty provided an important mechanism for France to show its sincerity in declaring that it would permanently end its test programme. By signing the treaty protocols on 25 March 1996, France legally bound itself not to test either in the Polynesia territories or other Pacific territories which it controls, or anywhere in the ocean areas within the designated treaty boundaries. In this sense, the treaty fulfilled its legal promise of securing the region against any further tests.

A further significant contribution to the region is the ban on nuclear-weapons stationing. While there were no immediate prospects of such stationing, some conservative political groupings in the region wholeheartedly embraced nuclear deterrence as an integral part of the Australian alliance with America, and from time to time actively canvassed the possibility of offering Australian territory as a base for US forces. As in the case of the US bases elsewhere, this may well have entailed the possibility of nuclear-weapons storage. The treaty has, at least, precluded this option, and, as already mentioned, functioned to lock conservative parties and governments into a permanent commitment to prohibit nuclear-weapons stationing. This can only benefit the long-term security of the region by lessening the chances of its becoming involved in any future nuclear conflict.

A further important regional benefit was its role as a catalyst in encouraging the negotiation of similar zonal arrangements amongst the neighbouring Association of South-east Asian Nations (ASEAN). As Greg Fry noted, the establishment of NWFZ in both the South Pacific and Southeast Asia would enable Australia and Indonesia to signal 'to each other their intention to defuse any nuclear competition that could otherwise arise between them. The signals would be backed by the assurance that it would be difficult for each to go against a regional treaty that they had signed'.[19]

The ASEAN states began pursuing their own NWFZ concept following Rarotonga and brought negotiations to a successful conclusion during 1995.[20] Indonesia's recent decision to develop a nuclear power industry has reawakened concerns in Australia on both environmental and weapons-acquisition grounds.[21] The NWFZ commitments in both regions will now provide some mutual reassurance and confirmation through verification and control procedures that any nuclear developments are of a peaceful character only.

The treaty has also been ultimately successful in achieving universal support and coverage among states in the original zone of application. However, since it was opened for signature, some of the Micronesian states north of the Equator have joined the SPF, such as the FSM and Marshall Islands. At the time the treaty was negotiated, these states' territories were not included, primarily because of potential conflict with US strategic interests in the region and US requirements under its respective Compact of Free Association agreements with particular Micronesia States. Once such states have joined the Forum, it is feasible for the treaty to be amended to include such states in its boundaries, although the legal or political necessity of gaining US approval may continue to be a constraint. On the other hand, now that the US has itself signed the treaty, there could be less US opposition to Micronesian states joining, particularly in the context of reduced US reliance on overseas land-based stationing and storage of nuclear weapons.

In terms of Lange's metaphor, it would seem reasonable to argue that the treaty has already served as the first step on a ladder, at least in the sense of contributing to the Southeast Asian NWFZ (SEANWFZ) as a second step. It may also be seen as part of a wider agenda of confidence-building measures (CBM), including regional support for the UN conventional arms register, military and defence information exchanges, and transparency measures, that are currently being considered, if not acted upon, at various regional forums, both governmental and academic. In that sense, the treaty itself has served as a valuable and important CBM facilitating further regional and inter-regional discussions and initiatives.

On the other hand, the movement to ensuing rungs on the regional disarmament ladder has been slow, to say the least, and it could be argued that many opportunities have been lost, either by way of extending and strengthening the treaty, or by way of developing new regional arms control treaties to address related problems of concern, notably missiles, non-land-based forms of deployment, other weapons of mass destruction, and landmines. If the treaty is functioning as the first step on a ladder, the climbers seem to be ascending in slow motion, and sometimes one might be forgiven for thinking that they are not moving at all, or are even about to fall back.

Global Impact

Turning to the treaty's impact on global arms control and disarmament, there is again some evidence to suggest that it has played a significant role beyond its own region. Firstly, it has provided a symbolic and practical precedent for other regions; and, secondly, it has begun to prove its value as a means for the region to participate in an emerging coalition of NWFZ states seeking to apply global political and diplomatic pressure on the nuclear-weapons and threshold states.

As only the second such zone in an inhabited region after the 1967 Tlatelolco Treaty, the Rarotonga Treaty served to demonstrate the continued relevance of zonal approaches even during the Cold War period, and the potential for regional groupings to develop their own arms control initiatives with or without the initial support of the major nuclear powers. As in the case of the Tlateloco Treaty, the Rarotonga Treaty was ultimately successful in securing legally binding negative security guarantees from all five NWS, despite the time it took for this to be achieved.

Not only did the Rarotonga Treaty provide a stimulus to the negotiation of a similar zone in the neighbouring region of Southeast Asia, but, as Andrew Mack argues, served as an important precedent for the African NWFZ treaty.[22] This was demonstrated by the fact that Australia was invited to send an official observer from the very outset of the negotiations, and by many similarities in the content of the two agreements. Australia's observer noted, in fact, that the African negotiators drew heavily on the Rarotonga Treaty and contained similar language.[23]

The second aspect of the Rarotonga's global role was brought into focus during the final bout of French testing in late 1996 when the idea of establishing informal diplomatic linkages between regions which had banned nuclear weapons began to be implemented in the form of meetings between Latin American and South Pacific UN diplomatic missions in New York to coordinate efforts on a UN General Assembly anti-testing resolution.

The positive global contribution of Rarotonga as a precedent and encouragement to other regions, and as part of a growing coalition of regional groupings seeking the total elimination of all nuclear weapons, is partly offset by limitations in the comprehensiveness of its measures. Such failure can only be seen as a weakness in the non-nuclear fabric that the Rarotonga is seeking to create and a missed opportunity in efforts to reduce the role of nuclear weapons globally. It is worth noting that the SEANFZ Treaty, by comparison, does seek to prevent the use of nuclear weapons from anywhere in the designated zone, including not only land territories but also the 200-mile exclusive economic zones [Article 1(a) and Draft Protocol Article 2].

Environmental Controls

Environmentally, the Rarotonga Treaty's contribution is less clear. Certainly, it went beyond the Tlatelolco Treaty to include controls over nuclear waste-dumping (setting a precedent which the African NWFZ treaty followed), and included a strong preambular commitment to 'keep the region free of environmental pollution by radioactive wastes and other radioactive matter'. However, closer analysis of its environmental provisions suggests some surprising limitations. The Treaty does not, for example, prevent land dumping of radioactive waste. This was on the grounds that if ocean dumping is prohibited, then logically some allowance must be made for land dumping. However, this begs the question of where such wastes should be dumped, given that the major potential dumpers are outside the region, and some have already applied pressure on small island states to permit land-based dumping. Further, for a treaty that sought, as one of its prime objectives, a cessation to French testing in the region, it is curiously silent on the question of disposing of the radioactive wastes generated at the test site. There is nothing in the treaty to prevent the French continuing to store or dispose of the waste on the site itself, with all the future hazards that might entail or, for that matter, on any other island in the South Pacific. It might be thought that the treaty relies upon the complementary South Pacific Regional Environmental Programme (SPREP) convention to deal with this problem, but that too fails to regulate land-based dumping. The issue is far from hypothetical since officials and concerned scientists have frequently voiced concern about French waste disposal practices at Moruroa.[24]

Aside from the obvious environmental benefit of preventing further testing in the region, the treaty's control over ongoing dumping of nuclear wastes would seem to be more symbolic than substantive, serving only to complement the SPREP ocean anti-dumping regime rather than to protect small island states and regional communities from the long-term risks of land-based nuclear waste dumping.

Role as Legal Model and Precedent

The final criterion on which the Rarotonga Treaty's contribution might be assessed is its role as a legal model and precedent. Certainly, it has already served as a precedent for the two new zones in Southeast Asia and Africa, in the same way that the Rarotonga negotiators made use of the earlier Tlatelolco Treaty as a guide and precedent. However, to say that it has been referred to as a precedent begs the question of exactly what precedent it establishes, or to put it another way, to what degree it offers a conceptual and legal NWFZ model that remains relevant and applicable in the new post-Cold War era.

Unfortunately, its basic design shows many of the hallmarks of the Cold War period in which it was negotiated. It was constructed, as so many other partial arms control measures of the period were, with the aim of giving least offence to the nuclear powers, in particular the United States. This was especially evident not only in its failure to regulate sea-based nuclear-weapons deployment, use and transit, but also its unwillingness to consider missile delivery systems.

In the current proliferation context, some of these regulatory omissions leave emerging threats relatively untouched. Potential proliferators are generally involved in simultaneous development of several types of weapons of mass destruction, including chemical, biological and nuclear weapons, and associated missile delivery systems. A zone that confines itself to nuclear warheads may well be inadequate in a context, like the Middle East, where there are multiple threats, not only from nuclear weapons but also chemical and biological weapons, and missiles. In this context, the Rarotonga model falls far short of the comprehensive controls required in the new proliferation environment. Even in the relatively stable regional environment of the South Pacific, the missile issue is not hypothetical since China already possesses missiles that can reach targets in the South Pacific, and Indonesia may soon acquire them.

In the case of chemical and biological warheads, these are already covered by universal conventions, but, as in the case of the NPT, these universal conventions have weaknesses and gaps that regional zone agreements could help overcome. As Jan Prawitz has argued, the more appropriate concept now would seem to be weapons of mass destruction-free zones.[25] In the case of the Middle East, a recent study has advanced a detailed and carefully phased proposal for such an expanded weapons of mass destruction-free zone in the region.[26]

Further, the Rarotonga model has some deficiencies in both its compliance mechanisms and in the kind of commitments sought from the NWS. In terms of compliance and control, it may even be seen as a step backwards from the Tlatelolco precedent, since it fails to create a separate enforcement organisation like OPANAL. Instead it relies on existing regional bodies which already have full agendas and are unlikely to possess the necessary technical expertise for ensuring compliance. Yet another compliance anomaly, as Ramesh Thakur has noted, is that the treaty's control system under Article 8 applies only to the treaty parties, not to the protocol parties; as a result, there is no proper system for verifying and ensuring compliance by NWS signatories to the protocols.[27]

Future Directions

The weaknesses of the Rarotonga Treaty as a precedent and model are understandable enough in the context of the Cold War climate in which it was negotiated and the pragmatic concern of some regional states, particularly Australia and New Zealand, to accommodate the strategic interests of the United States. In the case of Australia, there is some evidence to suggest that a prime motivation in both the timing and design of the initiative was a concern to channel more radical and comprehensive island state denuclearisation proposals into a measure that preserved key US and Australian nuclear interests.[28] Yet, despite the limited nature of the treaty, there can be little doubt that it has already played a valuable and important role as a regional confidence-building measure that has encouraged the establishment of a similar zone in neighbouring Southeast Asia and served as a building block in wider global efforts to declare the whole southern hemisphere a NWFZ and work towards the total elimination of all nuclear weapons.

In the post-Cold War context of reduced ideological tensions, heightened awareness of proliferation threats and new regional forums, there are new opportunities to strengthen the Rarotonga Treaty itself and/or to negotiate follow-on regional agreements that would outlaw all weapons of mass or indiscriminate destruction.

One step that could and should be taken in the wake of the major regional and world developments since the treaty was first negotiated is the convening of a review conference that would both assess progress in the treaty's implementation, consider amendments and recommend further initiatives.

While the treaty does not require mandatory periodic reviews, it does envisage the establishment of a Consultative Committee (Article 10 and Annex 3) for the purpose of 'consultation and cooperation on any matter arising in relation to this Treaty or for reviewing its operation'. This Committee, comprised of one representative plus advisers from each member state, and able, failing consensus, to make decisions by a two-thirds majority vote, is also empowered under Article 11 to 'consider proposals for amendment' and, in the case of any proposal agreed to by consensus, circulate it for acceptance by all Parties. This Consultative Committee is obliged to convene 'at the request of any Party', and it would be a relatively simple matter for any concerned regional state to ensure that the Committee is convened. Ideally, of course, the initiating state would seek the cooperation of all other parties in the convening of the Consultative Committee.

While the agenda of such a review conference would itself be a matter for regional negotiation, and consultations with relevant government and non-government organisations, the following possibilities might well be considered:

- Extension of the zone north of the Equator to cover all the Micronesian members of the South Pacific Forum. Now that the US has itself signed the protocols and revised its general approach to NWFZ, the potential for opposition on the grounds of possible conflict with US-Micronesian Compacts of Free Association is lessened. The FSM, in particular, participated as an observer in the negotiations of the Rarotonga Treaty and has, from time to time, expressed interest in joining the zone. The inclusion of the Marshalls would be particularly appropriate given the past history of US atmospheric testing in these islands. The anti-dumping provisions of the treaty would also be highly relevant given past and current proposals for radioactive waste dumping in or around Micronesia. The northwards extension of the zone would also be useful symbolically as a further encouragement to northern hemisphere states. Despite the 'South Pacific' labelling of the treaty, it should be noted that the zone already strays north of the Equator to include all of Kiribati's far-flung islands, and that it contains an explicit provision [Article 12(3)] permitting the redrawing of the treaty boundaries to include any new SPF members who wish to join the treaty so long as this is approved by the Forum itself.

- Strengthening of the provisions (or inclusion of an additional protocol) to prohibit long-range nuclear-capable missile delivery systems; and addition of a further protocol preventing any country from testing missiles in the zone. This is becoming all the more urgent as some regional and metropolitan states move to acquire or further develop such missiles.

- Amendment of the verification and control system in line with those of Tlatelolco and Pelindaba to include a specialist verification agency and referral to the UN Security Council and General Assembly in the case of violations that cannot be resolved at a regional level.

- Amendment of the control system to include the concept of societal verification whereby 'whistleblowing' individual citizens and NGOs can legitimately register complaints without suffering repression (as Mordechai Vanunu has suffered in Israel).

- Institution of a regular reporting system covering all relevant developments and activities in the region.

- Amendment of anti-dumping provisions to cover unregulated forms of land-based radioactive waste dumping and to bring the SPNFZ provisions into line with other international conventions and legislation in this area. In particular, such amendment needs to ensure that there are adequate controls over the removal of land-based nuclear waste that has already been created, such as the wastes in or around the French testing sites at Moruroa and Fangataufa, British sites in Australia and Christmas Island, and American sites in Micronesia.

- Institution of formal linkages with other established NWFZ, including regular consultations, cooperative action to further the wider aims and objectives of the treaties at the UN and in other international and regional forums, exchanges of information and data relevant to treaty verification and compliance, establishment of broader zones (such as a southern hemisphere NWFZ), and the establishment of an international NWFZ secretariat.

- Strengthening of non-use guarantees to include the use or threat of use of nuclear weapons *within* as well as *against* the zone.

- Extension of the zone, or negotiation of follow-on agreements, to cover all weapons of mass or indiscriminate destruction, including chemical and biological weapons, anti-personnel mines, and fuel air explosives. Such extension would serve to complement and enhance the effectiveness of the Chemical and Biological Weapons conventions and the Convention on Conventional Weapons.

Conclusion

The Rarotonga Treaty has already made significant contributions at both a regional and global level. It provided encouragement to the negotiation of a similar zone in the neighbouring region of Southeast Asia and is both a practical and symbolic element in a broader initiative to establish a southern hemisphere NWFZ. Further, it has demonstrated the power of regional groupings to take active steps towards arms control and disarmament in their own regions, with or without the initial support of the nuclear powers.

Nevertheless, there are many ways in which it can and ought to be strengthened, taking into account the new post-Cold War environment and emerging threats of proliferation across a range of weapons categories. In particular, the time would seem to be ripe, if not overdue, for the convening of a review conference that would discuss and negotiate a range of possibilities for either strengthening the treaty or developing follow-on treaties and confidence-building measures.

Through such a review, David Lange's original hope that the treaty would serve as the first rung on a ladder leading to wider regional and global disarmament may yet be vindicated.

Notes

1. South Pacific Forum, media conference in Rarotonga, 6 August 1985, author's notes.
2. Michael Hamel-Green, 'Regional Arms Control in the South Pacific: Island State Responses to Australia's Nuclear Free Zone Initiative', *Contemporary Pacific* 3 (Spring 1991), pp. 59–84.
3. Australia, Cook Islands, Fiji, Kiribati, Papua New Guinea, Nauru, New Zealand, Niue, Solomon Islands, Tonga, Tuvalu, Vanuatu, Western Samoa.
4. United States, White House, Office of the Press Secretary, *United States, France and the United Kingdom to Sign Protocols of the South Pacific Nuclear Free Zone Treaty* (Joint Statement), Press Release, Washington DC, 22 March 1996; France, *Discours Prononce Par Le President du Gouvernement Territorial de la Polynesie, M. Gaston Flosse, a L'occasion de la Ceremonie de Signature du Traite de Rarotonga,* official transcript, Suva, 25 March 1996; UK, British Embassy Suva, *Statement Made By HE Michael Peart, British Ambassador to Fiji, After Signing the Protocols to the SPNFZ on 25 March 1966*, Press Release, Suva, 25 March 1966.
5. *Age* (Melbourne), 26 March 1996, p. 9; *Peace and Disarmament News*, July 1966, p. 11.
6. United Nations, Conference on Disarmament, *Comprehensive Study of the Question of Nuclear-Weapon-Free-Zones in All its Aspects* (New York: UN General Assembly, 30th Session, Supplement No. 27A, A/10027/Add.1, 1975), pp. 31–4, 37–40.
7. J. Dorrance, *United States Security Interests in the Pacific Islands,* mimeo (Washington DC: US State Department, 1983), pp. 11–12.
8. Michael Hamel-Green, *The South Pacific Nuclear Free Zone Treaty: A Critical Assessment* (Canberra: Peace Research Centre, Research School of Pacific Studies, Australian National University, 1990), p. 1.
9. Rod Alley, *Nuclear-Weapon-Free Zones: The South Pacific Proposal* (Muscatine, Iowa: Stanley Foundation, Occasional Paper 1, 1977).
10. For detailed discussions of the SPNFZ initiative and treaty, see: R. Alexander, *Putting the Earth First: Alternatives to Nuclear Security in Pacific Island*

States (Honolulu: Matsunaga Institute for Peace, University of Hawaii, 1994), pp. 165–204; Greg Fry, *A Nuclear-Free Zone for the Southwest Pacific: Prospects and Significance*, Working Paper 75 (Canberra: Strategic and Defence Studies Centre, Australian National University, September 1983); Greg Fry, 'Regional Arms Control in the South Pacific', in Desmond Ball and Andrew Mack, eds, *The Future of Arms Control* (Sydney: ANU Press/Pergamon, 1987), pp. 137–56; Greg Fry, 'The South Pacific Nuclear Free Zone', in *SIPRI Yearbook 1986* (Oxford: Oxford University Press, 1986), pp. 499–507; Hamel-Green, *The South Pacific Nuclear Free Zone Treaty*; Andrew Mack, *Nuclear-Free Zones in the 1990s* (Canberra: Department of International Relations, Australian National University, Working Paper 1993/10, December 1993); South Pacific Forum Secretariat, *South Pacific Nuclear Free Zone*, Memorandum prepared for the 1995 NPT Review Conference (Suva, 1995); Ramesh Thakur, 'A Nuclear-Weapon-Free South Pacific: A New Zealand Perspective', *Pacific Affairs* 58 (Summer 1985), pp. 216–38; Ramesh Thakur, 'The Treaty of Rarotonga: The South Pacific Nuclear-Free Zone', in D. Pitt and G. Thompson, eds, *Nuclear-Free Zones* (Beckenham, Kent: Croom Helm, 1987), pp. 23–45.

11. In a recent discussion of this issue, Jan Prawitz noted that 'Transit through zonal high seas areas or through territories which are dependencies of nuclear-weapons powers could not be permitted without making the zonal regime of such areas an illusion.' See Jan Prawitz, 'The Concept of NWFZ', conference paper, 45th Pugwash Conference 'Towards a Nuclear-Weapon-Free World', Hiroshima, 23–29 July 1995, p. 30.

12. J. S. Roy, 'South Pacific Nuclear Free Zone', *Department of State Bulletin* 87(2126) (September 1987), pp. 52–3.

13. United States, White House, News Briefing by Robert Bell, Special Assistant to the President and Senior Director for Defense Policy and Arms Control of the National Security Council, official transcript, Washington DC, 22 March 1996.

14. United States, *Proposed Understanding and Declarations*, mimeographed attachment to US statement at time of 25 March 1996 US signature of protocols to Rarotonga Treaty, Suva, Fiji.

15. France, Letter from the French President, Prime Minister and Minister for Foreign Affairs, to South Pacific Forum Secretariat, authorising France's plenipotentiary, Gaston Flosse, to sign the Rarotonga Treaty protocols, Paris, 6 March 1996.

16. United Kingdom, Letter from Michael Peart, Ambassador to Fiji, to South Pacific Forum Secretariat, 25 March 1995.

17. People's Republic of China Embassy, Canberra, *Statement issued by Ambassador Ji Chaozhu on behalf of the Chinese Government, February 1987*.

18. Mikhail Gorbachev, 'Message to the Heads of States and Governments of the countries–members of the South Pacific Forum in connection with the

ratification by the USSR of Protocols II and III to the Treaty of Rarotonga', *Soviet News Bulletin* (USSR Embassy, Canberra), No. 4, 1 February 1988.
19. Fry, 'Regional Arms Control in the South Pacific', pp. 57–9.
20. *Arms Control Reporter*, January 1996, pp. 458.A.1-2, 458.D.1-8; ASEAN, *ASEAN Update* Vol.1/96, January–February 1996, pp. 2,10–12.
21. For example, Australia's former Governor-General and Foreign Minister, Bill Hayden's, recent comment that 'if an effort to develop nuclear weaponry capability was under way or had been achieved by others in our region', then Australia should be in a position to match such countries' capabilities 'in the shortest possible time'; *Weekend Australian*, 30–1 March 1996, pp. 1–2.
22. Mack, *Nuclear-Free Zones in the 1990s*.
23. Ibid.
24. The Australian Scientific Advisory Group that reported to the South Pacific Environment Ministers Meeting in Brisbane on 16–17 August 1995 indicated that despite lack of data, there were grounds for suspecting serious environmental impacts, including potential leaching into the ocean of radioactive materials and induced subsidence and landslides of the atoll structure. *Peace and Disarmament News* (Australian Department of Foreign Affairs and Trade), September 1995, p. 18. More recently Roger Clark, a Leeds University geologist, and Dr Manfred Hochstein of the University of Auckland, have questioned French waste management policy at Mororoa; *Age* (Melbourne), 25 October 1996, p. 12.
25. Prawitz, 'Concept of NWFZ', p. 25.
26. J. Prawitz, and J. F. Leonard, *A Zone Free of Weapons of Mass Destruction in the Middle East* (Geneva: United Nations Institute for Disarmament Research, 1996).
27. Thakur, 'The Treaty of Rarotonga', p. 41.
28. Hamel-Green, *The South Pacific Nuclear Free Zone Treaty*, pp. 55–71.

4
Southeast Asia – The Treaty of Bangkok

Carolina G. Hernandez

Nuclear-weapon-free zones (NWFZ) seek to prevent the spread of nuclear weapons and nuclear war. In Southeast Asia, such a zone constitutes, together with other mechanisms, arrangements and documents, the attempt on the part of the Association of South-east Asian Nations (ASEAN) to insulate the sub-region from great power rivalry in order to maintain a stable regional order for sustained economic growth and the peace and security of its peoples. ASEAN has had a 29-year history of promoting this goal. The 1995 Southeast Asian NWFZ (SEANWFZ) Treaty is only the most recent in a series of efforts to ensure its realisation.

Since its establishment in 1967, ASEAN has continuously sought the promotion of regional stability through political, economic and functional cooperation among its members and between them and an increasing number of dialogue partners. A stable Southeast Asia was seen as an assurance of insulating the sub-region from superpower rivalry during the Cold War, and from great power competition and hegemony in the post-Cold War era. In 1967 the five original ASEAN members decided to set aside their bilateral differences and conflicts for this purpose. In the course of 29 years, ASEAN has sustained political and security cooperation as an instrument for defusing and mitigating post-colonial Southeast Asian security problems. Intra-ASEAN conflicts such as *konfrontasi* between Indonesia and Malaysia, Singapore's expulsion from the Federation of Malaya and the Sabah dispute between Malaysia and the Philippines were set aside in the interest of regional reconciliation and stability. The ASEAN (Bangkok) Declaration, the Association's basic document, underscores this goal of promoting political, economic and functional cooperation to achieve regional security and stability. The 1971 Kuala Lumpur Declaration responded to the major security challenges facing ASEAN at that time, such as growing communist insurgencies, internal tensions and civil strife, the danger of being dragged into superpower conflicts occurring in the region and the demands of sustaining the members' political and economic agendas. Specifically, it reaffirmed the members' political resolve and collective commitment to secure the recognition and respect for Southeast Asia as a zone of peace, freedom and neutrality (ZOPFAN) in which external powers do not intervene.[1]

ASEAN's first summit produced the (Bali) Declaration of ASEAN Concord which provided for the goals and principles of cooperation, including plans of action in economic and functional cooperation, as well as the development of a distinct ASEAN identity. The summit also adopted the Treaty of Amity and Cooperation (TAC) which enshrines the principles of interstate relations, including mutual respect for each other's territorial integrity and national sovereignty, non-interference in each other's domestic affairs and the peaceful settlement of disputes. Since then, these principles have guided the conduct of intra-ASEAN relations as well as ASEAN relations with the outside world, sometimes with serious criticism from abroad and from important segments of civil societies within ASEAN itself.

The Bali summit also expressed an unequivocal rejection of military alliance or a confrontational response to the prevailing communist challenge faced by ASEAN members. The care with which ASEAN avoided any hint that its members were forming a military alliance is indicated by the fact that from the start, regional stability has been interpreted as a product of political, economic and functional co-operation and security conceived as comprehensive, multidimensional and multilevel. This resulted in the misperception that the primary goal of ASEAN is economic integration and the slow progress in market sharing, until the decision to adopt and implement an ASEAN Free Trade Area (AFTA) during the fourth summit in Singapore, has been interpreted as failure in achieving this goal.

The TAC also provided for a mechanism for the settlement of disputes in the form of the High Council. ASEAN has not used this mechanism of dispute settlement. Instead it has shelved for an indefinite period the settlement of divisive issues such as those over territory and borders until the appropriate time, in the belief that when settlement is ripe the dispute would be solved. In the meantime, acrimony and hostility bred by forcing the issue and putting other members in the difficult and sensitive position of having to choose between two ASEAN partners are avoided as they are seen as only counter-productive. This approach has made ASEAN the object of criticism not only from some quarters within the association, but especially from the West. This notwithstanding, ASEAN's record has shown that these approaches to the problem of regional peace, security and stability worked.

The principles of cooperation embodied in these various ASEAN documents were reaffirmed during the second ASEAN summit in Kuala Lumpur in 1977. Since then, ASEAN has worked to implement the members' collective commitment to ASEAN cooperation and the formation of a collective ASEAN identity. At the third summit in Manila in 1989, ASEAN sought to improve the process and scope of ASEAN cooperation, particularly in the economic and security realms. It was in 1984, during the interregnum between the second and third summits, that the concept of SEANWFZ was introduced. An effort to substantiate the creation in Southeast Asia of a zone of peace, freedom and neutrality, SEANWFZ may also be seen as ASEAN's contribution to regional arms control and disarmament as expressed in particular in the Nuclear Non-Proliferation Treaty (NPT, 1968). The fourth ASEAN summit in Singapore in 1992 directed the ASEAN foreign ministers to look into and elaborate the idea of SEANWFZ.

It was not until the fifth summit in Bangkok in December 1995 that ASEAN finally adopted the Treaty on the Southeast Asian Nuclear-Weapon-Free Zone. The six ASEAN members were joined in signing the treaty by Vietnam, which became an ASEAN member in July 1996, and Cambodia, Laos and Myanmar, all of which are observers in ASEAN, having previously acceded to the TAC. They are now applicants for ASEAN membership and the informal summit in Jakarta in December 1996 decided that the three countries will be simultaneously admitted into ASEAN at some future time.

Background to SEANWFZ

The adoption of the treaty is a major achievement in itself. ASEAN is aware that the realisation of a zone of peace, freedom and neutrality is a long process due to the fact that in 1977 and until the present, two ASEAN members (the Philippines and Thailand) remained allies of the United States in bilateral agreements under the San Francisco system of military alliances; another two (Malaysia and Singapore) were joined with Australia, New Zealand and Britain in the Five Power Defence Arrangements (FPDA); and the Philippines still hosted US military forces in its bases. ASEAN pragmatism also enabled its members to accommodate these bilateral military links as an imperative of the times. In this regard, foreign military bases on Southeast Asian soil were viewed as temporary and did not have to stall the declaration of commitment for the establishment in the sub-region of such a zone.

In the meantime, between the second and third summits, the incremental fleshing out of ZOPFAN led to the introduction in 1984 of the SEANWFZ concept. Until the late 1980s ASEAN consensus on this matter was not firm enough to warrant its adoption, although its members lent varying levels of support for the concept. There seemed to be a consensus among elites in Brunei, Indonesia, Malaysia and the Philippines that it was desirable to commit to the establishment of a SEANWFZ even as a long-term goal; to be effective, it had to include all the ten states of Southeast Asia (ASEAN 6, Cambodia, Laos, Vietnam and Myanmar); it would give substance to the goal of ZOPFAN; it must not include a ban on the peaceful uses of nuclear power; such a zone would be supportive of arms control and disarmament, especially the NPT; and it was not readily implementable for various reasons, including ASEAN's lack of nuclear expertise for setting up an effective monitoring system and the financial costs such a system entails.[2] It is assumed that the four ASEAN countries shared their elites' perspectives on this issue.

In addition, some of the elites in these four member countries expressed the view that a prospective treaty should take into account the existing defence and security arrangements of member countries; it would need to be flexible on the issue of port calls or transit of nuclear-powered or nuclear-armed ships (Brunei elite views);[3] some real obstacles lay in the adoption of a treaty in the form of the unstable conditions in Indochina due to the Cambodian conflict, territorial disputes in the Spratlys and the presence of military facilities in some ASEAN countries (Indonesian elite views);[4] and there was the need to negotiate even informally with other Southeast Asian countries and to obtain the recognition for SEANWFZ by external powers (Malaysian elite views).[5] While the Philippine constitution is the first in the region to include an anti-nuclear provision, opinion on its interpretation was divided because of the political polarisation around the issue of the US military facilities in the country. Nevertheless, the Philippines could be presumed to favour the idea of setting up such a zone as it was a signatory to a number of agreements supportive of the concept of a NWFZ. Among them are ASEAN's Manila Declaration of 1987 which directed its members to intensify their efforts for an early establishment of a SEANWFZ, the NPT and some 39 international and regional agreements on detente, denuclearisation and disarmament.[6]

On the other hand, Singaporean views, while in agreement that the NWFZ should cover all of Southeast Asia, include only nuclear weapons and not the peaceful uses of nuclear energy and respect the existing military or security commitments of some ASEAN members, still saw too many obstacles towards its establishment. In addition to those identified by their Indonesian counterparts, Singaporean elites thought that US and Japanese objections to such a treaty would be a major stumbling block in obtaining major power recognition of the zone.[7] Singapore's elites were thus hesitant supporters of the idea.

Thai elites appeared similarly reluctant primarily because the Cambodian conflict was still in full steam at that time. As ASEAN's frontline state on this issue with Vietnam, Thailand was not fully convinced of the wisdom of a premature adoption of SEANWFZ. It thought that prior attention should be given to the resolution of the Cambodian conflict and that the enlistment of US and Soviet support, essential to the zone's success, was compromised by their military presence in the Philippine bases and in Cam Ranh.[8] Consequently, Thailand sought the support of others in ASEAN to wait until such time as all the members of ASEAN were ready to put their energies and commitment behind it before deciding to adopt and implement such a treaty.

Not surprisingly, the Indochinese states, led by Vietnam, were unanimous in their support for SEANWFZ. They saw many positive developments that warranted the establishment of SEANWFZ as a first step towards the realisation of ZOPFAN. These included superpower detente, Sino-Soviet detente and progress towards a political settlement of the Cambodian conflict. Such a zone would render military bases in the region irrelevant to its security needs, a goal towards which countries should move in order to establish an effective NWFZ.[9] Most of the obstacles to the adoption of SEANWFZ had disappeared by the mid-1990s. The US military facilities in the Philippines were dismantled after the rejection in 1992 by the Philippine Senate of a new treaty between the two countries. A political settlement of the Cambodian conflict was effected following the Vietnamese troop withdrawal from Cambodia. Soviet implosion made its bases in Cam Ranh untenable. ASEAN reconciliation with Vietnam followed the Cambodian political settlement. The end of the Cold War facilitated superpower disarmament in Europe. In Asia–Pacific, territorial disputes in the Spratlys remain, military alliances between some ASEAN members and great powers continue to be in force and new security arrangements, such as that between Australia and Indonesia, have been forged. Nevertheless changes in the regional strategic environment also led many of the states in Southeast Asia to allow US troops and naval ships and military aircraft to make port calls for refuelling, repair and other purposes as a hedge against post-Cold War uncertainties and to compensate for the loss of the Philippine bases. On the whole, however, Southeast Asian states felt comfortable in finally adopting the decision to sign the SEANWFZ Treaty in December 1995.

The adoption of the treaty must have been influenced by NWFZ in other parts of the world. Latin American states created such a zone through the Treaty of Tlatelolco in 1967 while the members of the South Pacific Forum established one, through the 1985 Treaty of Rarotonga, that stretches from Latin America to Australia's west coast and from the Antarctic to the Equator. North and South Korea agreed to denuclearise the Korean peninsula in 1992, although the agreement continued to await implementation. In June 1995 the text of the Treaty of Pelindaba between the members of the Organisation of African Unity (OAU) was agreed on the establishment of a NWFZ in Africa.[10] (The Treaty was formally signed in April 1996.) The latest of such efforts is the December 1995 SEANWFZ Treaty.

SEANWFZ and Regional Security and Stability

The adoption of the SEANWFZ Treaty is seen as a milestone in the region's nuclear history. It represents a regional vehicle that can enhance the protection against the dangers of nuclear weapons, nuclear testing, radioactive contamination and pollution. It is the region's contribution to nuclear non-proliferation, denuclearisation and disarmament as sought by the NPT. The Treaty was shaped by the signatories' desire to promote the realisation of the principles of the United Nations Charter to take concrete action to contribute to the progress of disarmament of nuclear weapons, maintain regional peace and security, pursue the ASEAN Declaration on ZOPFAN, the NPT, the Final Document of the Tenth Session of the General Assembly encouraging the establishment of NWFZ, the 1995 review and extension of the NPT on the cooperation of all nuclear-weapons states (NWS) and their recognition and support for relevant protocols as important for the effective implementation of NWFZ, and the determination to promote regional environmental protection from radioactive wastes and radioactive materials.[11]

SEANWFZ covers the territories of all ten Southeast Asian states and their continental shelves and exclusive economic zones (EEZs). These territories include land, international waters, territorial sea, archipelagic waters, their seabed and subsoil, as well as the airspace above them. The nuclear weapons banned from the zone are any explosive device that can release nuclear energy in an uncontrollable manner, but they exclude the means of transport or delivery of unassembled or partly assembled nuclear devices.[12]

While nuclear research is not specifically prohibited, the Treaty bans the development, manufacture, acquisition, possession, control, stationing, transport, testing or use of nuclear weapons. It also bans dumping and discharging of radioactive materials either at sea of in the atmosphere.[13] While peaceful use of nuclear energy is allowed, it can be done so only under strict nuclear safety regulations established by the International Atomic Energy Agency (IAEA) whose assessments are to be made available upon request by other parties to the Treaty. This feature is unique to SEANWFZ, as is the provision that the export of special fissionable material to any NWS is subject to IAEA safeguards, although SEANWFZ also requires that such export to non-NWS be subject to safeguards as required under Article 3(1) of the NPT.[14] SEANWFZ carries a redundant provision in requiring states parties to conclude safeguards agreements with the IAEA within 18 months of the Treaty's coming into force, since as parties to the NPT the ten Southeast Asian states are already obliged to do so.[15]

Article 7 of the Treaty grants a state party the right 'to decide whether to allow visits by foreign ships and aircraft to its ports and airfields, transit of its airspace by foreign aircraft, navigation through its territorial sea of archipelagic waters in a manner not governed by the rights of innocent passage, archipelagic sea lanes passage or transit passage'.[16] A Commission consisting of all parties is established to oversee the Treaty's implementation and ensure compliance. It makes its decision by consensus, or failing this, by a two-thirds majority vote of states present and voting. All parties are members of the Commission's Executive Committee which has been assigned specified functions, including the setting up of fact-finding missions and concluding agreements with the IAEA and other international organisations when authorised by the Commission.[17]

A control system is also established to ensure compliance. Like other NWFZ and other mechanisms of non-proliferation, effective compliance is crucial to success. The control system consists of IAEA safeguards, report and exchange of information, request for clarification and fact-finding missions.[18] Non-compliance is subject to IAEA rules and procedures and, in cases affecting international peace and security, to the UN Security Council and General Assembly.[19] The Treaty comes into force upon the ratification of seven signatories and is open to review after 10 years of operation.[20] Withdrawal from the Treaty is allowed in case of a substantive violation of the basic understandings by another party after a 12-month notice has been given.[21] A protocol providing for negative security assurances for the parties to the Treaty is open for accession of the five NWS.[22] Unfortunately, there were no specific undertakings provided for in the protocol for NWS except to bind them not to contribute to the commission of any act constituting a breach of the Treaty.

Critique

Critics of the treaty, while recognising its contribution to nuclear disarmament, consider it to be more of a political statement by its signatories on their commitment to nuclear disarmament. It is perceived as being limited in at least four areas.[23]

First, it does not absolutely prohibit the transit of nuclear weapons or devices through the territorial seas of its members. As already cited, Article 7 allows states parties to determine for themselves whether to grant transit rights through their territories to foreign ships and aircraft. This option granted to a state party the right to determine whether or not it would allow the entry into or passage of nuclear armed ships and aircraft through its land, air and water domains even as the flag state, such as the US for example, insists on neither confirming nor denying whether these ships or aircraft indeed carried nuclear weapons.

Second, while the treaty bans the dumping of radioactive wastes in the zone, there is 'no prohibition on nuclear activities which could produce such wastes, or any other non-essential uses of radioactive wastes'.[24] Provided shipments of plutonium or any other radioactive materials have clearance or exemption levels recommended by the IAEA, they may presumably be allowed to enter the zone.[25]

Third, the treaty does not ban the production of nuclear power plants. These plants could pose dangers to nuclear proliferation because nuclear wastes from reactors, critics allege, contain weapons-usable plutonium which could be used in nuclear-weapons production when reprocessed. These wastes can also be diverted to countries such as North Korea that are aspiring to develop nuclear weapons.

Fourth, the Treaty also runs the risk of being weakened by its full recognition of the rights of innocent passage or transit passage of international straits, archipelagic sea lanes and high seas, and undertakings that accommodate the provisions of the 1982 UN Convention on the Law of the Sea (UNCLOS) and the freedom of the seas recognised in the UN Charter. This means that ships carrying nuclear weapons can continue to enjoy these rights in these various UNCLOS regimes.

It is not difficult to understand why the SEANWFZ Treaty continues to accommodate the obligations of some of its signatories under existing bilateral or multilateral security arrangements with external powers. These treaty obligations have to be recognised in the establishment of the zone because the security arrangements they established continue to serve a strategic purpose in the highly fluid and uncertain regional and global post-Cold War environment. They are seen as guarantees of regional stability and security. At the same time, the temporary character and the need for their temporary accommodation is also well-recognised in ASEAN. Hence the notion that the implementation of ZOPFAN, of which the SEANWFZ is a part, is seen as a goal which may not be immediately realisable.

With regard to the disposition of radioactive wastes and other radioactive material according to IAEA standards and procedures, the absence of other regulatory mechanisms to determine safe or tolerable limits of radioactivity and disposal leaves the parties no recourse but to resort to the IAEA.

Other critics fault the SEANWFZ for not having an 'additional protocol binding the NWS to desist from nuclear testing within the zone of application'.[26] Their obligation consists merely of not contributing to any act that is violative of the Treaty. As well, the US reportedly refuses to sign the protocol to which NWS have been invited to join due to the zone's extension to the parties' continental shelf and EEZ which could hamper US ability to provide effective security operations when the need for them arises.[27] The US reluctance to accede to the protocol might stem from the negative security assurance which would commit the US not to launch nuclear weapons from within the zone even if it faced a nuclear attack from another nuclear power which had also acceded to the protocol,[28] and 'its interpretation of the freedom of the high seas and its self-defined rights for naval and military deployments for regional security in the Pacific'.[29]

Regarding the peaceful use of nuclear power, such a proposition remains controversial for the reasons critics above have cited. Yet the search for alternative sources of energy will become even more compelling in the next century.[30] The rapid growth of the Asia–Pacific economies, projected to continue into the future even though the rates of growth will probably decline, will mean that energy consumption for industrial, commercial and other peaceful uses will rise dramatically. Rising incomes will result in changing lifestyles that will help boost the demand for energy. The question that might be raised in this regard is: are there real alternatives to energy generation other than the nuclear path? This is a question that energy experts will have to address in an unequivocal and authoritative way. In the meantime, Southeast Asian states needed to safeguard their future by not banning what appears, for the moment at least, a viable alternative energy source. What seems curious, given the Treaty's recognition of the peaceful uses of nuclear power, is its failure to provide for the protection of such facilities should states parties set them up in the future.

Moreover, it must be noted that security being comprehensive in character and political legitimacy being a condition of domestic stability, Southeast Asian nations that continue to depend on economic performance as the principal basis of legitimacy will not be able to afford the undermining of their performance. In this sense, for all its weaknesses and limitations, SEANWFZ can contribute to regional security and stability. Finally, it is necessary for the NWS to recognise and support NWFZ if these are to become truly effective instruments of nuclear disarmament. Short of the achievement of the NPT goal of the eventual elimination of nuclear weapons and the relevant provisions of UNCLOS regarding the rights of innocent passage, or transit passage of straits, archipelagic sea lanes and high seas notwithstanding, NWFZ can only be fully respected if nuclear weapons were to be dramatically reduced and NWS abide by the spirit and intent behind the establishment of such zones. Instead of looking at the SEANWFZ Treaty as no more than a diplomatic or political statement, it should be encouraged and seen as a small but important contribution towards the promotion of regional peace and security as well as nuclear non-proliferation. It reiterates ASEAN's commitment to nuclear non-proliferation, establishes a regional verification system to ensure compliance by parties and sets a significant precedent in regional security cooperation that could be a model and encouragement for other sub-regions such as South Asia and Northeast Asia on nuclear non-proliferation.[31] However, to be effective, the recognition and support of the five declared NWS, particularly the US, should be actively and creatively sought by the parties to SEANWFZ.

Notes

1. Md Hussin Nayan, 'Openness and Transparency in ASEAN Countries', *Disarmament* 18:2 (1995), pp. 136–7.
2. Noel M. Morada, 'Towards a Conceptualization of a Southeast Asian Nuclear-Weapon-Free Zone', unpublished MA thesis, Department of Political Science, University of the Philippines, Diliman, October 1989, pp. 92–103.
3. Ibid., pp. 93–4.
4. Ibid., p. 95.
5. Ibid. p. 97.
6. Ibid., p. 102.
7. Ibid., pp. 103–4.
8. Ibid. pp. 105–6.
9. Ibid., pp. 106–8.

10. Jan Prawitz and James F. Leonard, *A Zone Free of Weapons of Mass Destruction in the Middle East* (Geneva: United Nations Institute for Disarmament Research, 1996), p. 3.
11. Culled from the Treaty's preamble.
12. Art. 1 - Use of Terms.
13. Art. 3 - Basic Understandings.
14. Tariq Rauf, 'Nuclear Disarmament and Non-Proliferation', paper presented at the ASEAN Regional Forum (ARF) Track Two Seminar on Non-Proliferation, Jakarta, 6–7 December 1996, p. 30.
15. Ibid.
16. Art. 7 - Foreign Ships and Aircraft.
17. Art. 5 - IAEA Safeguards; Art. 8 - Establishment of the Commission for the Southeast Asia Nuclear-Weapon-Free Zone; and Art. 9 - The Executive Committee.
18. Art. 10 - Control System; Art. 11 - Report and Exchange of Information; Art. 12 - Request for Clarification; and Art. 13 - Request for Fact-Finding Mission.
19. Art. 14 - Remedial Measures.
20. Art. 16 - Entry into Force and Art. 20 - Review. (The Treaty came into force on 27 March 1997 - Editor.)
21. Art. 22 - Duration and Withdrawal.
22. Art. 1, Protocol to the SEANWFZ Treaty.
23. Roland Simbulan, 'The Southeast Asian Nuclear-Free Zone Treaty: A treaty whose time has finally come', *Manila Chronicle*, 16 December 1995. The author is the National Chairperson of Nuclear Free Philippines Coalition and a faculty member of the University of the Philippines, Manila.
24. Simbulan, 'Southeast Asian Nuclear-Free Zone Treaty'.
25. Ibid.
26. Rauf, 'Nuclear Disarmament and Non-Proliferation', p. 31.
27. Paul N. Villegas, 'US to thresh out concerns on ASEAN's Nuclear-free stance with member states', *Business World*, 25 January 1996, p. 8.
28. Ralph A. Cossa, 'SEA Seeks Endorsement of its Nuclear-Free Zone,' *International Herald Tribune*, 23 August 1996.
29. Rauf, 'Nuclear Disarmament and Non-Proliferation', p. 31.
30. Masao Takuma, 'Japan's Nuclear Energy Program, Utilisation of Plutonium and Nuclear Non-Proliferation,' a paper presented at the above-cited ARF Track Two Seminar on Non-Proliferation.
31. Rauf, 'Nuclear Disarmament and Non-Proliferation', p. 31.

5
Africa – The Treaty of Pelindaba

Julius O. Ihonvbere

Some states appear to be willing to starve their people and to take enormous heat from the international community in order to obtain nuclear weapons.[1]

The Treaty of Pelindaba is an African success story even if it has taken 31 years to give birth to it. The Treaty represents some of the best news coming out of an Africa that continues to suffer its share of the tragic and destructive effects of conflict.[2]

The decision by nations to build or acquire nuclear weapons is influenced by a variety of factors, including location and the character of local politics and leadership. It can be expected that the processes of arriving at such a decision in a democratic political system will be significantly different from that of a dictatorship. In the latter an individual could take and pursue the decision to develop or acquire weapons of mass destruction (WMD), as has been the case in Iraq and Libya among others.[3] Beyond the individual or leadership factors however, are security concerns, the quest for regional prestige, the ambitions of particular regimes, the desire to move technological developments to a higher level, industrial determination and international prestige. For instance, one reason given by India for opposing the Nuclear Non-Proliferation Treaty (NPT) is that while it is designed to stop the 'spread of nuclear weapons to non-nuclear states', it fails to provide 'adequate security guarantees', and 'it fails to reduce or eliminate stockpiles of the weapon states and thus legitimates them'.[4] Thus the main consideration often advanced by states seeking to develop 'threshold' nuclear-weapons capability is security. India's neighbour Pakistan invokes exactly the same reasons, as do South Africa and Israel. Certainly, a decision to acquire or develop WMD (biological, chemical or nuclear), especially in recent times with increasing international opposition to nuclear weapons, can be very costly, dangerous and negate rather than assist the search for power, influence and prestige.

The existence of several international agreements, treaties and mechanisms designed to control export of nuclear technology, including the NPT, the International Atomic Energy Agency (IAEA), the London Nuclear Suppliers Group, the Missile Technology Control Regime (MTCR) and the Coordinating Committee on Export Controls (COCOM), have not prevented nations like Iraq, South Africa, India, Pakistan, Israel and North Korea from developing some capability or actually manufacturing the bomb. In fact, signatories to the NPT like Iraq and North Korea have violated its provisions often invoking security concerns.[5] The South African case is equally instructive. In spite of numerous sanctions and embargoes against the apartheid regime, it managed, through its nuclear-weapons manufacturing outfit, Advena, to 'develop an extensive array of nuclear-weapons manufacturing capabilities'.[6] Since the major nuclear-weapons states (NWS) use similar arguments of 'deterrence' and 'security' and have been very slow to heed global calls for disarmament, it has been difficult to construct a global disarmament regime and ensure absolute non-proliferation.[7]

The end of the Cold War, however, has increased international interest in disarmament as many argue that the ideological battles of the past which have now disappeared make the building and stockpiling of WMD, especially nuclear weapons, unreasonable. The new globalisation places emphasis on economic, environmental and social problems and opportunities. Even the developed economies are increasingly under great economic and social pressures as crime, unemployment, bankruptcies, inflation and environmental problems constrain the ability to focus unduly on defence and security issues in an increasingly complex and competitive yet 'shrinking' world. Unfortunately, the new global dispensation has not given assurances that the world is out of the dangers posed by nuclear weapons.

Recent developments in Japan also confirm the fact that individuals and cults could get into the WMD business, especially by building

Africa – The Treaty of Pelindaba

biological and chemical weapons systems. In spite of developments in the global system and the new emphasis in economic and social concerns, the new discourse on denuclearisation is yet to link it effectively and seriously to the urgent need to eliminate or, at least, reduce national and global inequalities. The frequent references to 'peaceful uses' of nuclear technology as an alternative to the status quo hardly go far enough to define what 'peaceful uses' actually mean, who would benefit from it, and what sort of sacrifices, institutions and relations are required to institute an alternative global regime to ensure a critically different agenda.

Beyond South Africa, the African continent was never seen as posing a fundamental threat to global peace based on the possession of nuclear weapons. Even the South African capability, which was shrouded in much secrecy, did not qualify the continent as a major risk compared to some other developing regions.[8] Africa has historically been concerned with the dangers of nuclear weapons. Consequently, since political independence in the 1960s, African leaders have pursued denuclearisation with vigour. To be sure, there were always visible discrepancies between their official declarations, on the one hand, and the ability to mobilise the required political will to see through a denuclearisation programme. Thus, while on the one hand proposing and campaigning for a denuclearised Africa, on the other hand some African states have pursued independent nuclear programmes (South Africa, Algeria and Libya); made a lot of noise about acquiring a so-called 'black bomb' (Nigeria); or forged alliances with nations with nuclear capabilities (Kenya and the client states of the former Soviet Union).

Nigerian leaders, buoyed by the huge oil rents which followed the 1973 oil price increases by the Organisation of Petroleum Exporting Countries (OPEC), argued for the nuclear option in the 1970s and 1980s. Without due attention to the technical, technological, environmental, security and other implications, Nigeria established an Atomic Energy Commission in 1976. In 1980 Foreign Minister Iya Abubakar declared that 'Nigeria will develop nuclear technology for peaceful purposes and eventually become a nuclear power . . . Nigeria is a great country and it needs a strong, invincible and unassailable defence capability. It is only when she has become a nuclear power that she can boast of that status'.[9] In the same year President Shehu Shagari narrowed down the reasons why Nigeria needed nuclear weapons thus: 'Nigeria might acquire nuclear weapons to protect herself if racist South Africa persisted in acquiring the deadly weapons to threaten the continent'.[10] Clearly the need to balance the power of apartheid South Africa rather than economic or other scientific benefits was the main motivation behind Nigeria's quest for nuclear technology. Of course contradictions, conflicts, and crises arising from acute corruption and mismanagement, coups and counter coups, ethnic and religious violence, misplaced priorities, infrastructural and institutional decay, and very poor leadership have mediated, even contained, any plans for the development and manufacture of nuclear weapons by Nigeria.[11]

What is perhaps more interesting is the very limited appreciation of the dangers of nuclear weapons in Africa. The issues of denuclearisation are hardly part of national discourses. As well, even when leaders speak of the so-called peaceful uses of nuclear technology, they hardly reflect a serious understanding of the chronic socio-economic and political distortions in their respective economies. For many African leaders, the nuclear weapon is not only a status symbol, but also an instrument for consolidating their repressive and generally corrupt dictatorships. Dictators in Zaire, Equatorial Guinea, Uganda, Nigeria, Togo and elsewhere in the continent, at one time or the other, have seen the development or acquisition of WMD as the most reliable way to resolve border problems, contain internal opposition and consolidate the stranglehold over their societies.

In this study, we examine the background to the quest for denuclearisation; the factors which delayed it for over three decades; the imperatives for a nuclear-weapon-free zone (NWFZ); the South African angle to the quest for a NWFZ; the 1996 Treaty of Pelindaba; and the future of Africa as a NWFZ.

Background to Africa's Quest for Denuclearisation

African states attained political independence in the 1960s as poverty stricken, underdeveloped, foreign dominated and marginal actors. Colonialism had severely distorted and retarded social formations and rendered the continent technologically backward. The region was also extremely vulnerable to external penetration, pressures, domination and exploitation. The structures and relations of dependence on the outside world continued to influence and determine internal and external socio-economic and political relations. These debilitating conditions informed the military, strategic and foreign policy calculations of African states in an increasingly complex global division of labour and power. The idea of getting involved in the Cold War between the East and the West scared African leaders who realised that they lacked the military, economic and technological capacities to play such 'high politics'. Not surprisingly, African states subscribed to nonalignment in order to stay away from the Cold War.[12]

The establishment of the Non-Aligned Movement (NAM) not only facilitated the construction of a new political platform for underdeveloped nations to assert themselves against the emergence of nuclear regimes, but also gave emerging African states a forum in which to articulate their views. This of course did not prevent all forms of economic, ideological and cultural alignments and realignments with the great powers with consequences for domestic construction of political relations. Following the September 1961 joint statement by the United States and the Soviet Union embodied in the 'McCloy-Zorin Statement' an 18-member Conference on Disarmament (CD) was set up by the UN General Assembly to pursue, among other objectives, the goals of a general and complete disarmament and collateral measures to contain proliferation. The CD included three African states (Nigeria, Egypt and Ethiopia), an acknowledgment of the importance of non-nuclear and nonaligned positions on disarmament. This period marked the beginning of international redefinition of disarmament as going beyond mere reduction in the stockpiles of nations or the reduction of conventional armaments to the more concrete issues of establishing NWFZ; non-proliferation; building trust among NWS; and the economic, environmental, and social implications of nuclear-weapons development. The UN not only began to focus on the issue of development but also began to declare 'Disarmament Decades' alongside its declaration of 'Development Decades'. Though the Organisation of African Unity (OAU) was established by independent African states in 1963 as an expression of a collective pan-Africanist will, it concerned itself initially with the liberation of colonies, the termination of minority rule and apartheid in Southern Africa and the resolution of boundary disputes.

Africa's security perceptions had changed by 1960 when the French government carried out nuclear tests in the Sahara desert.[13] These tests, which had direct implications for severe contamination, also had the potential for sparking off a proliferation problem in the continent by getting some African states interested in nuclear weapons. This would then drag the continent into the Cold War. This test by the French gave most African states the impetus to oppose nuclear proliferation and to appreciate first hand how vulnerable the continent was to nuclear disaster or contamination. In fact some African states like Nigeria, as demonstration of total opposition to such tests and nuclear proliferation, broke diplomatic relations with France. African leaders seized on every opportunity to complain loudly about how the 'remarkable development of science and technology, instead of being placed at the service of peoples, has, on the contrary, been used to produce arms in frightening numbers and of incredible sophistication, thus constituting a constant menace to the survival of the human race'. They therefore insisted that the arms race could not 'guarantee any other than an illusory security', while the proliferation of arms in particular would pose 'a dangerous threat to the security and stability of the African continent and stand in the way of our progress towards development and the well-being of our peoples'.[14] Since the OAU had not yet been established, concerned African leaders led an initiative at the UN General Assembly which adopted Resolution 16/1652 on 24 November 1961 declaring Africa a denuclearised zone. The resolution drew attention to the implications of the arms race; the dangers of nuclear-weapons proliferation; the dangers of further nuclear tests; the importance of nonalignment with the nuclear powers; and the need to focus scarce resources on the challenges of growth and development. Specifically, the UN resolution called on member states to 'refrain from carrying out any nuclear tests in Africa, and from using the continent to test, store, or transport nuclear weapons'.[15] With its formation in 1963, the OAU took off from the General Assembly resolution and the issues of declaring the continent a denuclearised zone became a central part of its programmes, agitations and policies.

In August 1963 African representatives at the UN were urged to unite in the struggle to declare Africa a denuclearised zone and to support a partial nuclear test ban treaty. At the Cairo inaugural conference following the establishment of the OAU in 1963, African leaders reaffirmed their commitment to keeping the continent as a NWFZ. In 1964 the OAU adopted the 'Declaration on the Denuclearisation of Africa'. This was the very first regional 'unilateral renunciation of the right to develop nuclear weapons'. Thus in some sense the 'concept of the nuclear-weapon-free zone as a major component of a non-proliferation regime owes a great deal to the African initiative'.[16] The declaration also emphasised the peaceful uses of nuclear technology in the interest of development. The OAU called for an end to the arms race; the destruction of existing nuclear weapons; the removal of foreign military bases in the continent; and the urgent need for a disarmament agreement among the nuclear powers under international supervision. The OAU leaders also called on the UN to convene an international conference aimed at concluding an international treaty on the denuclearisation of Africa.

This was endorsed by the UN General Assembly in Resolution 20/2033 which asserted that 'the denuclearisation of various areas of the world would help to achieve the desired goal of prohibiting the use of nuclear weapons', and that 'the denuclearisation of Africa would be a practical step towards the prevention of the further spread of nuclear weapons in the world and towards the achievement of general and complete disarmament and of the objectives of the United Nations'. It reiterated the earlier demands of the OAU and called on the NWS 'not to transfer nuclear weapons, scientific data or technological assistance to the national control of any state, either directly or indirectly, in any form which may be used to assist such states in the manufacture or use of nuclear weapons in Africa'.

At the 1979 meeting of the OAU Council of Ministers, the final resolution specifically addressed the 'threat posed to the security of Africa as a result of [South Africa's] nuclear capability through extensive material and technological assistance which it received from its Western partners'. It reiterated earlier OAU resolutions on the denuclearisation of Africa, condemned the collaboration between Israel and South Africa; and called for the 'peaceful uses of nuclear energy'. Thus it can be said that the 'problem of South Africa' was critical for forming the attitude and responses of the OAU to the denuclearisation of the continent.

In 1984 the OAU called for regional conferences on security, disarmament and development. One such conference, supported by the UN, was held in Lome, Togo in August 1985. It is interesting to note that at this meeting the primary concerns of delegates and African leaders included the dangers posed to Africa by nuclear proliferation; the seeming reluctance of the nuclear powers to pursue comprehensive disarmament; the gradual incorporation of the continent into the Cold War; the support which South Africa was enjoying in its nuclear programme from Western nations and suppliers; and the urgent need for the region to confront deepening economic and environmental problems rather than pursue a nuclear agenda. In his opening remarks, Prvoslav Davinic argued very forcefully that the preference for WMD and other conventional weapons in place of promoting development 'constitutes one of the greatest challenges facing mankind today', and that 'national security cannot be found at constantly higher and higher levels of armaments'.[17]

Though the UN General Assembly approved OAU resolutions on Africa's anti-nuclear agenda, nothing was done internationally to ensure the denuclearisation of the continent. As well, though the Cold War was already well underway, Africa did not constitute an immediate threat to either power bloc and the powers did not see any reason to take the region more seriously, after all, 'Africa [had] neither recorded a Chernobyl-type nuclear accident, nor even a Goiania-type radiological incident as in Brazil; and no African country [had] been found in gross violation of its safeguards agreements'.[18] As well, though nationalist movements and independent states had all opted for nonalignment, African states were still under the full economic control and manipulation of foreign powers:

> In a period of intense rivalry such as the Cold War, those powers were not at all prepared to remove the advantages and resources of Africa from their strategic considerations. A nuclear demilitarisation of Africa had consequences which those powers with bases on the continent were not prepared to accept.[19]

Clearly, therefore, Africans have expressed a long-standing interest in denuclearising the continent, largely as an expression of their priorities, but also as a demonstration of the region's comparative powerlessness in global geostrategic calculations. However, intentions were not enough. Rivalry between the superpowers, among other factors, delayed the adoption and ratification of a NWFZ for over three decades.

Impediments to Denuclearisation in Africa

In spite of Africa's quest to denuclearise the continent in the 1960s and the numerous resolutions by the OAU and the UN, the process made only very limited progress. There are four main reasons for this.

First, the nuclear powers had no interest in undermining their strategic advantages in the continent by pushing for denuclearisation and the closure of military bases. They, in particular the United States, simply ignored all the pleas and declarations from the OAU and the UN. US policies were dictated by self-interest and the desire to gain some strategic advantage over the Soviet Union irrespective of the costs. Its adventures in South Africa, Angola, Zimbabwe, Somalia and Namibia are pointers in this direction. Thus the strategic interests of the nuclear powers were put above those of the region.

The second reason had to do with the foreign interest in the exploitation of Africa's resources such as uranium in Chad and South Africa. Denuclearising the continent meant that access to these resources would become regulated and restricted. As well, with denuclearisation the strategic space age minerals of the continent could become more expensive. Thus the economic motivations of the nuclear powers overrode the security interests of Africa.

A third reason for the delay in the process of denuclearising Africa was the existence of racist and minority regimes in Southern Africa. This made it very difficult to reach agreement as these countries were not part of the OAU and many had strong links with Western powers in the hopes of sustaining their nefarious and notorious regimes. Thus the political conditions and balances needed to reach agreement on denuclearisation did not exist until the mid-1970s when countries like Zimbabwe and Angola became liberated from colonial bondage. In fact the particular case of apartheid South Africa continued to convince several African leaders that special actions needed to be taken to terminate apartheid. The situation or perception of how dangerous South Africa's apartheid regime was only became hardened with rumours about the nuclear programme of the apartheid regime.

Finally, political independence threw up a whole range of contradictions and conflicts within Africa. Personality conflicts, coups and counter-coups, ethnic conflicts, border disputes and religious upheavals — all combined to create uncertainty and suspicions in and among Africans. Some countries had leaders who did not appreciate the need for denuclearisation. Many felt that Western support for apartheid in South Africa made the need for a so-called 'black bomb' necessary. Some leaders had exuberant pan-Africanist ideas and were prepared to use every possible means to attain such goals. The net result was lack of consensus, inability to generate the political will to support resolutions and misdirected discourses on the need for denuclearisation and the peaceful uses of nuclear technology. Taken together, these factors delayed the efforts by the OAU to initiate and establish a NWFZ. To be sure, there were constant efforts at passing resolutions within the UN and the OAU. But the realities of global political balances, great power economic interests, security perceptions, the South African challenge and deepening internal contradictions vitiated such efforts.

Imperatives for a Nuclear-Weapon-Free Zone in Africa

The main imperatives for the establishment of a NWFZ in Africa have been the intense competition for ideological-cum-political control of Africa by the two superpowers, the US and the former USSR; the increasing nuclear capability of apartheid South Africa and its aggressive military incursions into the frontline states; the preponderance of conflicts in the continent; and the growing interest and influence of some NWS like Israel. However, by the late 1970s 'the goal of African efforts . . . was not the conclusion of a treaty, but rather the adoption of measures to prevent the goal of a nuclear-weapon-free zone from being irrevocably undermined by the growing nuclear capability of South Africa and its cooperation with non-African states'.[20] African leaders were united in the fact that the process of disarmament globally and for attaining the declaration of Africa as a NWFZ would be 'greatly facilitated by removing the system of apartheid maintained by the racist regime in South Africa, which [represented] a serious threat to the peaceful development of Africa and symbolise[d] the most appalling defiance of human dignity'.[21]

South Africa had not signed the NPT and was therefore not bound by international regulations. Its policy of apartheid had made it a pariah state in the global community and this only hardened its commitment to unorthodox ways of strengthening its security. South Africa was also illegally occupying Namibia and resisting the efforts of the South West African People's Organisation (SWAPO) in its struggle for independence. In the then Rhodesia (now Zimbabwe) a white minority regime led by Ian Smith continued to be supported and subsidised by apartheid South Africa in its so-called Unilateral Declaration of Independence (UDI). In Angola, Guinea-Bissau and Mozambique, South Africa continued to collude with Portugal to perpetuate one of the most uncivilised and brutal colonial regimes in history. When Portuguese colonialism was militarily defeated in the 1970s, South Africa continued its policy of subversion, attacks, harassment and destruction of lives and properties against the former Portuguese colonies and the frontline states. Finally, African states were very aware of the military might of South Africa, that it had established a very mobile and integrated military establishment whose sophistication and power far exceeded that of any other African nation. Its military arsenal was equally intimidating and its defence budget and security expenditures were clear pointers to the power of the South African military. African leaders were therefore left in no doubt that the continued existence of such a dangerous power in the continent posed a direct threat to the continent's security. What was more, the ideological battles between the Western and Eastern blocs in South Africa evidenced in Eastern support for the African National Congress (ANC) and Western direct and/or indirect support for the apartheid arrangement further convinced African leaders that the region would be dragged into the nuclear race by the great powers.

The South African nuclear programme had been initiated in 1957 when it exported uranium to the US and UK. In 1961 South Africa purchased the 20 MW Safari-I atomic reactor from the US. In 1968 it acquired the Safari-II reactor, and a pilot uranium enrichment facility was established in Valindaba through the assistance of West Germany in 1971. Five years later South Africa signed a contract with France to establish two power reactors. In 1979 the American Vela Satellite allegedly picked up signals of what was believed to be a South African nuclear test on the Atlantic Ocean. South Africa denied it but African states were fully convinced that it was a South African project with Western collaboration. Later, Israel was to become involved in South Africa's nuclear programme. It is instructive that though South Africa had not acceded to the NPT, was operating a cruel and inhuman system of apartheid, had been isolated by the international community through several collective and unilateral sanctions, Western nations, especially Germany, France and the US, went ahead to support a nuclear programme for whatever purposes. Western nations even went as far as refusing to support the demand by African states for South Africa to be removed from taking the African seat on the board of governors at the IAEA.

In 1977 the Soviet Union announced that it had discovered a nuclear test site in the Kalahari Desert. African leaders concluded that it had been constructed by South Africa to test its nuclear weapons. This only confirmed African suspicions about South Africa's nuclear programme and led to a frenzy in the continent. While some argued that Nigeria had to develop a counter bomb, many felt that the answer was not to encourage a nuclear arms race in Africa but to work to dismantle whatever South Africa had constructed. In 1979 the UN General Assembly mandated a Group of Experts from France, the Philippines, Nigeria, Sweden, the Soviet Union and Venezuela to study South Africa's nuclear plans and capability. The Group concluded that 'there is no doubt that South Africa has the technical capability to make nuclear weapons and the necessary means of delivery'.[22] Unfortunately, this was not sufficient to get the Security Council to do much about dismantling or terminating South Africa's nuclear agenda. Part of the reason was the strong economic and cultural ties between the apartheid regime and the Western nations and their corporations.

The South African Challenge

The most critical development in the eventual establishment of a NWFZ which was signed by all African states in 1996 can be found in the announcement by President F. W. de Klerk in March 1993 to a stunned world that South Africa actually had nuclear weapons; it had manufactured six nuclear fission devises; this had been done in secret without foreign assistance; the nuclear weapons had been dismantled and destroyed; and South Africa was now prepared to accede to the NPT and work towards the declaration of Africa as a NWFZ. In an address to a special joint session of parliament, de Klerk announced that 'at one stage South Africa did develop a limited nuclear deterrent capability'. He further informed parliamentarians that in 'early 1990 final effect was given to decisions that all the nuclear devices should be dismantled and destroyed'. According to de Klerk, the non-nuclear components of the weapons were destroyed while the highly enriched uranium (HEU) components were melted down. This act of denuclearisation, according to de Klerk, marked a new beginning in South Africa for 'international cooperation and trust'. As demonstration of this new era, in 1995 South Africa gave full and active support to the indefinite extension of the NPT.[23]

African leaders were shocked at the confirmation of their long-held fears because they had no previous information as to how far South Africa had gone. As well, there were those who doubted the claims by de Klerk that outside help had not gone into the development of the weapons. The romance between apartheid South Africa and Israel convinced many that outside help had gone into the project. While it was known that the United States and France, among other countries, 'provided South Africa with civilian nuclear technology and assistance that did not directly abet the bomb program', it was equally known that 'this cooperation nonetheless increased the technical competence of South Africa's nuclear engineers, scientists and technicians'.[24] David Albright has noted that a 'can do' mentality contributed to South Africa's achievements in the area of nuclear-weapons development: 'because of its technological capabilities . . . South Africa depended less on imports than Iraq or Pakistan did.' Nevertheless, support from the outside world, especially the US, was also critical. Staff members of its nuclear programme were trained in Europe and in the US; the United States supplied its Safari-1 reactor as well as about 100 kilograms of weapon-grade uranium fuel between 1965 and 1975; and when sanctions became rather strong in the 1970s, South Africa designed a clandestine procurement plan and strengthened its secret collaboration with Israel for 'technology, knowledge, material, and equipment'. He concludes that by the 1980s:

> South Africa had imported machine tools, furnaces, and other equipment for its nuclear-weapons program. Most of these items were not proscribed by international nuclear export controls. But they were imported in violation of international sanctions imposed on the apartheid regime.[25]

Within the ANC and black South Africans there was speculation that the new South African position had been necessitated by a desire to avoid the nuclear weapons, along with the related technology, from being inherited by a black majority government. It was reported that the 'U.S. and other foreign governments had . . . been putting pressure on Pretoria to destroy any nuclear weapons technology and high grade uranium before a new government, most likely dominated by the ANC, comes to power. Washington is reported to have been particularly concerned with the ANC's link with Libya.'[26] Whatever the hidden reasons, the OAU and the entire world was relieved at the announcement. As J. W. de Villiers, Chairman of the Atomic Energy

Corporation of South Africa, has noted, 'South Africa represents the world's first instance of nuclear rollback, a state which has unilaterally and voluntarily relinquished nuclear weapons'.[27]

Why did South Africa, which had been *the* obstacle to the denuclearisation of Africa, suddenly have a change of heart? Five major reasons can be adduced for this dramatic development.

First, the end of the Cold War altered the strategic considerations which had hitherto informed the calculations of the nuclear powers. South Africa was no longer sure of unalloyed support from its Western partners who were more interested in the economic resources of the country.

The second reason had to do with the general change in the political landscape of the region. Hostilities had more or less ended in Angola as Jonas Savimbi was prepared to be part of a democratic contestation for power. As well, 50 000 Cuban troops had withdrawn from Angola thus reducing the security threat perceived by the apartheid regime. Namibia had become free. The frontline states were becoming democratic, one-party regimes and life presidents were being ousted in democratic elections, international non-government organisations (NGOs) were becoming very influential in the region and the content and context of politics were experiencing dramatic reconfiguration. South African leaders realised that they needed to follow the trend or remain isolated. One way of winning the support of Africa and the world, and demonstrating that it had actually turned a new leaf, was not just the termination of apartheid but also the dismantling of a dangerous nuclear programme.

The third reason was the official ending of apartheid, the recognition of the ANC and other opposition parties, the release of Nelson Mandela from prison after 27 years and the commencement of negotiations for a transition to democratic rule. These developments would have been meaningless if the nuclear programme had not been terminated. These developments terminated the armed struggle, ended military support for the ANC from the frontline states and Eastern bloc nations and reduced or eliminated the general security threats perceived by the apartheid regime. This situation rendered redundant the need for a nuclear deterrence capability.

The fourth reason why South Africa changed its policy had to do with its desire to join the pan-African and international community with a clean slate and to take advantage of the benefits of the NPT and the safeguards provided by the IAEA. The election of de Klerk in 1989 established a new, more moderate and realistic direction in South Africa's domestic and foreign policies. Thus, following the dismantling of its nuclear programme, it called for comprehensive inspections, made full disclosures far beyond what was required and acceded to the NPT in July 1991. It also accepted and signed the safeguards agreement of the IAEA.

Finally, South Africa needed to win the confidence of African states and the OAU. The dismantling of the institutions and structures of apartheid was one way of doing this. The second way was the dismantling of is nuclear programme. Countries like Nigeria and Libya had used South Africa as the reason why they were interested in a nuclear programme to protect the rest of the continent against the minority regime. With its new position on nuclear-weapons development, South Africa single-handedly exploded the myth of the 'black bomb' and opened the way to the declaration of Africa as a NWFZ.

To be sure, the declaration and accession to international agreements did not completely erase questions about South Africa's nuclear programme. Which countries aided South Africa in its weapons programme? Were the nuclear weapons developed for peaceful, defensive or aggressive purposes? How did South Africa develop the technology and acquire the components without detection? Is it true that Western nations, with all the satellites and other sophisticated methods of detection, were unaware that South Africa's nuclear programme had developed to such an extent as declared by de Klerk? Has South Africa safely disposed of the fissionable materials and the components it had stockpiled over the years? While these questions are important, even critical, the South African example is clear demonstration of the fact that security can be provided by nuclear disarmament rather than by the proliferation and accumulation of 'unlimited destructive capability'.[28]

To the South African issue and new commitment, the desire of African states and the long-standing commitment of the OAU to denuclearisation, we must add the deepening economic crisis in Africa as an impetus for pursuing a NWFZ. By the end of the 1970s Africa was in serious economic trouble.[29] Infrastructure and public institutions were in decay. Poverty had become endemic. Political elites and governments were not just under pressure but were facing stiff and violent challenges from their peoples. Foreign aid and investments were down. States were failing as ethnic and other forms of violence became commonplace. The debt crisis had reached unprecedented proportions as debt servicing took large chunks of foreign exchange earnings and most African states became 'debt distressed'. Hunger, malnutrition, disease and disillusionment had come to inform the daily lives of the majority of Africans. Africa came to account for about half of the world's and three-quarters of the least developed nations' refugees as AIDS, violence, coups, counter-coups, religious violence and institutional decay ravaged even the hitherto more prosperous and stable states like Nigeria, Zambia, Kenya, Senegal and Malawi. Economic reform programmes packaged and imposed by the International Monetary Fund (IMF) and World Bank had failed woefully as badly delegitimised, non-hegemonic, unstable and inefficient states faced new challenges and pressures from within and without.[30] The end of the Cold War had affected the dictators in the continent who also faced new demands for human rights, social justice, accountability, democracy and democratisation. In societies which had been constructed and run as dictatorships, these new demands required expensive, risky and very challenging restructuring of socio-economic and political relations.

Beginning in 1980 African states decided to redefine and expand the meaning of security from military and nuclear to social, cultural and economic dimensions. The adoption of the *Lagos Plan of Action for the Socio-Economic Transformation of Africa 1980–AD2000* (LPA) marked the beginning of a new agenda.[31] This document was to serve as a blueprint for the socio-economic transformation of the African continent through policies which would build self-reliance, mobilisation, growth and development. The LPA (like other documents since then) was a confession of the failure of past strategies which relied on violence, intolerance, repression, human rights abuses, one-party and one-person rule, military juntas, outlandish military expenditures and irresponsible policy making. As Tilahun W. Selassie has lamented, 'With their war for political independence won, 53 African states are now fighting a more difficult war against hunger, malnutrition, disease and economic deprivation. For that they sorely need a peaceful environment'.[32] Thus, at the continental level, there was an increasing realisation of the urgent need to move from 'nuclear security to human security' by mediating contradictions, opening up suffocated political spaces, mobilising resources and articulating holistic regional and national programmes for growth and development.[33]

The Treaty of Pelindaba: An Evaluation

At the sixty-second ordinary session of the OAU Council of Ministers in Addis Ababa in June 1995, a resolution was adopted in favour of the implementation of a treaty declaring Africa a NWFZ. This resolution adopted the draft Pelindaba Treaty prepared by the Group of Experts. The OAU heads of state and government approved the Council's resolution at its thirty-first ordinary session in late June 1995 and also approved the offer of the Mubarak Government in Egypt to host the signing of the treaty. The signing of the Treaty of Pelindaba in Cairo on 11 April 1996 was therefore the outcome of strong initiatives from leading African states like South Africa, Egypt and Nigeria, as well as of the factors outlined earlier. The treaty itself was named after the headquarters of the South African Atomic Energy Corporation where the draft treaty was finalised on 2 June 1995.[34] Thus, complementing the treaties of Tlatelolco and Rarotonga, the Treaty of Pelindaba 'effectively bans the manufacture or use of nuclear weapons throughout the southern hemisphere'.[35] Forty-nine of the 53 African states signed the treaty while two – Madagascar and Seychelles – abstained. Liberia and Somalia could not sign because domestic upheavals prevented them from being represented.

The immediate background to the treaty can be traced to the strategy meeting of African states at the United Nations in 1990 on how to actualise the 1964 Declaration on the Denuclearisation of Africa. After the meeting, the African leaders led an initiative in December 1990 for the establishment of a Group of Experts with the specific mandate 'to examine the modalities and elements for the preparation and implementation of a convention or treaty on the denuclearisation of Africa' (General Assembly Resolution 45/56A). At the 54th and 55th ordinary sessions 1991 and 1992, the OAU Council of Ministers took note of the changing global order, developments within Africa, especially in Southern Africa, and concluded that the time was conducive to the implementation of the July 1964 Cairo declaration on the denuclearisation of Africa. In December 1992 the mandate of the Group of Experts was extended to include the 'drawing up of a draft treaty or convention on the denuclearisation of Africa' (Resolution 47/76). To ensure that the Group's work was comprehensive, its membership was broad-based including representatives of the various sub-regions, the OAU, the Economic Commission for Africa (ECA), the UN and the IAEA. Representatives of similar NWFZ from the Pacific and Latin America were invited as observers. Representatives of the NWS as well as of Portugal and Spain were invited to special meetings which dealt with the interests of extra-regional states. After six meetings over five years in Addis Ababa, Lome, Harare, Windhoek and Johannesburg, a draft treaty was produced in Johannesburg in June 1995.[36] Within a few months, it had gone through all the authority levels of the OAU and was signed in 1996.

The Treaty is significant in several ways. In its preamble, the Treaty acknowledged previous efforts and initiatives by the UN and OAU towards the establishment of a NWFZ in Africa. It noted that NWFZ were a 'most effective means for preventing the proliferation, both horizontal and vertical, of nuclear weapons'.[37] The document stated its ultimate goal as the attainment of a 'world entirely free of nuclear weapons', and noted that the African Nuclear-Weapon-Free Zone (ANWFZ) 'will constitute an important step towards strengthening the non-proliferation regime, promoting cooperation in the peaceful uses of nuclear energy, promoting general and complete disarmament and enhancing regional and international peace and security'. The framers of the Treaty saw the initiative as a major contribution to global disarmament efforts and that the NWFZ will 'protect African states against possible nuclear attacks on their territories'. The Treaty also noted that the NWFZ does not in any way contradict or negate the right to utilise the positive aspects of nuclear science and technology. In short, the preamble to the Pelindaba Treaty is a heavily loaded statement of the hopes, expectations, commitments and trust which African states have in the global system. It is also in some measure a rather overly optimistic expression of confidence in the rational calculations of the nuclear powers since it assumes that just by declaring itself a NWFZ, it will always be respected by the powers and protected by the provisions of the treaty.

At a general level, the signatories all pledged 'not to conduct research on, develop, test, or stockpile nuclear explosive devices; to prohibit the stationing of nuclear devices on their territory; to maintain the highest standards of protection of nuclear materials, facilities, and equipment; and to prohibit the dumping of radioactive waste'.[38] Articles 3–6 deal with non-proliferation which African states take very seriously. The Treaty covers not just nuclear weapons but also 'nuclear explosive devices' which are defined in Article 1 as any device capable of releasing nuclear energy irrespective of whether it is for peaceful or aggressive purposes. These provisions deal specifically with prevention of stationing, renunciation of nuclear explosive devices, prohibition of testing and, for those which are already in possession of nuclear weapons, the declaration, dismantling and destruction of such devices.[39]

In calling on members to renounce nuclear weapons completely, the Treaty provided a comprehensive definition of covered areas including research, development, manufacture, stockpiling or control. Members are not to seek assistance or provide assistance to others within and outside the region in any of these areas. However, this is unique to the African treaty and seems to have drawn a lot from the South African experience. This all-encompassing and inflexible provision seems to have been mediated in Article 4 which deals with the stationing of nuclear weapons. The members agree to prevent the stationing of nuclear weapons on their territories but could reach no agreement on foreign aircraft and ships with nuclear devices or weapons visiting their ports. Article 4(2) leaves that decision to the discretion of individual members. This is unfortunate as a more definitive and stringent provision could have closed all loopholes. Article 5, however, prohibits any form of testing of nuclear weapons in any member territory. Treaty members are also prohibited from assisting others or performing any sort of test anywhere else. This provision strengthens Article 1 on 'nuclear devices' thus making the ban complete.

Article 6 of the Pelindaba Treaty is unique to Africa. It deals with the declaration, dismantling and destruction of nuclear explosive devices. The article also deals with the conversion of such devices. Clearly informed by the South African experience with a secret nuclear agenda, Article 6 requires member states to openly declare their capability to manufacture such nuclear explosive devices, and if they already had one to dismantle and destroy not just the weapons but also the facilities for production. Article 7 responds directly to the growing incidents of toxic waste dumping in Africa. Though the OAU had responded to this with the Bamako Convention on the Ban of the Import into Africa and Control of Transboundary Movement and Management of Hazardous Wastes, this article required member states to uphold the provisions of that convention.[40] The treaty also requires that signatories not 'assist or encourage the dumping of radioactive wastes and other radioactive matter anywhere within the African nuclear-weapon-free zone'. This article strengthens the position adopted in the preamble to the effect that the OAU was 'Determined to keep Africa free of environmental pollution by radioactive wastes and other radioactive matter'. Withdrawal from the treaty requires a written explanation to the Secretary-General of the OAU of reasons which must not only be 'extraordinary', but also capable of infringing or abridging the 'supreme interests', of a member country.

While the treaty is clear on ensuring that Africa is respected and acknowledged as a NWFZ, Article 8 stipulates that

> as part of their efforts to strengthen their security, stability, and development, the Parties undertake to promote individually and collectively the use of nuclear science and technology for economic and social development. To this end, they undertake to establish and strengthen mechanisms for cooperation at the bilateral, subregional, and regional levels.

The Treaty encourages its signatories to take advantage of the benefits of the IAEA. Clearly therefore, the treaty expects African states to pursue the peaceful utilisation of nuclear science and technology at collective rather than national levels. Hence the name African NWFZ was carefully chosen to reflect the desire to keep nuclear *weapons* out of the region. As Olu Adeniji has rightly observed, African states 'were determined . . . not only [to] provide a legally binding renunciation of a nuclear arms race, but also [to] create an enabling environment of mutual trust and cooperation in the peaceful uses of nuclear energy and nuclear technology for economic and social development'.[41]

This provision raises critical issues which are not yet part of the discourse on denuclearisation, especially in Africa: does 'peaceful uses' mean the same thing as 'developmental uses'? The latter refer to the deliberate and socially-based articulation of an agenda which utilises the science and technology of nuclear development to alter society, relations of production, patterns of accumulation and the improvement in the living conditions of the majority. It cannot remain an elitist affair designed to empower transnational corporations and members of the elite class in their various activities. The inequalities, tensions, contradictions and divisions which such utilisation would breed could be as dangerous as the direct use of WMD. Thus it is not enough to simply declare a need to use nuclear technology for 'peaceful uses'. Institutions and structures must be put in place to support such a project and demonstrate an open commitment to altering the appropriation of the information, knowledge and results by a small clique at the expense of the larger society. For Africa, with its gross inequality in the distribution of resources, power and opportunities, this reconceptualisation is very critical. Pelindaba does not address this issue sufficiently enough. As well, global discourses on denuclearisation have not tried to move away from the so-called peaceful uses to be more definitive about developmental uses.

To maintain safeguards, regulations and control, Article 9 outlines processes for the verification of peaceful uses of nuclear energy 'under strict non-proliferation measures to provide assurance of exclusively peaceful uses'. It also requires signatories to 'conclude a comprehensive safeguards agreement with IAEA for the purpose of verifying compliance'. Article 10 requires signatories to maintain very high security over nuclear installations, equipment and facilities in order to check theft, vandalism, illegal handling and proliferation. Article 11 prohibits attacks on the nuclear installations of member states. The Treaty does not however specify what would happen if such an attack were to occur. The truth is that Africa is counting on the conscience of the world to protect it from such an attack since no African state has retaliatory capacity. Article 12 establishes an African Commission on Nuclear Energy and requires member states to submit annual reports on their nuclear programmes or activities to the Commission. Member states are also enjoined not to serve as sources of fissionable materials or other equipment to other non-NWS without ensuring full compliance with IAEA safeguards. This provision regulates and places a high degree of responsibility over commercial transactions.

Three Protocols accompany the Pelindaba Treaty. The first covers assurances from the NWS that they would not use or threaten signatories with nuclear weapons or against any territory within the zone. The second requires the NWS not to test nuclear weapons within the zone nor to assist in the testing of such weapons or other explosive devices anywhere within the zone. The third requires extra-zonal states with claims to territories within the zone to apply the provisions of the Treaty to such territory. Britain, France, the US and China signed two protocols pledging to cooperate.[42] Washington saw its signing of the two protocols as a clear demonstration of commitment to the 'Principles and Objectives for Non-Proliferation and Disarmament' adopted in May 1995 which indefinitely extended the NPT as well as evidence of America's 'strong support for a nuclear-weapon-free zone throughout the African continent'.[43]

The Future of Africa as a NWFZ

It is instructive that with the signing of the Treaty of Pelindaba in 1996, the nuclear debate in the continent seems to have been mediated, if not completely terminated. For one thing, it is now realised just how dangerous South Africa was as no African government had a clear idea as to how far it had gone with its nuclear programme. One of the main responses to fears about South Africa's nuclear programme had been for counter-nuclear programmes by, possibly, Nigeria, since it was large enough and had the resources for such an expensive project. It is now clear that such a race would not have enhanced Africa's security, could have forced South Africa to expand its own programme and might have culminated in some unfortunate accident or confrontation.[44] With the Pelindaba Treaty, all African states have committed themselves to nonproliferation, to focusing on the challenges of economic development, and to non-cooperation with outside interests in the development of nuclear capability.

Pelindaba has brought South Africa fully within the African security spectrum. It has acceded to all international programmes and protocols and joined other African states to define the continent as a NWFZ. South Africa has joined the Zangger Committee. This means that all future nuclear exports requiring safeguards will be listed. It has also joined the Nuclear Suppliers Group as well as the MTCR. Nelson Mandela has given very clear and strong commitments to Africa and the world that South African scientists and engineers as well as its resources will never again be devoted to the development and manufacture of WMD. In May 1993 the South African Parliament, in a strong move to support Mandela's position, passed legislation prohibiting South Africans from being involved in any way in the development and manufacture of nuclear weapons. In 1995 President Bill Clinton approved a new 'South Africa-U.S. Agreement on the Peaceful Use of Nuclear Energy' which replaced the earlier one of 22 August 1957.[45] Without doubt, this is a critical agreement which goes a long way to cement or demonstrate South Africa's commitment to a NWFZ in Africa. But is this an equal agreement? The United States still has nuclear weapons and South Africa has none. Nonetheless, the main security threat within the continent, which had been a source of worry for the OAU and African leaders since the early 1960s, has been eliminated with the Treaty of Pelindaba and other bilateral and multilateral agreements.

Pelindaba has redirected the nuclear debate in Africa from deterrence and confrontation to peaceful and developmental uses. While the line between peaceful and non-peaceful uses could be quite thin, as the region experiences more political liberalisation, there are reasons to assume that democratic, transparent and accountable regimes will engage more in dialogues, consensus and economic and social development. With the provisions of the Treaty emphasising 'collective' as against national uses of nuclear technology, we can envisage more interest in and attention to the peaceful uses of nuclear technology. It is quite encouraging to see how far South Africa was willing to go in its disclosure statements, its role in the indefinite extension of the NPT, its role in the establishment of the NWFZ and its offer to host the headquarters of the African Nuclear Energy Commission. As well, when South Africa announced its unilateral and voluntary denuclearisation, it also converted its hitherto secret nuclear-weapons facility known as the Kentron Circle Facility (now known as Advena) to a 'commercial facility offering high-tech products for aerospace, mining, medical, and other industries. Advena has become an experiment in the conversion of nuclear weapons-related expertise to . . . commercial production . . . for domestic and export markets'.[46] In this way, Africa, through South Africa, is showing an excellent example of the good that could come from nuclear science and technology.

The Treaty of Pelindaba, along with other similar treaties, poses a fundamental challenge to the great powers not only to respect the NWFZ but also to take the issue of disarmament more seriously in the interest of global peace. The treaties serve as a major impediment to proliferation and would serve to make it much more difficult for the nuclear powers to engage in the traditional tactic of promoting proliferation while resisting disarmament. Clearly, a regional approach is critical to the realisation of a denuclearised world. The security threats experienced in other third world regions in terms of heavily armed neighbours really do not exist in Africa where most 'threats' and sources of instability are domestic. Yet Pelindaba must not and cannot exist on its own. The UN, the developed nations, the ECA and the OAU, as well as regional organisations like the Economic Community of West African States (ECOWAS), must give support to the goals of a NWFZ and the challenge of development and democracy.

For the 21st century, the focus of African states should be on the faithful adherence to Treaty provisions, maintaining safeguards and exploiting the numerous benefits of nuclear science and technology. Developing countries, in their quest for growth and development, are going to keep looking for forms of nuclear technology to accelerate this process. In this era of globalisation, it is even more imperative for them to seek to exploit the unprecedented expansions of the frontiers of science and technology. When the IAEA was created in 1957, it was designed to prevent proliferation and maintain a uniform international system of safeguards. More specifically, according to Article II of the IAEA's statute, it was expected that it would 'accelerate and enlarge the contribution of atomic energy to peace, health and prosperity throughout the world. It shall ensure so far as it is able, that assistance provided by it or at its request or under its supervision or control is not used in such a way as to further any military purpose'. Clearly therefore, its goal was the curtailment of the expansion of nuclear-weapons production and the expansion of its peaceful applications.[47] Between the entry into force of the NPT in 1970 and its indefinite extension in 1995, more states have come to accept IAEA safeguard standards as well as punitive actions against violators.

The ANWFZ is not and must not be seen as an end in itself. It can at best be perceived as a means to harnessing the advantages of nuclear science and technology, safeguarding the region from the predatory activities of proliferators and redirecting attention away from aggressive security considerations to basic human needs and the constraints of dependence, domination, marginalisation and underdevelopment. As Benson Agu has noted, 'African countries encounter many problems in the areas of health care, agriculture and industry whose solutions could benefit from the use of nuclear techniques, if the countries were in a position to apply them'.[48] Unfortunately, only a handful of nations are able or are in a position to take advantage of the peaceful uses of nuclear science and technology. Thus, policies within and amongst African states must focus on the uses of nuclear technology for power generation, food production, disease eradication, industry, natural resources exploration and development, environmental monitoring, food irradiation technology, cancer therapy and other aspects of medicine and research.

Notes

1. George H. Quester, 'Toward an International Nuclear Security Policy', *Washington Quarterly* 17 (Autumn 1994), pp. 1–2. (UTCAT version).
2. Sola Ogunbanwo, 'History of the Efforts to Establish an African Nuclear-Weapon-Free Zone', *Disarmament* 19:1 (1996), p. 19.
3. Libya is said to have constructed an underground chemical-weapons facility at ai Tarhunah, about 80 km southeast of Tripoli, the country's capital. Though the US signed the two protocols of the ANWFZ 'without reservations', its officials have continued to make statements to the effect that nuclear weapons could be used to destroy the Libyan facility. See William M. Arkin, 'Nuking Libya', *Bulletin of the Atomic Scientists* 52 (July–August 1996), p. 64.
4. Deepa Ollapally, 'US–India Tensions: Misperceptions on Nuclear Proliferation', *Foreign Affairs* 74 (January–February 1995), p. 1. For a discussion of the Middle East see Shai Feldman, 'Middle East Nuclear Stability: The State of the Region and the State of the Debate', *Journal of International Affairs* 49 (Summer 1995), pp. 205–30.
5. See Alexander Kalyadin and Elina Kirchenko, 'Nonproliferation After the New York Conference', *International Affairs* 7 (1995), pp. 27–33.
6. David Albright, 'A Curious Conversion', *Bulletin of the Atomic Scientists* 49 (June 1993), p. 10.
7. See T. V. Paul, 'Strengthening the Non-Proliferation Regime: The Role of Coercive Sanctions', *International Journal* 51 (Summer 1996), pp. 440–65.
8. There are about 485 nuclear power stations in the world (operational or under construction). 'Africa can boast only two power plants in South Africa . . . With the clear exception of South Africa, and possibly Egypt, it is obvious that Africa's nuclear science and technology is only at its nascent stage.' Tilahum W. Selassie, 'The African Nuclear-Weapon-Free Zone and Sustainable Development on the Continent', *Disarmament* 19:1 (1996), pp. 41–2.
9. Quoted in *West Africa* (London) 3303 (10 November 1980), pp. 2222–3.
10. Ibid.
11. See Julius O. Ihonvbere, *Nigeria: The Politics of Adjustment and Democracy* (New Brunswick, NJ: Transaction Publishers, 1994); Toyin Falola and Julius Ihonvbere, *The Rise and Fall of Nigeria's Second Republic, 1979–1984* (London: Zed Books, 1985); and Tom Forrest, *Politics and Economic Development in Nigeria* (Boulder: Westview, 1995).
12. African leaders were also very aware of the Cuban missile crisis of 1962 which almost resulted in a nuclear war. It became clear to the African leaders that horizontal and vertical proliferation of nuclear weapons could only culminate in the mutual destruction of the world.
13. For a very good discussion of Africa's security issues and perceptions see G. Afroka Nweke, *African Security in the Nuclear Age* (Enugu, Nigeria: Fourth Dimension Publishers, 1985).

14. Atsu-Koffi Amega, 'Welcome Remarks', in *Conference on Security, Disarmament and Development: Meeting of Experts* (New York: United Nations, 1986), p. 15.
15. Ogunbanwo, 'History of African Nuclear-Weapon-Free Zone', p. 14.
16. Oluyemi Adeniji, 'The Concept of Disarmament in the African Context', in *Conference on Security, Disarmament and Development*, p. 35. It is argued by African leaders that this initiative on NWFZ encouraged other developing regions and led to the conclusion in 1967 of the Treaty of Tlatelolco.
17. Prvoslav Davinic, 'Opening Remarks', in *Conference on Security, Disarmament and Development*, p. 10.
18. Benson N. C. Agu, 'Denuclearization: Enhancing African Regional Co-operation in Peaceful Nuclear Applications', *Disarmament* 19:1 (1996), p. 21.
19. Ibrahim Sy, 'A Nuclear-Weapon-Free-Zone in Africa', *Disarmament* 16:3 (1993), p. 95.
20. Ibid.
21. Davinic, 'Opening Remarks', p. 11.
22. Sy, 'A Nuclear-Weapon-Free Zone in Africa', p. 96.
23. 'A Newly Opened Book', *Time* 141 (5 April 1993), pp. 16–17. de Klerk had also announced that South Africa's nuclear programme was exclusively for 'Deterrence.' Essentially, according to de Klerk, it was meant to 'blackmail' Western powers, especially the United States into coming to South Africa's help in the event of a Soviet-backed attack against the then apartheid regime.
24. J. W. de Villiers, 'Why South Africa Gave up the Bomb', *Foreign Affairs* 72 (November–December 1993), p. 4. (UTCAT version).
25. David Albright, 'South Africa and the Affordable Bomb', *Bulletin of the Atomic Scientists* 50 (July–August 1994), pp. 37–8.
26. 'De Klerk: South Africa had the Bomb', *Africa Report* 38 (May–June 1993), pp. 6–7.
27. de Villiers, 'Why South Africa Gave up the Bomb', p. 1. de Villiers linked the development of South Africa's nuclear programme to Western economic interests in the country's uranium which dates back to involvement of the United States and the United Kingdom in the Manhattan Project. His statement simply supports the assertion that the line between 'peaceful' and 'non-peaceful' uses of nuclear-weapons technology is very thin indeed.
28. Selassie, 'The African Nuclear-Weapon-Free Zone', p. 42.
29. See Julius O. Ihonvbere, 'Africa in the 1990s and Beyond: Alternative Prescriptions and Projections', *Futures* 28:1 (1996), pp. 15–35 and *Africa and the New World Order* (New York: Peter Lang Publishing, forthcoming); and Adebayo Adedeji, ed, *Africa Within the World: Beyond Dispossession and Dependence* (London and Akure: Zed Books and ACDESS, 1993).
30. For the Zambian example see Julius O. Ihonvbere, *Economic Crisis, Civil Society and Democratization: The Case of Zambia* (New Brunswick, NJ: Transaction, 1996).

31. See OAU, *Lagos Plan of Action for the Economic Development of Africa 1980–2000* (Geneva: International Institute for Labour Studies, 1981). This document confessed that 'Africa is unable to point to any significant growth rate, or satisfactory index of general well being, in the past 20 years.' (p.1). For a critical evaluation, see the introduction to Julius O. Ihonvbere, ed, *Political Economy of Crisis and Underdevelopment in Africa: Selected Works of Claude Ake* (Lagos: JAD, 1989).
32. Selassie, 'The African Nuclear-Weapon-Free Zone', p. 39.
33. See UN Development Programme, *Human Development Report 1994* (London: Oxford University Press, 1994) and Economic Commission for Africa, *African Charter for Popular Participation in Development and Transformation* (Addis Ababa: ECA, 1990).
34. 'Pelindaba' roughly translated means 'the discussion has been completed.' See Ogunbanwo, 'History of African-Nuclear-Weapon-Free Zone', p. 14.
35. Bereng Mtimkulu, 'Africa Bans the Bomb - Treaty of Pelindaba Signed', *Bulletin of the Atomic Scientists* 52 (July–August 1996), p. 11.
36. All the six meetings of the Group were financed by the UN through its regular budget. Without doubt, the UN was the fundamental force behind the establishment of a NWFZ in Africa. Since the 1960s, it provided the political impetus which gave legitimacy to African initiatives in addition to its own resolutions. If the UN did not appear to have moved faster, this can be attributed to the lack of support from the NWS and the Security Council.
37. Pelindaba Text of the African Nuclear-Weapon-Free Zone Treaty, Addis Ababa, 21-3 June 1995. Reproduced in *Disarmament* 19:1 (1996), pp. 139–47.
38. Mtimkulu, 'Africa Bans the Bomb', p. 11.
39. Ibid., p. 4.
40. For a discussion of one major incident of toxic waste dumping See Julius O. Ihonvbere, 'The State and Environmental Degradation in Nigeria: A Study of the 1988 Toxic Waste Dump in Koko', *Journal of Environmental Systems* 23:3 (1993–4), pp. 1–21.
41. Olu Adeniji, 'The African Nuclear-Weapon-Free Zone Treaty - The Pelindaba Text and its Provisions', *Disarmament* 19:1 (1996), p. 4. See also 'Fact Sheet: African Nuclear-Weapon-Free Zone Treaty', *U.S. Department of State Dispatch* 7 (15 April 1996), p. 194.
42. Russia attended the signing ceremony but refused to sign because it objected to the presence of a US military base on the island of Diego Garcia which is a British possession in the Indian Ocean.
43. 'United States to Sign Protocols of the African Nuclear-Weapon-Free Zone', Statement by the Press Secretary, White House, 11 April 1996.
44. Even in the NWS there are increasing doubts as to the 'decades-old role of nuclear weapons as cornerstone of Western defence policy'. In the case of the United States, it is increasingly being concluded that 'nuclear weapons diminish rather than enhance US security.' Robert McNamara noted in 1992

that only a return to a non-nuclear world could guarantee security. See Michael McGuire, 'Eliminate or Marginalize: Nuclear Weapons in US Foreign Policy', *The Brookings Review* 13 (Spring 1995), p. 36. See also Kenneth N. Waltz, 'Nuclear Myths and Political Realities', *American Political Science Review* 84 (September 1990), pp. 733–44.
45. William J. Clinton, 'Message to the Congress on the South Africa-United States Agreement on the Peaceful Use of Nuclear Energy', *Weekly Compilation of Presidential Documents* 31 (2 October 1995), p. 1746. Though the 1957 agreement was scheduled to expire in 2007, and had been suspended in the 1970s by the United States when South Africa commenced its nuclear-weapons development and manufacturing programme, changes in the global order, the African continent and within South Africa dictated a drastic review. The new agreement also puts in important safeguards which were absent in the 1957 agreement: 'full-scope safeguard; perpetuity of safeguards; ban on 'peaceful' nuclear explosives; a right to require the return of exported nuclear items in certain circumstances; a guarantee of adequate physical security; and a consent right to enrichment of nuclear material subject to the agreement.'
46. Albright, 'Curious Conversion', p. 8. Albright also revealed that when South Africa's nuclear programme was terminated, Advena employed about 300 people. This was reduced within a year to about 110 staff and in April 1992, 23 of Armscor's (Advena's parent industry) 26 subsidiaries were taken over by a commercial venture known as Debel (Pty) Limited.
47. The fact that the technologically advanced nations could independently develop nuclear weapons meant that they were not obligated to allow the IAEA to regulate or control their facilities. This meant that the IAEA was more suited to the control and regulation of less developed nations.
48. Agu, 'Denuclearization', p. 31.

PART THREE
Four Prospective Zones

6
A Northeast Asian Nuclear-Weapon-Free Zone: A Korean Perspective

Bon-Hak Koo

The idea of establishing a nuclear-weapon-free zone (NWFZ) in a populated region was conceived primarily to prevent the emergence of new nuclear-weapons states (NWS). Countries which are confident that their enemies in the region do not possess nuclear weapons may not be inclined to acquire such weapons themselves. This is why the Nuclear Non-Proliferation Treaty (NPT) encourages the creation of NWFZ.[1]

Though the Cold War strategic confrontation between superpowers has gone, arms buildup rather than arms control has been a salient phenomenon in post-Cold War Northeast Asia. In fact East Asia has emerged as the world's largest arms-buying region by registering over 30 per cent of all major weapons purchases in the 1990s. More worrisome in the region is the possibility of nuclear proliferation. Thus it is important to constrain the proliferation of nuclear weapons for preserving the peace and stability of the region.

International efforts to constrain proliferation of nuclear weapons have been pursued at three different levels: global, regional and bilateral. The International Atomic Energy Agency (IAEA) safeguards system, the NPT and the Comprehensive Test Ban Treaty (CTBT) are the main instruments of non-proliferation at the global level. The treaties of Rarotonga and Tlatelolco and the European Atomic Energy Community (Euratom) are examples of regional proliferation barriers.

The Argentina-Brazil Accounting and Control Commission (ABACC) and the Joint Declaration on the Denuclearisation of the Korean Peninsula represent examples of bilateral constraints.

In efforts to constrain nuclear proliferation, global regimes like the IAEA safeguards system and the NPT are the most important mechanisms because they provide a philosophical background for the non-proliferation of nuclear weapons. So far at least they have successfully constrained the proliferation of nuclear weapons. However, the global regimes contain fundamental problems such as inequality between the 'nuclear haves' and the 'nuclear have nots'.

The global non-proliferation regimes are supported by mechanisms at the regional level, of which NWFZ are good examples. They have been examined or established in many regions including Europe, the Middle East, Africa, Southeast Asia, South America and the South Pacific. Recently, NWFZ have become a focal point of international non-proliferation efforts. On 15 December 1995 the first NWFZ treaty in Asia – the treaty on the Southeast Asian NWFZ – was signed at the Association of South-east Asian Nations (ASEAN) summit meeting in Bangkok. On 11 April 1996 the African NWFZ treaty – the so-called Pelindaba Treaty – was signed in Cairo. And on 11–12 October 1996 a conference on a limited NWFZ in Northeast Asia was convened in Bordeaux, France in which both civilians and officials participated.[2]

A NWFZ in Northeast Asia has been proposed at different times and in different forms by the former Soviet Union, the Russian Federation and North Korea. These proposals have not received any serious response from the relevant countries in the region. However, the recent proposal made by the Center of International Strategy, Technology and Policy of the Georgia Institute of Technology has attracted considerable interest from the regional countries.

This chapter aims to explore the utility and limitations of a NWFZ and evaluate various NWFZ proposals for Northeast Asia and their applicability in the context of the interests of the countries of the region.

NWFZ: Concept, Utility, Limitations

A NWFZ is a geographical region from which, by treaty or formal convention, nuclear weapons are permanently banned. The precise terms of existing and proposed zonal arrangements vary depending on regional characteristics, but such agreements typically outlaw the possession, deployment and use of nuclear weapons (defined as explosive devices) in a designated area. States parties to the zone pledge not to develop, test, produce, acquire or otherwise possess nuclear weapons; not to permit any outside state to store, install or deploy nuclear weapons on zonal territory; and neither to give nor receive assistance for the development and production of nuclear weapons. In addition, NWS, even though their territories are not located within the zone, are asked to make a formal commitment to respect the nuclear-weapon-free status of the zone and not to use or threaten to use nuclear weapons against any states in the zone.[3]

The concept of NWFZ emerged from the assessment that the complete abolition of nuclear weapons is not possible in the current international situation. It is relatively easier to constrain the possession and production of nuclear weapons in a limited region, thus contributing to the peace and security of the region.

The motives behind the calls for a NWFZ vary from region to region. The motivation common to all zones is the belief among states that they would be more secure if their region were free of nuclear weapons. The US-Soviet arms race prompted many countries to fear that they could fall victim to the consequences of nuclear war despite their own non-nuclear status. For example, the Cuban missile crisis in October 1962 was a watershed event in the development of NWFZ because the non-NWS in Latin America realised how close the world had come to nuclear war, and how the presence of nuclear weapons in their region put them directly at risk. In the wake of that crisis, these states moved to negotiate the Treaty for the Prohibition of Nuclear Weapons in Latin America (Tlatelolco Treaty) which bans nuclear weapons from the entire Latin American region.[4]

The NWFZ prohibits deployment, production, acquisition, stockpiling and development of nuclear weapons in the region. Thus it requires more comprehensive obligations than those of the NPT. The NPT recognises five NWS and their privileges as NWS. However, a NWFZ demands of all states in the region that they not develop, acquire, stockpile and produce nuclear weapons.

A NWFZ has three main characteristics:

- the non-possession principle – a renunciation by participating states of the zone of the production and acquisition of nuclear weapons or other nuclear explosive devices, as well as direct or indirect control of such weapons or devices;

- the non-deployment principle – an obligation not to permit the deployment of foreign nuclear weapons within the limits of the region; and
- the non-use principle – the nuclear powers must strictly respect the nuclear-weapon-free status of the zone and refrain from using or threatening to use nuclear weapons against the states of the zone.

However, the non-deployment obligation presents various kinds of difficulties for the countries involved. So does the related issues of nuclear-weapons transit and the question of non-use assurances.[5]

In 1975 the UN General Assembly defined a NWFZ as 'any zone recognised by the General Assembly of the United Nations, which any group of nations in free exercise of their sovereignty, has established by virtue of a treaty or convention'. Under the General Assembly definition, the treaty must provide for the 'total absence of nuclear weapons to which the zone shall be subject' and 'an international system of verification and control is established to guarantee compliance with the obligation deriving from that statute'.[6]

This definition set out the legal requirements for the establishment of a NWFZ. Regional states are free, when agreeing to a treaty or convention establishing a NWFZ, to decide what specific measures within this broad framework they consider appropriate to the circumstances and requirements of their particular region.[7] The UN definition also requires NWS to respect the total absence of nuclear weapons from such areas, not to contribute in any way to a violation of the zone's nuclear-weapon-free status, and to refrain from using or threatening to use nuclear weapons against NWFZ member states.[8]

NWFZ have a particular role to play in the regions free of nuclear weapons. NWFZ can promote the security of non-NWS both by obtaining pledges from NWS regarding the non-use of weapons against them and by discouraging or preventing the deployment of nuclear weapons within their own regions. They may also play an important arms control role: the withdrawal of nuclear weapons stationed outside the territories of the NWS under the terms of the treaty establishing a NWFZ would have a considerable arms control impact.

However, the establishment of NWFZ is not easily achieved and there is little likelihood of many more treaties establishing NWFZ.[9]

As noted in chapter 1 above, consensus was reached in the UN in 1975 on the principles by which states should be guided in setting up NWFZ. The agreed principles notwithstanding, there can be no fixed form of NWFZ because of dissimilar geographical circumstances and different political, economic and strategic considerations. The differences may concern the following: the scope of obligations assumed by the parties; the responsibilities of extra-zonal states; the security assurances provided by the NWS; the geographical area subject to denuclearisation; the measures of verification and enforcement; and the conditions for the entry into force of the arrangement and its denunciation.[10]

The concept of a NWFZ is only a means towards a complete removal of nuclear weapons. It cannot substitute for a national security policy, nor can it remove the threat of nuclear war. It is primarily a confidence-building measure which needs to be matched to the specific circumstances of the region in question and to the links which exist between that region and broader systems of international order. Therefore a NWFZ is a possible instrument in support of such broader purposes.[11]

A NWFZ in Northeast Asia

Rationale

The establishment of a NWFZ in the Northeast Asia should serve to protect the population of the region from the scourge of a nuclear arms race. Such a measure could add one very important safeguard against the onset of escalating tensions resulting from the stationing of nuclear weapons by any third party. This could enhance the possibility of zonal states remaining outside the immediate dangers of a nuclear-weapons exchange, as well as protecting them from a policy of nuclear blackmail by such powers.

A NWFZ in Northeast Asia could eventually assist in the process of establishing a new environment of confidence-building between the countries in the region. With the reduction of nuclear ambiguity and the removal of the necessity of forging a strategy for unilateral deterrence, the foundation could be created for the establishment of legal commitments to maintain Northeast Asia free of nuclear weapons. The spirit of confidence that would emerge between and among states of the region could possibly spill over to other fields and eventually help in restoring political stability.[12]

During the Cold War, since proposals regarding establishing a NWFZ were mostly developed by communist countries, most Western countries, including the US, tended to reject the idea. However, after the end of the Cold War confrontation between the superpowers and the subsequent reduction of nuclear weapons in the US and Russia, the demand to consider the issue of denuclearisation in Northeast Asia to consolidate the peace and security of the region has increased.

Several reasons can be identified for investigating a NWFZ in Northeast Asia today. First, nuclear weapons may cause tensions and conflict among regional countries. In Northeast Asia, the US, Russia and China possess nuclear weapons, Japan has both the technological and material bases to develop nuclear weapons, and North Korea is suspected of pursuing a clandestine nuclear-weapons programme. In this regard, peace and security cannot be consolidated in Northeast Asia without resolving the nuclear issues.

Second, there is a nuclear imbalance in Northeast Asia. Since the US and Russia withdrew tactical nuclear weapons from the region, China has not reduced nuclear weapons and some of these are targeted at regional countries. This not only makes the region insecure, but also negatively affects confidence-building among regional countries.

Third, it is necessary to assuage growing anxieties of the non-nuclear countries regarding the nuclear programme of the problem countries. North Korea's announcement of withdrawal from the NPT, and the continuing suspicions about its nuclear programme, necessitate a fundamental solution for the nuclear stability in Northeast Asia. Also, suspicions of the Japanese nuclear programme must be allayed.

Fourth, a regional assurance for the denuclearised Korean peninsula is urgently needed. The success or failure of the denuclearised Korean peninsula depends on support from the regional countries, especially from the three nuclear powers.

Nevertheless, there are more restraining than facilitating factors for a NWFZ in Northeast Asia in the current security environment. The Western countries' negative attitude towards a NWFZ is the most serious one. During the Cold War, Western countries were suspicious of the sincerity of the communist countries' NWFZ proposals. In addition, the strategic importance of nuclear weapons made Western countries reject NWFZ proposals. The United States may worry that establishing a denuclearised zone might not only jeopardise the US deterrent power, but also hinder free access to allied ports and bases by American ships and aircraft carrying nuclear weapons. Japan also worries that denuclearisation of the region might divest the American nuclear umbrella from Japan. Another restraining factor is the intention of the non-nuclear countries to develop nuclear weapons. Since three of the six regional countries possess nuclear weapons, the non-NWS find it hard to resist, or at least to renounce, the nuclear temptation.

However, the changing security environment since the end of the Cold War facilitates the establishment of a Northeast Asian NWFZ (NEANWFZ). First, the end of the Cold War reduced the effectiveness of nuclear weapons as a means of deterrence. Second, the withdrawal of American and Russian nuclear weapons from Northeast Asia contributes to creating a favourable environment for a NWFZ in the region. Third, a growing global concern for nuclear proliferation provides a rationale for the establishment of a regional NWFZ. Fourth, the denuclearisation declaration on the Korean peninsula, though it has not been implemented yet, provides a turning point towards a NWFZ in the region. The current security environment is thus surely more conducive to the establishment of a NEANWFZ than any other since the end of the Second World War.

Proposals

In 1959 Nikita Khrushchev, the former General Secretary of the Communist Party of the Soviet Union (CPSU), proposed a NWFZ in Northeast Asia. The Soviet proposal included not only denuclearisation of the Korean peninsula, but also a NWFZ in the entire Asia–Pacific region. The proposal, however, was initiated as a means of political propaganda as part of the Soviet foreign policy of peaceful coexistence. In the Cold War situation prevailing at that time, the proposal did not attract any interest from the US, Japan and South Korea.

Nevertheless, the establishment of a NWFZ in the Asia–Pacific region is at the core of the Russian arms control proposal in Asia. The former Soviet Union and Russia have been active in the cause of establishing a NWFZ in Northeast Asia. Since Khrushchev first proposed a NWFZ for the Asia–Pacific region in 1959, it has been an important element in the arms control proposals of the former Soviet Union. In the 1980s, the proposal by the former Soviet Union on the denuclearisation of the Korean peninsula totally supported the North Korean denuclearisation proposal. In March 1984 Konstantin Chernenko, General Secretary of the CPSU, officially supported the North Korean proposal in his meeting with Kim Il Sung in Moscow. The former Soviet Union consistently supported the North Korean proposals from that date onwards.

Mikhail Gorbachev more or less took a concrete stand on a NWFZ in Northeast Asia. In proposing an 'All Asian Conference' in May 1985, Gorbachev advocated a comprehensive test ban in Asia–Pacific and the Indian Ocean; the non-use of nuclear weapons in the Asian continent; the non-use of nuclear weapons by nuclear powers against non-nuclear countries; and the unconditional participation in the NPT by non-nuclear countries in the region. Furthermore, in his Vladivostok announcement of July 1986, Gorbachev proposed the establishment of a denuclearised zone on the Korean peninsula, Southeast Asia and the South Pacific.

In proposing a NWFZ, Moscow aims at the following objectives. First, with the USSR/Russia being faced with the necessity to reduce nuclear weapons, a NWFZ in Northeast Asia would be helpful in maintaining a nuclear balance in the US-Russian relationship. A NWFZ would neutralise the US nuclear superiority in the region. Second, a NWFZ could prevent Chinese nuclear arms build-up. With the end of nuclear confrontation with the US, this became more important. Third, a NWFZ could prevent nuclear proliferation in Northeast Asia. Nuclear proliferation can create tensions and conflict among regional countries which is not beneficial to the Russian national interest. Fourth, a NWFZ could check Japanese nuclear armament. The current objective of the Russian regional denuclearisation proposal may well be directed at Japan, because Moscow regards the prospect of a nuclear-armed Japan as a serious threat to Russian security. In this regard, it is expected that Russia will strongly and continuously support a NWFZ in Northeast Asia.

In August 1976 North Korea proposed a NWFZ on the Korean peninsula at the Conference on the Korean peninsula which was held in Tokyo. But the real aim was to secure the withdrawal of the US forces stationed in South Korea.

In March 1981, in a joint communique with the Japanese Socialist Party, North Korea proposed the abolition of all nuclear weapons in Northeast Asia; the prohibition of the development, testing, production, possession, transport and use of nuclear, chemical and biological weapons in the region; the withdrawal of all foreign troops from the region and the abolition of any military alliance treaty with extra-regional countries; and the establishment of a NWFZ on the Korean peninsula and around the East Sea.

On 31 May 1990 North Korea promulgated an 'Arms Control Proposal for the Peace of the Korean Peninsula', which included a NWFZ on the Korean peninsula; the immediate withdrawal of nuclear weapons deployed in South Korea; the prohibition of the production and acquisition of nuclear weapons; and banning the transit and passage of aircraft and vessels carrying nuclear weapons through or over the territory of North and South Korea. On 23 October 1991, at the Fourth North–South High-Level Talks, Yeon Hyong-mook, the Prime Minister of North Korea, proposed the establishment of a 'Nuclear-Free Zone on the Korean Peninsula'.

In addition to Russian and North Korean proposals, there have been NWFZ proposals on the Korean peninsula or in Northeast Asia by scholars. In 1972 Allen Whiting proposed a NWFZ in Northeast Asia. He proposed the withdrawal of all nuclear weapons from the region within a 2400km radius from Tokyo. However, his proposal urged withdrawal of only US nuclear weapons, without mentioning nuclear weapons of the Soviet Union and China.

In 1975 William Cunningham proposed a NWFZ on the Korean peninsula. He suggested the establishment of a NWFZ by agreement of the six countries concerned: the US, Soviet Union, China, Japan, and North and South Korea. This proposal was aimed at preventing Japan's possible acquisition of nuclear weapons by establishing a NWFZ on the Korean peninsula.

In 1975 Morton Halperin proposed a NWFZ on the Korean peninsula. His proposal included an international guarantee of the NWFZ status. This proposal was too optimistic in requiring the US, Soviet Union and China to reach such agreement to guarantee the NWFZ status of the peninsula.

In 1966 and 1979 Maeda Hayasi proposed banning the use of weapons of mass destruction including nuclear, biological and chemical weapons by North and South Korea; an international guarantee of the ban by the four countries surrounding the Korean peninsula; compliance with the non-nuclear principle by Japan; and the guarantee of the status of such a zone by the United Nations.

A Limited Nuclear-Weapon-Free Zone

The Center of International Strategy, Technology and Policy of the Georgia Institute of Technology initiated a study on a NWFZ in Northeast Asia after President George Bush's 1991 announcement of the withdrawal of all tactical nuclear weapons from US overseas bases. The initial proposal was to set up a circular zone around the Korean peninsula with a radius of 1200 nautical miles and to withdraw all nuclear weapons from the zone. This was subsequently revised; the original circle became an eclipse by excluding a considerable part of the Chinese and Russian territory and including part of Alaska.

The proposal envisaged a gradual and phased withdrawal of tactical nuclear weapons, but made exceptions for Russian and Chinese strategic missiles. The exceptions were not only to secure a stable deterrence capability of the two countries in the region, but also to obtain Russian and Chinese support for the proposal.

The proposal was realistic and achievable, in that it suggested practical measures to implement a NWFZ in the region. It contained measures on how to abolish or move tactical nuclear weapons from the zone while leaving strategic nuclear weapons intact. However, tactical nuclear weapons are movable by cars, vessels and aircraft, so they can easily be redeployed from outside the zonal boundary. The proposal also contained reservations on submarine-launched nuclear weapons.

A NWFZ in Northeast Asia: Problems and Prospects

The issues that will need to be addressed regarding NEANWFZ are the abrogation of nuclear development and inspection of nuclear facilities of the non-NWS; the opening of the nuclear facilities and deployment by the NWS; the prohibition of new deployment of nuclear weapons by the NWS; the removal of nuclear weapons from the region; banning the passage and transit of nuclear weapons in the zone; negative security assurances (that is, pledges not to use or threaten to use nuclear weapons within the zone) from the NWS to the non-NWS; and removing the nuclear umbrella provided for the non-NWS.

Regional countries' attitude towards a NEANWFZ is summarised in Table 6.1. On the questions of abrogating nuclear development programmes and opening the nuclear facilities of non-NWS to international inspection, nuclear powers like the US, Russia and China will take a positive position. Non-NWS such as North Korea and Japan will need to avoid taking a negative position.

Table 6.1: Attitudes Towards a NEANWFZ

	USA	Russia	China	Japan	North Korea	South Korea
Abrogation of nuclear option, compliance with inspection	Y	Y	Y	NK	NK	Y
Transparency on nuclear weapons and deployment	N	Y	N	Y	Y	Y
No nuclear-weapons deployment by NWS	Y	Y	N	Y	Y	Y
Removal of nuclear weapons	Y	NK	N	Y	Y	Y
Banning passage/transit of nuclear weapons	N	N	N	Y	Y	N
Negative security assurances	NK	NK	Y	Y	Y	NK
Removal of nuclear umbrella	N	Y	Y	N	Y	N

N = No, NK = Not known, Y = Yes

The US and China will be opposed to opening up information about their nuclear deployments. China might also oppose any prohibition of new deployment of nuclear weapons by the NWS and the removal of nuclear weapons from the region. All the NWS in the region will be opposed to the banning of passage/transit of nuclear weapons through the zone. While the NWS might show reluctance regarding negative security assurances, the removal of nuclear umbrellas will elicit negative responses from the non-NWS sheltering under them.

The Negative Aspects

For the successful implementation of a NWFZ, regional countries need to have a common understanding of the necessity of establishing such a zone. In the backdrop to the Treaty of Tlatelolco, Latin American countries recognised that nuclear war could have broken out in the midst of the Cuban missile crisis of 1962. They could have been victims of nuclear war even though they themselves did not possess nuclear weapons. Countries in the South Pacific made a concerted effort to prevent France from testing nuclear explosives which could jeopardise their living environment. By contrast, there has not been any kind of such common recognition or feeling for the need of a NWFZ among Northeast Asian countries.

For a NWFZ to be successfully implemented, it must not conflict with the security interests of regional countries. The treaties of Tlatelolco and Rarotonga could reduce the risks of nuclear war and the damage caused by nuclear tests, but without erecting any impediments to the security interests of member countries.

Traditionally, the US has been unenthusiastic about NWFZ. The US might consider that any NWFZ would restrain its global strategy by limiting passages or operations of its aircraft and vessels in the region. A NWFZ may require the removal of the nuclear umbrella provided for Japan and South Korea. In that case a NEANWFZ could heighten conflict among regional countries and lead to the reduction of US influence in the region. In the post-Cold War environment, the US is still the core of stability in Northeast Asia through the security alliances with Japan and South Korea. A NWFZ may weaken its security system in Northeast Asia, and hence heighten conflicts and instability in the region. In this perspective, the NWFZ may not accord with the US security interest in the region.

China, though it proposed a NWFZ in the late 1950s, now maintains a negative position towards a NEANWFZ. Recently, China declared the suspension of its nuclear tests, though it implemented tests until last year. China has been trying to modernise its nuclear-weapons systems and has not paid any serious attention to reducing its stockpile of tactical or strategic nuclear weapons. A regional NWFZ could cause a reduction in the Chinese tactical and theatre nuclear weapons targeted at regional countries and also restrain Chinese nuclear activities. In addition, pledges of the non-use of nuclear weapons and negative security assurances towards the regional countries could curtail Chinese political influence in the region. In this regard, China will be reluctant to agree to establishing a NWFZ in the region. Since tactical and theatre nuclear weapons of the US and Russia in the Northeast Asian region have been reduced, China does not need to hesitate to establish a NWFZ in the region for reasons of present security needs. Nevertheless, China is apprehensive of the Japanese nuclear potential, and this anxiety affects Chinese calculations on a NEANWFZ. For these reasons China will maintain its traditional position on a NEANWFZ. China will also object to the idea of abolishing or removing nuclear weapons actively deployed in the region. In sum, China worries that a NWFZ could prove burdensome in forcing a revision of its military strategy in the region; require the redeployment of Chinese intermediate range ballistic missiles; hinder Chinese nuclear-weapons testing and development programmes; and reduce China's influence in the region.

Although Japan has not shown a clear position on a NWFZ in Northeast Asia, it seems to maintain a negative position for the following reasons. First, Tokyo might believe that a NWFZ in Northeast Asia would jeopardise the US nuclear umbrella for Japan. Japan is almost totally dependent for its security upon the US security commitment. Thus the US nuclear deterrent is critical in defending Japanese security. Second, a NWFZ could hinder Japan's own nuclear capability. Japan presently eschews the development of nuclear weapons. However, considering that the nuclear capability for peaceful purposes can easily be transformed to serve military purposes, a NEANWFZ might emplace additional constraints on Japanese nuclear capability in peacetime.

Japan maintains a dual attitude towards NWFZ. On the one hand, it supports the establishment of NWFZ in principle, but on the other hand it is opposed to its establishment in the Northeast Asian region. Japan has shown an exceptional position towards a NWFZ within the United Nations framework. Though Western countries maintained a negative attitude towards nuclear arms reduction during the Cold War era, Japan consistently voted for plans to establish NWFZ in Africa, the Middle East, South Asia and the Indian Ocean. Japan also voted for the Treaty of Tlatelolco and the Treaty of Rarotonga.

Northeast Asia is the region where the interests of three nuclear powers are in competition and conflict. Therefore, it is hard to expect unanimous support for a NWFZ both from NWS and non-NWS. Support from NWS is necessary for the successful implementation of a NWFZ. Russia supports a NWFZ in Northeast Asia, but the US, China and Japan do not seem to be active in supporting a NWFZ in the region, and the position of non-NWS is not optimistic. So the prospects for a NWFZ in Northeast Asia are not bright.

The Positive Aspects

The international security environment has been changing since the end of the Cold War towards being more cooperative, thus providing a favourable atmosphere in the Northeast Asian region. In the longer term, this will positively affect the arms control mood in the region. In addition, non-proliferation efforts by the international community also exercise positive affects on a NWFZ in the region.

A NWFZ is beneficial in keeping peace and stability in the regional and global contexts. It can also contribute to confidence-building among the participating countries. However, it is very difficult to implement the idea among regional countries where confidence among them has not yet matured. The current security environment of Northeast Asia is not benign enough for the materialisation of the idea of a NWFZ. The post-Cold War security environment of Northeast Asia is still uncertain and regional countries are paying much attention to building up their armed forces. Arms reduction rather than pre-emptive nuclear-weapons disengagement is the salient phenomenon in Northeast Asia. In this circumstance, a regional NWFZ may not be acceptable to some regional countries.

In the US perspective, a NWFZ may contribute to restraining the emergence of new NWS in Northeast Asia. Washington may believe that if a NEANWFZ can abort the North Korean nuclear development programme, then it could also facilitate the task of keeping Japan from developing nuclear weapons. Currently, the US has withdrawn all tactical nuclear weapons from the region. Thus in the case of a limited NWFZ, the US may not need any additional withdrawal or removal of tactical nuclear weapons in the Asia–Pacific region. Thus it may be somewhat interested in a limited NWFZ in Northeast Asia.

For South Korea, it is more urgent to implement successfully the Joint Denuclearisation of the Korean peninsula which was signed in 1992 between North and South Korea. Though all American nuclear weapons have been withdrawn from South Korea, as long as the military threat from North Korea continues, South Korea cannot give up the US nuclear umbrella and will not deny transit rights to US ships and aircraft carrying nuclear weapons.

If the denuclearisation of the Korean peninsula is successfully implemented, then South Korea would welcome a regional NWFZ. However, since the US, Russia and China possess nuclear weapons, the zonal concept should be introduced in a gradual manner in order not to provoke negative responses from the NWS. Establishing a limited deployment zone in a small area around the Korean peninsula. may be acceptable as an initial step. Then if the limited zone is successful, the geographical scope may be expanded to include Japan, adjacent waters and parts of China and Russia. Nevertheless, as in the Treaty of Rarotonga, transit rights should not be restrained.

Conclusion

There is no consensus in theory or practice on whether a NWFZ should extend to portions of the high seas, to straits used for international navigation, and to international air space; nor on whether it should affect the right of innocent passage through territorial waters. Similarly, there is no agreement on whether the transit of nuclear weapons through a NWFZ by outside powers should be permitted. There is also the question of whether 'peaceful' nuclear explosions are allowed within a NWFZ and whether negative security assurances offered by the nuclear powers are a prerequisite to a zone's effectiveness and should apply without reservations.[13]

From the review of the concept of NWFZ, general requirements might be as follows: a renunciation by the participating states of the zone of the production and acquisition of nuclear weapons or other nuclear explosive devices, and an obligation not to permit the deployment of foreign nuclear weapons within the limits of the zone. It is necessary to ensure that such zones are really free from nuclear weapons. The relevant agreements should not contain any loopholes for violations of the nuclear-weapon-free status of the zones. The nuclear powers must strictly respect the NWFZ status and refrain from using or threatening to use nuclear weapons against the NWFZ states parties.

However, many allies of NWS accept policies of non-deployment of nuclear weapons in peacetime, but oppose the idea of extending it in advance to apply also in times of crisis or war. Another basic constraint embodied in the NWFZ concept is the commitment (by the NWS) not to use nuclear weapons against the zone and (by member states) not to allow the use of such weapons from zonal territory. But since nuclear weapons may well be within the NWFZ some of the time, they may also be there at the outbreak of war, in which case there would be strong incentives for them to be fired from inside the zone territory.[14]

Nevertheless, the international structure of Northeast Asia still hinders materialisation of the concept of a NWFZ in the region. In this regard, the following conditions must be satisfied for a regional NWFZ to be realised. First, the nuclear threat by nuclear powers against non-nuclear countries must be eliminated. In other words, the nuclear powers must provide binding negative security assurances. Second, the nuclear powers must come to an agreement on 'no-first-use'. Third, the nuclear powers must agree to a reduction of their nuclear weapons. Chinese participation in this agreement is essential for the success of denuclearisation. Fourth, Chinese reduction and repositioning of theatre nuclear weapons, corresponding to the reduction of American and Russian tactical nuclear weapons, must be effected. Fifth, suspicions about the Japanese nuclear programme must be allayed. Lastly, the North Korean nuclear programme should be transparent. If the above mentioned conditions are satisfied, then the goal of a NWFZ in Northeast Asia can be achieved.

Notes

1. Jozef Goldblat, 'Nuclear-Weapon-Free Zones', in John Simpson and Darryl Howlett, eds, *The Future of the Non-Proliferation Treaty* (New York: St. Martin's, 1995), p. 86.
2. The conference was organised by the Center of International Strategy, Technology and Policy, Georgia Institute of Technology, under the leadership of Dr. John E. Endicott.
3. Shannon Selin, *Canada as a Nuclear-Weapon-Free Zone: A Critical Analysis*, Issue Brief no. 10, Canadian Centre for Arms Control and Disarmament, August 1988, p. 2.
4. Jon Brook Wolfthal, 'Nuclear-Weapon-Free Zones: Coming of Age?', *Arms Control Today* 23 (March 1993), p. 3.
5. Sverre Lodgaard, 'Nuclear Disengagement Zones and No First Use Doctrines as Arms Control Measures', in Desmond Ball and Andrew Mack, eds, *The Future of Arms Control* (Sydney: Australian National University Press, 1987), p. 128.

6. UN General Assembly Resolution 30/3472B, 11 December 1975.
7. Helen Leigh-Phippaard, 'Nuclear-Weapon-Free Zones: Problems and Prospects', *Arms Control* 14 (August 1993), p. 95.
8. Wolfthal, 'Nuclear-Weapon-Free Zones' p. 4.
9. Leigh-Phippaard, 'Nuclear-Weapon-Free Zones', pp. 93–4.
10. Goldblat, 'Nuclear-Weapon-Free Zones', pp. 86–7.
11. Johan J. Holst, 'A Nuclear-Weapon-Free Zone in the Nordic Area: Conditions and Options', in Kari Mottola, ed, *Nuclear Weapons and Northern Europe* (Helsinki: Finnish Institute of International Relations, 1983), p. 5.
12. Mahmoud Karem, *A Nuclear-Weapon-Free Zone in the Middle East: Problems and Prospects* (New York: Greenwood, 1988), p. 9.
13. Selin, *Canada and a Nuclear Weapon-Free Zone*, p. 2.
14. Lodgaard, 'Nuclear Disengagement Zones', p. 129.

7
A Northeast Asian Nuclear-Weapon-Free-Zone: A Japanese Perspective

Naoko Sajima

In the wake of the disappearance into history of the global and bipolar confrontation between the United States and the former Soviet Union, regional dynamics have become more prominent. This has partially eroded some common norms of behaviour in international politics which was formerly provided by the Cold War tension. Thus the need has arisen to develop a new logic to live in a world in which there is no common threat. In order to work out policy options, a discussion with friends and allies on whether these options can be pursued jointly might be indispensable. Even among the Northeast Asian countries, where the legacies of the confrontation of the Cold War still remain, options to redesign strategies and defence policies should be debated, hopefully at their own initiative. And for that purpose, the circumstances must be made more propitious to encourage such intra-regional debate.

Japan was in the fortuitous position of being able to take advantage of a credible US extended deterrence during the Cold War period. Now it has become necessary for Japan to review its comprehensive security approach in the new regional context. The idea for the establishment of a Nuclear-Weapon-Free Zone (NWFZ) in Northeast Asia should be now one of the proposals subjected to a vigorous debate.[1]

A Northeast Asian NWFZ: A Japanese Perspective

Attempts to establish a NWFZ are not new. In 1957, speaking at the United Nations General Assembly, Polish Foreign Minister Adam Rapacki proposed the idea of a NWFZ in Central Europe. In 1958 he again proposed two different revised plans, but these were not accepted by the United States and its allies.

To date, several NWFZ have been established in uninhabited areas: Antarctica in 1959; Outer Space in 1967; the Seabed and the Ocean Floor and in the Subsoil Thereof in 1971; and the Moon and other Celestial Bodies in 1979. However, only four zones have been established in inhabited areas: Latin America in 1967; the South Pacific in 1985; Southeast Asia; and Africa. Though treaties establishing the last two were signed in December 1995 and April 1996 respectively, neither zone was operational as of the end of 1996.

In this chapter, I will first describe the prerequisites, or at least the foreseeable requirements, of NWFZ by examining the conditions of the four existing zones. Second, I will critically assess the conditions of Northeast Asia. Third, I will then boldly try to sketch a strategic option and a constructive scenario for the future. In this chapter, the following five countries are considered as Northeast Asian nations: Russia, China,[2] North and South Korea, and Japan. While the United States is indeed a nuclear power, it will not be considered as a Northeast Asian nation.

Characteristics of Existing Nuclear-Weapon-Free Zones

It is possible to abstract four characteristics that are common to the four extant NWFZ in populated regions of the world. First, they are all located in regions far removed from the Cold War 'frontlines'. While these regions were vulnerable to 'East-West proxy wars', the nuclear threat to them was negligible. The Rapacki Plan may not have been viable because Central Europe was the main Cold War frontline.

Second, the treaty members of extant NWFZ are relatively new and small, both in scope of economic power and international influence. In some cases they chose nuclear-weapon-free options based more on reasons of economy or international prestige than strategic calculation. They then used the resulting united block of nuclear-weapon-free nations as diplomatic tools or cards. The Latin American countries first tried to establish their zone when the Cuban missile crisis of 1962 alarmed them and forced them to unify in common opposition to the grave nuclear threat. When the South Pacific nations speedily negotiated the Treaty of Rarotonga in the mid-1980s, the new Cold War tension was critically high and the Soviet Union appeared to be encroaching on their sovereignty. By unifying in a nuclear-free zone they rejected the East-West confrontation and asserted their independence. The Southeast Asian and African zones are evidence of messages from the political leaders of their member nations to the outside world that they intend to seize the regional security initiative in the post-Cold War environment.

Third, each of the zones was established through the cooperation of nations already linked by an existing multilateral framework, although with differing objectives. The Latin American countries which established the first NWFZ have a long history of regional cooperation since the first pan-American Congress in 1889. The Treaty of Tlatelolco was born through the experience of the Latin American parliament which was established in 1964. The Treaty of Rarotonga was formulated by the South Pacific Forum. In Southeast Asia, the possibility of a NWFZ was first argued in the form of the Zone of Peace, Freedom and Neutrality (ZOPFAN) which was declared in 1971, when foreign ministers of the Association of South-east Asian Nations (ASEAN) met in Kuala Lumpur. While it was slow to emerge as an institution, ASEAN's regional responsibility has become more prominent since the end of the Cold War. Finally, the African zone established by the Treaty of Pelindaba had its origin in the nuclear-free declaration of the Organisation of African Unity (OAU) in 1964.

The fourth common characteristic of existing NWFZ is a solid antinuclear consensus, if not among the citizens then at least among the political leaders of member nations. The Treaty of Tlatelolco was clearly motivated by the spread of anti-nuclear sentiment after the Cuban missile crisis. The Treaty of Rarotonga was supported by a strong public opinion against the French nuclear tests which had been conducted for years at the Moruroa and Fangataufa atolls in the South Pacific. Additionally, since Australia and New Zealand were both controlled by Labour governments, the timing was right for change.[3] The Treaty of Rarotonga might also appear to be more a reaction against the radioactivity generated by nuclear testing than against the nuclear weapons themselves. The nations of Southeast Asia and Africa have long desired neutrality and the non-interference of the nuclear powers. For them, a common priority was national autonomy with resilience. Malaysian Prime Minister Dr Mahathir bin Mohamad said before signing the treaty, 'we should not be listening to outside advice about out security needs, we should be on guard against becoming a pawn in global politics'.[4]

Conditions in Northeast Asia

By contrast, the current conditions in Northeast Asia are very different. First, there are still two nuclear powers in the region, China and Russia. Moreover, the last vestiges of Cold War confrontation still exist on the Korean peninsula. Accordingly the United States continues to provide its nuclear umbrella, through alliances, to non-nuclear Korea and Japan. And because both China and Russia have huge territories, the Northeast Asian strategic theatre is directly related to other regions. Conditions of Northeast Asia are always related to the global nuclear strategy of those countries. For instance, it is believed that part of the equipment that the former Soviet Union had shifted to areas east of the Urals from areas subject to the Conventional Forces in Europe (CFE) Treaty before signing it, as well as part of the Russian forces' equipment withdrawn from Eastern Europe, are now being deployed in the Far East.[5] Since these nations are geographically anchored, this situation will never change. Consequently, though the dissolution of the Soviet Union brought an important change to the power structure in Northeast Asia and though its military capability has been badly damaged by political and economic turmoil, in reality, from a global and longer-term perspective, it did not cause any strategic changes in the Northeast Asian region. Since in the foreseeable future the two nuclear powers China and Russia are likely neither to change their respective defence strategy by abandoning nuclear weapons nor fragment into smaller political units, a NWFZ comprising all regional countries will never appear in Northeast Asia.

Second, the size of the Northeast Asian nations is not the same as those of other NWFZ nations. Russia is large on every dimension and Japan has the second largest economy in the world. Their international influence is global rather than regional. And though its economy is still developing, China has a large population, huge territory and extraordinary psychological influence through the so-called overseas Chinese in the world. Even small strategic changes in these countries have an enormous influence on neighbouring countries which have close psychological, economic, military and political links.

Third, in thousands of years of history, the Northeast Asian nations have never experienced a multilateral framework among themselves. While most of them now belong to many international regional organisations such as the ASEAN Regional Forum (ARF) and the Asia–Pacific Economic Cooperation (APEC), these are for a wider region. The Northeast Asian countries did not initiate those regional forums for themselves. While the development of regional institutions has been slow, nuclear deterrence has been surprisingly well managed so far. The balance of power theory is still considered practical.

Moreover, there are still many obstacles to the multilateral approach. In the case of the common security idea, it is predicated on the assumption that while an adversarial relationship may exist among states, the adversaries share a common interest in avoiding wars because of the shared perception that a war between them will cause intolerable damage to both sides. This is not realistic in Northeast Asia. As for collective security, it is a mechanism by which member states aim at maintaining peace by uniting their strength against the common threat. This is not suitable in the ambiguous circumstances of Northeast Asia in the post-Cold War era. Cooperative security attempts to build up a solid structure of peaceful relations among nations by measures which are not confrontational or coercive, such as confidence and security-building measures and security dialogues. The critical issues are not dealt with by the members and do not directly contribute to conflict resolution. It might not be suitable either to Northeast Asia where many critical issues remain, such as territorial disputes which are intertwined with complicated historical legacies.

Fourth, an anti-nuclear stance is not seen as a common sentiment among the Northeast Asian people. This despite the fact that the region was the first and remains the only one in which atomic bombs were used, and the Japanese, who suffered them first, continuously recall the tragedy and firmly renounce the use of nuclear weapons. Neither Russia nor China is willing to renounce nuclear weapons. Furthermore, North Korea continues to be suspected of developing nuclear weapons. South Korea, wary of continual North Korean threats of forcible reunification, is reluctant to give up the protection of the US nuclear umbrella. Because of examples like a recent novel which deals with unified Korea and ends with the scene of attacking Japan with nuclear weapons, South Koreans do not have any allergy to nuclear issues.[6] A long-time observer and analyst of Korean affairs says that Seoul is likely acting primarily on public sentiment rather than established legal principles.[7] If so, the indifference of the Korean people to nuclear issues is a further obstacle to a NWFZ.

Nuclear-Weapon-Free Zone: A Strategic Option?

The above four factors may help to explain why nuclear deterrence has been so well managed in Northeast Asia so far. The strategic circumstances might be affected seriously by even a small change of these conditions, because it relates to the concerns of the global powers. The well managed peace might not be easily damaged. Indeed in Northeast Asia it has long been recognised that deterrent arsenals need to be credible, though it would be better if peace (even in a limited sense) could be guaranteed without the undeniable dangers of nuclear weapons.[8]

Do the conditions mentioned above preclude any future scenario for a nuclear-weapon-free world in Northeast Asia? Must we continue to depend on nuclear weapons as a necessary evil? Are there any prospects of reinvigorating the idea of a nuclear-weapon-free peace in the region when circumstances have changed?

In a sense we cannot ignore the possibility of the situation becoming more favourable: 'before proliferation gets out of hand, or a new Cold War begins, we must take every opportunity we can to move the nuclear states towards implementing their obligations to bring about a nuclear-weapon-free world'.[9]

Perhaps the most readily imaginable change in the region is in the Korean peninsula. The peaceful reunification of Korea and the establishment and maintenance of peace in the peninsula is not unimaginable. After a chaotic period of transition, the reunification of the Korean peninsula might lead to a state of lasting peace. At that stage the idea of a NWFZ might become a more attractive strategic option. As Mel Gurtov has observed:

... in light of the U.S. emphasis on nonproliferation, and its well-known efforts over the years to persuade South Korean leaders to forego the nuclear option, any movement toward an independent South Korean nuclear capability would surely be opposed, not only by Washington but just as strongly by Tokyo, Beijing, and others.[10]

Shinichi Ogawa suggested that the establishment of a Northeast Asian NWFZ (NEANWFZ) has to be initiated by Japan and South Korea first, because both countries have already adopted non-nuclear principles. And even if the NEANWFZ is established legally only in Japan and Korea, he argues that it will be beneficial for Japan, for several reasons.[11]

First, it may restrict the nuclear activities of both China and Russia even in a limited sense. For instance, when China and Russia strongly oppose the nuclear arming of Japan and South (and North) Korea and sincerely wish to assure the denuclearisation of Japan and Korea, they betray a sense of unease about the status of nuclear-weapons proliferation within the Northeast Asian region. Allaying their fears permanently about the nuclear intentions of Japan and Korea should produce a corresponding relaxation of their own nuclear postures in Northeast Asia.

Second, Japan and South Korea have the capability to establish their own inspection system for each other within the framework of a NWFZ. As already shown by the cases of Iraq and North Korea, the current inspection system in the Nuclear Non-Proliferation Treaty (NPT) framework is inadequate. A NWFZ will be able to reinforce or rectify the deficiency of the current system. Accordingly it will be able to prevent the appearance of a nuclear-armed unified Korea which is the worst scenario for Japan.

Third, it may contribute to the dilution of mutual suspicions between Japan and Korea. Ogawa himself does not clearly mention this. Because the lack of faith in each other's sincerity is deeply rooted in people's minds, it may seem difficult to reverse even by the establishment of a NEANWFZ. However, at least it can contribute to the development of the architecture of new strategic thinking rather than elimination of the mutual lack of faith.

Fourth, the establishment of a NEANWFZ would not only prevent the appearance of a nuclear-armed unified Korea, but it would also be likely make it pro-US. This would be a favourable outcome for Japan. It would be beyond the capacity of a non-nuclear unified Korea to establish a regional military balance with its own conventional forces. Instead it would be more realistic for unified Korea to enter into a security relationship with the US than be neutral or reliant on China.

Fifth and finally, the establishment of a NEANWFZ could ease regional and international suspicions about Japan's accumulation of plutonium and produce a more comfortable environment for the development of the peaceful use of nuclear energy. In sum, it is possible that a NEANWFZ could become a meaningful option for Japan in future.

As well, the establishment of NEANWFZ could arise from strong incentives in Japanese domestic politics. Because of Japan's social norms of strong antipathy towards nuclear weapons, the Japanese people will fervently welcome the NWFZ. Consequently, the idea and its achievement will be politically attractive for the leaders.

A NEANWFZ may in fact be the best conceivable future option for Japan. Whether the process will be successful or not, even to start the arguments on the NEANWFZ will contribute to Japan's long-time external objectives.[12] Japan continues to be viewed with suspicion and mistrust by neighbouring countries, particularly by China and Korea, due to the history of Japan's imperialistic expansion in China (1894–1945) and Korea (1873–1945). It is therefore by no means easy for Japan to build a comfortable relationship with these two countries. Moreover, Japan's repeated apology to these countries has been undermined more than a few times by Japanese cabinet ministers' inappropriate and shallow comments denying or limiting Japan's war responsibilities. It is not really feasible for Japan to develop any regional policies indigenously. Instead it is necessary for Japan to rely on outside credibility, namely that of the United Nations and/or the US, for taking security initiatives in the region. The mutual security treaty with the US and the presence of US forces in Japan have often been justified for that reason. (The significance of the US-Japan security treaty is of course much broader than just this.)

A NEANWFZ could promulgate a new credible framework for Japan and the region in the post-Cold War era. And hopefully, if through the process towards NEANWFZ Japan can end the widespread speculation abroad that it might arm itself with nuclear weaponry which is in contrast to the domestic reality,[13] then not only the utility of nuclear energy but also the openness and transparency of Japan's non-nuclear policy will be welcomed. And it will surely strengthen the trust-building in the region.

Indeed, even beyond the constitutional restraint, indigenous nuclear-weapons development is not a feasible choice for Japan from a rational perspective. There is no advantage whatsoever for Japan in acquiring nuclear weapons. Because the most important task of nuclear weapons is deterrence, this is attained by taking into calculation the danger of the possible exchange of damage between the nuclear powers. Therefore, considering Japan's position, with its geographical limitations, the second largest economy in the world, very dense population and highly centralised political and economic systems, it is obvious that Japan would be extremely vulnerable to an exchange of damage by nuclear warheads.

Clearly, it might be an appropriate attitude for Japan to start considering arguments about the realisation of a NWFZ. It might also be postulated that, after the reunification of Korean peninsula, when the US military presence might become uncertain, the establishment of a NWFZ could secure Japan from this uncertainty to some extent. Currently, from the Japanese perspective, the Japan-US strategic partnership must not be disturbed by any means. There may seem to be some obstacles to the coexistence of the US nuclear strategy and the NWFZ at the moment. But because the idea may contribute to the effectiveness of the NPT regime, it will not impede the global strategy of the US and at the same time will contribute to the defence of Japan. For this purpose, for instance, issues such as innocent passage norms might be factored into the discussion even for the time being.[14]

In any case, the situation must be initiated gradually and cautiously, since such a strategic change may produce many unexpected and unpredictable consequences.

Scenarios for the Future

Nevertheless, I would like to try to present several contingencies which could possibly point the way to constructive NWFZ scenarios for the future.

First, *if* the Korean peninsula was to be unified by South Korean initiative and led to the establishment of a democratic nation which respects the rule of law as crucial part of society. The Joint Declaration on the Denuclearisation of the Korean Peninsula in 1991 said that the 'South and North shall not test, manufacture, produce, receive, possess, store, deploy or use nuclear weapons', and that both of them 'shall not possess nuclear reprocessing and uranium enrichment facilities'.[15] However, if a nation of seventy million people were to be unified by despotic means, it would be likely to choose nuclear weapons as a convenient option in its defence policy.

Second, *if* while overcoming the legacy of the past a unified democratic Korea and Japan establish bilateral security relations and agree to a NWFZ for both countries. Although indirect alliance relations have existed through the United States for more than forty years; although bilateral economic, cultural and social relations are expanding; and although the two countries now share similar democratic institutions in the strategic context: there are still too many obstacles for them to share a common security.[16] Alternatively, however, if a unified Korea chose to pursue a more independent strategy and tried to strike a balance between China and Japan, then a bilateral Japan-Korea NWFZ would be beyond their capacity. It could further complicate regional situations.

Third, *if* Russia and the United States were to jointly further the nuclear arms reduction process and agree to the withdrawal of nuclear weapons from limited areas, including Northeast Asia. For that purpose, the global nuclear disarmament process must be encouraged and credible transparency in the region must be attained through confidence-building measures developed through multilateral security frameworks.

Fourth, *if* the established situation should compel or naturally encourage China to change its nuclear policy and agree to limit the area of its nuclear-weapons deployment. For this scenario to eventuate, China must maintain political stability and follow the international rules of behaviour. However, should China choose a unilateral track and become a 'rogue' actor in the region, Korea and Japan will probably continue to seek the protection of the US nuclear umbrella.

Conclusion

Many people, after living in the shadow of nuclear disaster through the Cold War, cannot quite believe, even though the worst threat has passed, that there can ever be anything approaching full nuclear disarmament or a complete system of safeguards. Nevertheless, the long struggle to end nuclear testing, however discouraging, cannot be allowed to destroy the hope that even more can be achieved. Most importantly, the negotiation of the Comprehensive Test Ban Treaty (CTBT) has provided valuable experience on most matters – including, crucially, verification procedures – which might stand in the way of agreement on the wider question of nuclear disarmament.

On 13 March 1996 Japan's Prime Minister Ryutaro Hashimoto expressed the view that, if the conditions of international law can be met and the relevant nuclear powers can agree with it, a NWFZ might contribute to the nuclear non-proliferation process. He also said that he would carefully watch the development of the Southeast Asian NWFZ.[17] If the way to solving this problem is to take things one step at a time, then Japan could perhaps take the first step. On 31 October 1996 a policy agreement, including a continuous study for the realisation of a NEANWFZ, was reached by the leaders of the Liberal Democratic Party, the Social Democratic Party and the New Party Sakigake which may serve as a symbolic statement for maintaining the appearance of a tripartite coalition.[18]

Whilst foreign observers may question Japan's reasons for desiring a non-nuclear policy, there are several reasons for its firmness and importance.[19] Japan must continually remind the world community that it has not forgotten the precious sacrifices of Hiroshima and Nagasaki.

Nevertheless, all NWFZ require the cooperation of the nuclear powers. Without that, the treaties will never have any practical meaning at all. The NWFZ process must not be only for the self-satisfaction of a group of small nations. Rather, it must be the culmination of a concerted belief by all nations, small and large, weak and powerful, that nuclear weapons pose a great danger to humankind.

Notes

1. For instance Shinichi Ogawa, 'Nihon oyobi chosennhannto no hikakuchitaika' ('Denuclearisation of Japan and Korean Peninsula'), *Gaikojiho* 1340 (July–August 1997), pp. 18–33; Kumao Kaneko, 'Japan Needs No Umbrella', *Bulletin of the Atomic Scientists* 52 (March/April 1996), pp. 46–51.
2. In this paper, Taiwan is excluded as a regional state but considered an independent actor in the region as a part of China.
3. Both lost office in 1975. The Australian Labor Party came back to power in 1983, the New Zealand Labour Party in 1984.
4. In 'SEANWFZ Treaty', http://www.iijnet.or.jp/asia/inform/seanwfz.htm.
5. Japan Defense Agency, *Defense of Japan* (Tokyo: Japan Times, 1995), p. 45.

6. About the recent boom of anti-Japan publications in South Korea, see details in Katsuhiro Kuroda, *Kankoku-Hannnichi Syndrome* ('Anti-Japan Syndrome in Korea'), (Tokyo: Akishobo, 1995).
7. *Asian Wall Street Journal,* 29 August 1996.
8. Cf 'Policy with regard to nuclear weapons should focus on maximising the benefits of nuclear deterrence, whilst minimising the potential harm'; Ron Smith, 'Nuclear Weapons: The Good and the Bad', *New Zealand International Review* 21 (January/February 1996), p. 26.
9. Alyn Ware, 'The Nuclear Bomb: A Weapon in Search of a Target', *New Zealand International Review* 21 (July/August 1996), p. 26.
10. Mel Gurtov, 'South Korea's Foreign Policy and Future Security: Implications of the Nuclear Standoff', *Pacific Affairs* 69 (Spring 1996), p. 23. Or see his view in 'Prospects for Korea–U.S.–Japan Triangular Security Relations', in Manwoo Lee and Richard W. Mansbach, eds, *The Changing Order on Northeast Asia and the Korean Peninsula* (Seoul and Boulder: Institute for Far Eastern Studies and Westview, 1993), pp. 126–8.
11. Ogawa, 'Nihon oyobi chosennhannto no hikakuchitaika' pp. 26–8.
12. See Kaneko, 'Japan Needs No Umbrella'.
13. For details see Matake Kamiya, *Will Japan Go Nuclear? Myth and Reality* (Wellington: Centre for Strategic Studies, Working Paper No. 1/95, 1995).
14. On a recent argument of the innocent passage norms, see *Far Eastern Economic Review,* 29 February 1996, p. 30.
15. 'Joint Declaration on the Denuclearisation of the Korean Peninsula', initialed on 31 December 1991, signed on 20 January 1992, and entered into force on 29 February 1992; quoted in *Korean and World Affairs* 16 (Spring 1992).
16. According to the public survey, 82.6 per cent of Koreans do not think that they can establish credible relations with Japan; *Yomiuri Shimbun,* 21 September 1996.
17. Quoted in *Gunshuku mondai shiryou* 187 (June 1996), p. 9.
18. *Nikkei Shimbun,* 1 November 1996.
19. See Kamiya, *Will Japan Go Nuclear?*

8
The Case for a South Asian Nuclear-Weapon-Free Zone

Samina Yasmeen

Thirty years ago, on 16 February 1967, Latin American countries concluded the Treaty for the Prohibition of Nuclear Weapons in Latin America. Nine years later, in December 1975, the United Nations General Assembly passed a resolution which identified nuclear-weapon-free zones (NWFZ) as 'constitut[ing] one of the most effective means of preventing the proliferation, both horizontal and vertical, of nuclear weapons and for contributing to the elimination of the danger of a nuclear holocaust'.[1] Since then the world has witnessed the formation of NWFZ in the South Pacific, Southeast Asia and Africa.[2] Suggestions are also being made for a NWFZ encompassing all countries of the southern hemisphere. Meanwhile, South Asia remains locked in an undeclared nuclear deterrence involving its two major states, India and Pakistan. The question arises as to whether these two states need to follow examples set by other countries and establish a NWFZ in South Asia.

This paper attempts to answer this question. It argues that the inherent dangers of an inadvertent nuclear conflict in the region underscore the need for a NWFZ in South Asia. However, the goal can only be achieved in stages which take into account the political and strategic realities of the region. To this end, the paper is divided into three parts. The first part discusses the rationale for a nuclear-weapon-free South Asia; the second part discusses various ideas that have been put forth for creating such a zone; and the last part identifies stages and steps

The Case for a South Asian Nuclear-Weapon-Free Zone 153

that may assist in the ultimate creation of a South Asian nuclear-weapon-free zone (SANWFZ).

The Rationale for a Nuclear-Weapon-Free South Asia

Since their independence in August 1947, India and Pakistan have been locked in an adversarial relationship which is dominated by the mythology of the enemy across the border. For India, Pakistan is a theocratic, manipulative and unaccommodating state which refuses to accept the reality of its secondary status within the South Asian context. Pakistan, in turn, views India as a bullying, expansionist, duplicitous and domineering state which fails to acknowledge the equality of Pakistan's status with that of India. Not that alternative images of the 'other' do not exist, but they are dominated and overtaken by scholarly and folk images which perpetuate the notion of an adversary across the border. These images also contribute to and are reinforced by a never-ending cycle of negative actions taken by India and Pakistan against each other.[3] At the lower end of the spectrum, these actions have led, for example, to the harassment of diplomatic staff from the two states, inconvenience caused to visitors from across the border and refusal to grant visas to ordinary citizens. At the upper end of the spectrum, the mythology of the enemy has manifested itself in three major wars and uncompromising attitudes adopted on the Kashmir issue.

The nuclear stalemate between India and Pakistan is another manifestation of, and contributor to, the negative images of the 'other' as well as an adversarial relationship. The initial impetus to the nuclearisation of South Asia, however, did not come from the region itself. Instead, it was triggered by an extra-regional development – China's nuclear test of 1964. Coming soon after the Sino-Indian border war of 1962, the Chinese explosion intensified Indian fear of Chinese hegemony and prompted them to launch their own nuclear programme. Under the leadership of Dr Homi Bhaba, and then Dr V. A. Sarabhai, the Indian nuclear programme progressed quickly and resulted in India's first nuclear test in May 1974. Described by New Delhi as a 'peaceful nuclear explosion', this test was not followed by a vigorous overt policy of acquiring nuclear-weapons capability. Nonetheless, with a series of unsafeguarded nuclear facilities, India has accumulated significant quantities of fissile material which could be used to 'assemble a number of nuclear weapons in a relatively short time frame'.[4] Estimates of this capability vary. According to a study by the Stockholm International Peace Research Institute (SIPRI) on fissile material, by the end of 1993 India had accumulated stocks of about 350kg of weapons-grade plutonium.[5] SIPRI also estimated that by the end of 1995, India would have acquired 'enough plutonium for between 65 and 105 nuclear weapons'.[6] Meanwhile, India has reportedly been engaged in a programme to develop the capability to produce hydrogen bombs.[7]

Pakistan's nuclear programme has been a direct response to India's nuclear policy. Aware of Indian attempts to acquire a nuclear capability, some Pakistani groups argued for a similar capability in the mid-1960s. It was, however, not until Zulfiqar Ali Bhutto's rise to power in 1971 that these arguments yielded results. Assuming power against the background of a humiliating defeat in the Indo-Pakistan war of 1971 and the creation of Bangladesh, Bhutto initiated concerted moves for Pakistan to acquire nuclear capability. The Pakistan Atomic Energy Commission was placed under his supervision and soon Pakistan was in the market for a plutonium reprocessing plant. Meanwhile Dr Abdel Qadir Khan, a Pakistani scientist working in the Netherlands, convinced Bhutto of the desirability of following the 'uranium enrichment route' to acquiring a nuclear capability.[8] Jointly, these efforts proved costly for Pakistan. In April 1979 the United States cited Pakistan's nuclear efforts as a reason for suspending economic aid. The Soviet invasion of Afghanistan in December 1979 changed the picture. Interested in retaining Pakistan's support as a frontline state, the United States not only provided US $3.2 billion in economic and military aid but also turned a blind eye to Islamabad's plans to acquire a nuclear capability through uranium enrichment. By 1986, Pakistan had succeeded in enriching uranium to a degree that its senior scientists and leaders could give statements indicating that Pakistan had finally acquired a nuclear capability.[9] In September 1990 (post-Soviet withdrawal from Afghanistan), these developments once again cost Pakistan its aid relationship with Washington. Unable to certify under the Pressler Amendment that Pakistan did not possess the capability to produce a nuclear device, the US government suspended military and economic aid to Pakistan. Since then, the Pakistan government has claimed that it has ceased to enrich uranium beyond the point reached in 1990.[10] Despite these claims, SIPRI estimates that by 1994 Pakistan possessed 150–250kg of highly enriched uranium (HEU). As the only non-NPT state possessing this 'sizeable inventory of unsafeguarded HEU', Pakistan is considered as having the capability to produce at least 6–10 nuclear weapons. If it chooses to 'uncap' its enrichment programme, Pakistan is credited with the capability of producing 'about three nuclear weapons each year'.[11]

Despite acquiring nuclear capability, neither India nor Pakistan has openly admitted having a nuclear-weapons programme. The undeclared nuclear status of the two major South Asian states is viewed by some analysts as a stabilising factor.[12] This assessment of the nuclearisation of the region is related to the view that, irrespective of the regions where it takes place, nuclear proliferation is a stabilising rather than a destabilising development. Others draw upon the classical notions of rational deterrence theory which assumes that in conditions of 'mutual conditional viability', adversaries rationally refrain from engaging in a conflict for fear of invoking disproportionately higher and irrational response from their opponents. Within the South Asian context, deterrence theory is applied to suggest that a covert nuclear capability enables both India and Pakistan to threaten the use of a nuclear bomb, even if a 'dirty' one, if the other side chooses to use its own nuclear capability. Given that such a use would result in massive casualties and threaten the core of both societies, the mere threat of an irrational response is seen as inducing rationality among India and Pakistan. This rationality is also viewed as being extended to the domain of conventional wars; the fear of a war escalating to a nuclear conflict, it is often argued, would restrain the two states from engaging in even a conventional war. Implicitly, these arguments draw parallels between the US-Soviet rivalry during the Cold War era and the Indo-Pakistan hostility. If the two superpowers refrained from using nuclear forces and kept the war 'cold', the two South Asian adversaries could also follow suit.

These justifications and acceptance of the nuclearisation of South Asia,[13] however, are inherently flawed. They ignore the criticism levelled against deterrence theory. They also ignore the recent research on the human mind which clearly suggests that human beings, across all cultures, are capable of acting irrationally. These findings point out that it is possible for fear and anxiety to result in the 'emotional mind' taking over the 'rational mind' which, in turn, can lead to actions human beings are not rationally capable of or likely to take under normal circumstances.[14] The implied comparison with the United States and the Soviet Union is also problematic. To begin with, there is no conclusive evidence to explain why the two superpowers did not go to a nuclear conflict and kept the Cold War 'cold'. Even if one assumes that a direct linkage exists between their nuclear capabilities and the absence of war, the role played by communications, command and control networks cannot be ignored in creating a 'stable' nuclear environment. In South Asia, neither India nor Pakistan has a sufficiently developed command, control and communications network to create the same degree of stability as the one which prevailed between Washington and Moscow. Indeed, the close geographic proximity of the two states, and the short flight times of delivery vehicles, impose huge technical difficulties in devising an effective warning system necessary to mount a credible response to an attack.[15] The last decade indicates that, under tense situations, the two states can and do come close to losing nuclear stability. During Operation Brasstacks in 1986, India and Pakistan faced each other against the background of newly acquired nuclear capability. In 1990, as relations deteriorated over the revived Kashmir issue, both states were reportedly considering use of nuclear weapons. Although subsequent research has cast doubt on the validity of these reports,[16] it cannot be denied that crises could erupt in future and that brinkmanship could lead to actions which both sides may regret, including the possibility of a nuclear conflict.

The likelihood of a nuclear conflict among the presently undeclared nuclear states may increase if India and Pakistan continue their attempts to 'mate' their dirty nuclear bombs with dual-use delivery systems. The French Jaguar and Soviet MiG-23 and MiG-27 aircraft in the Indian inventory can be modified to carry nuclear weapons. The US supplied F-16 aircraft can similarly be refitted by Pakistan and used as a platform for delivering nuclear weapons.

Meanwhile, however, both India and Pakistan are also engaged in ballistic missile acquisition programmes. India has already successfully tested Prithvi I, a short-range ballistic missile with a range of 150km, and has 'integrated' it into the regiment of artillery. In January 1996, it also tested Prithvi II with a range of 250km which will be inducted into the airforce. India has also been developing an intermediate-range ballistic missile, Agni, with a maximum range of 2500 km. Although the programme has been recently suspended,[17] New Delhi still has the capability of resuming it if and when it chooses to do so. Across the border, Pakistan has been developing its own short-range ballistic missiles. The existence of such a programme was unknown until early 1989 when Pakistan revealed the existence of Hatf I and II with ranges of 80–100km and 300km respectively. Pakistan is also believed to be developing another missile, Hatf III, with a range of around 600km.[18] The missile is reportedly related to the Chinese M-9. China has also been allegedly supplying M-11 missile components and technology to Pakistan. If this process of ballistic missile acquisition is paralleled by miniaturisation of nuclear warheads, Indo-Pakistan nuclear rivalry – no matter how covert and ambiguous – could lead to a situation where the nuclear balance does not remain balanced. It may result in an unintended nuclear conflict.

The human costs of a nuclear conflict, if it occurs, would be monumental. Although detailed estimates on casualties resulting from an exchange of 'dirty' nuclear bombs is unavailable, other studies indicate the extent of possible devastation caused by such a conflict. According to Rashid Naim, a limited attack on military centres would cause 503 310 and 577 100 immediate deaths in India and Pakistan respectively. The estimated injuries during such an exchange would be approximately 701 300 for India and 579 641 for Pakistan. Counter-value targeting, on the other hand, could result in nearly 17 and 29 million deaths in Pakistan and India respectively.[19] It may be argued that the estimates assume a 'full scale exchange' between the South Asian adversaries and, therefore, do not present an accurate picture. These arguments notwithstanding, the fact cannot be denied that even a 'limited nuclear exchange' could result in casualties of 10 000–12 000 for Pakistan and India. The costs would be even higher if one takes into account the long term effects of a nuclear exchange between India and Pakistan, including effects on social and economic structures and damage to the ecological system. Given the nature of these costs, it can be safely argued that a SANWFZ, with its ultimate emphasis on non-possession, non-deployment and non-use of nuclear weapons, would protect one-fifth of the world's population from the harsh consequences of an unintended nuclear conflict.

Establishing a SANWFZ will also contribute towards the goal of 'comprehensive security' of Indian and Pakistani people. Together, India and Pakistan accommodate 1.04 billion people. With a life expectancy of 60–2 years, these citizens have adult literacy levels of 48 and 62 per cent in India and Pakistan respectively. Only 16 and 28 per cent of the total Indian and Pakistani population have access to sanitation facilities, with nearly half of them without access to proper health care and safe drinking water. The combined infant mortality rate in these states is 80 for every 1000 births per year, and 63 and 40 per cent of the Indian and Pakistani children under 5 years of age suffer from malnutrition. The per capita GNP in these two states is $320 and $430 for India and Pakistan respectively. These socio-economic indicators coexist with significant defence spending by both India and Pakistan.[20] In 1995, for example, India and Pakistan spent $8289 million and $3642 million on defence respectively. This amounted to per capita expenditure of $9 for India and $28 for Pakistan. Not discounting genuine security needs of both states, these expenditures reflect and are justified by the continuing hostility between the two states. Any development and agreement that reduces the hostility between India and Pakistan, therefore, may result in a reduction of defence expenditure. The establishment of a SANWFZ could be identified as one of the many confidence-building measures which could achieve such a goal. This, in turn, would enable the two states to divert resources away from defence and allocate them for improving socio-economic status of their citizens. Instead of focusing on 'security *vis-à-vis* the other', the elites of the two states will be able to focus on 'security in' their countries. Denuclearising South Asia may also improve the general context in which India and Pakistan conduct their relations and enable them to take more conciliatory positions on thorny issues such as the future of Kashmir.

SANWFZ Proposals

The idea of a SANWFZ is not new. It was mooted as early as September 1972 when the Pakistani representative to the International Atomic Energy Agency (IAEA) called for a treaty between the South Asian countries patterned along the lines of the Treaty of Tlatelolco.[21] Pakistan's Prime Minister, Zulfiqar Ali Bhutto, repeated the idea at the inaugural ceremony of the Karachi Nuclear Power Plant (KANNUP) in November 1972. To ensure that atomic energy did not 'become a symbol of fear for its people', he said, 'Pakistan would welcome if the entire subcontinent, by the agreement of the countries, could be declared a nuclear weapon free zone and the introduction of nuclear weapons banned'.[22] The Indian nuclear explosion of May 1974 added an element of urgency to the proposal. Pakistan suggested the idea of denuclearising South Asia to India and raised it with other regional leaders. The most cogent and articulate proposals, however, were presented at the United Nations.

On Pakistan's request, an item entitled 'Declaration and Establishment of a Nuclear-Free Zone in South Asia' was included in the agenda of the General Assembly's 29th session held in 1974.[23] During the discussions on the item in the First Committee of the General Assembly, Pakistan's representative outlined the 'cardinal features of the proposed nuclear-free zone in South Asia'.[24] These principles included an understanding by states of the region to refrain from producing or acquiring nuclear weapons, as well as an undertaking by the nuclear-weapons states (NWS) that they would not introduce nuclear weapons into the region and would not use or threaten to use nuclear weapons against members of the zone. The 'faithful implementation of their commitments by the parties' was to be ensured through a system of safeguards and verification.

The elaboration of the proposal indicated Pakistan's preference for the UN to play a significant role in realising the goal of declaring South Asia a NWFZ. Firstly, the UN General Assembly was to *proclaim* South Asia as a NWFZ. This was to be followed by consultations among the countries of the region and, at an appropriate time, with the NWS to give practical shape to the declaration of South Asia as a NWFZ. The UN Secretary-General was to be authorised to invite countries of the region to begin these negotiations, whereas the UN General Assembly was to be given the task of laying down 'appropriate guidelines in order to facilitate the process of negotiations and give it a sense of direction'. As discussion on the proposal progressed, Pakistan watered down its preference for a UN role. The draft resolution tabled at the First Committee, therefore, called upon the General Assembly to *endorse, in principle,* the concept of a NWFZ in South Asia. The organisation was also to invite 'the states of the South Asian region and such other neighbouring non-nuclear states as may be interested to initiate, without delay, necessary consultation with a view to establishing a nuclear-weapon-free zone' and urge them, in the interim, to refrain from any action contrary to the achievement of these objectives. The Secretary-General was to provide all necessary assistance and report to the next General Assembly session.[25]

With slight modifications, these proposals have formed the basis of Pakistan's subsequent draft resolutions and statements on establishing a SANWFZ.[26] The underlying motivations for the proposal, however, have undergone a change. Initially, the proposal was designed to prevent India from continuing its nuclear programme. Coming soon after the defeat in the 1971 war, Pakistan viewed the Indian nuclear test as paving the way for a drastic alteration in the strategic balance in India's favour. This imbalance was, in turn, perceived as containing the possibility of relegating Pakistan to a position of perpetual inferiority. The idea of declaring South Asia a NWFZ, therefore, was an attempt to halt this 'downward trend'. Hence, the proposed resolutions urged the regional countries to refrain from *any action* which was contrary to the achievement of a SANWFZ. Since Pakistan had already embarked on a nuclear programme itself, the proposed zone was also tacit bargaining with India to avoid entering into a nuclear arms race. In essence the strategy was similar to the one adopted by NATO *vis-à-vis* the Soviet Union on the placing of intermediate-range nuclear missiles in Europe in 1979. The Soviet Union was encouraged to withdraw its already-placed intermediate-range nuclear missiles in Eastern Europe for the promise of NATO not posing a similar, but yet nonexistent, threat to the Soviet Union. In a similar vein, Pakistan was indicating to India that by giving up its already acquired nuclear capability New Delhi could avoid facing a future threat of a nuclear neighbour.

Once Pakistan acquired undeclared nuclear capability in the 1980s, the proposal for declaring South Asia a NWFZ also acquired new logic. It was used, once again tacitly, as a bargaining chip against India. The sub-text of the resolutions introduced at the General Assembly seemed to suggest that if India agreed to give up its nuclear option, Pakistan would also oblige. Otherwise, the two states would remain locked in an undeclared nuclear race. More importantly, however, Pakistan's proposal for denuclearising South Asia has constituted part of its strategy of projecting itself as a 'pro-non-proliferation' state. Since the end of the Cold War, the United States has been increasingly concerned about horizontal nuclear proliferation in the Third World, especially South Asia. These concerns were heightened during the 1990 Indo-Pakistan crisis over Kashmir. Since then, the US has initiated moves to halt the spread of nuclear weapons in the South Asian region. It has suggested 'capping' the Indian and

The Case for a South Asian Nuclear-Weapon-Free Zone 161

Pakistani nuclear programmes as well as the possibility of 'rolling back' these programmes. The balance of emphasis on capping and rolling back has varied during the last six years but the ultimate American goal remains the same – controlling the spread of nuclear weapons. Pakistan, with its interest in resumption of an aid relationship with the US, has continuously projected itself as a 'reasonable' state which is willing to pursue non-proliferation – provided India agrees to the same goal in the region. In 1991, within the context of this general strategy, Pakistan floated the idea of a Five Power Nuclear Summit involving India, Pakistan, the US, Russia and China to discuss the possibility of denuclearising South Asia. In 1994, it also suggested nine-power talks on the issue. Meanwhile it has modified its proposals to the UN General Assembly to highlight the significance of such regional negotiations for denuclearising South Asia.

India has responded negatively to the idea of declaring South Asia a NWFZ. This rejection has been explained primarily in terms of the procedures suggested for the creation and territorial boundaries of a SANWFZ. During the discussion in the First Committee of the UN General Assembly in 1974, for example, the Indian representative argued that:

> ... the first prerequisite to the creation of such a zone is an agreement among the countries concerned ... As regards Pakistan's proposal ... no consultation among the states in the region took place before the item was inscribed [on the UN agenda]. Therefore, it would be premature, indeed it would be prejudging future consultations, to declare South Asia a nuclear-weapon-free zone or even to endorse the concept.

The representative also questioned the notion of a 'South Asian zone'. He argued that differing conditions across the world must be taken into account while assessing the feasibility of creating a zone. 'Africa and Latin America', he argued, 'are separate and distinct continental zones, geographically and politically. In that sense, *South Asia cannot be considered a zone*'.[27] So strong was the Indian criticism that it presented an alternative draft resolution to the First Committee the same year which stated that 'the initiative for the creation of a nuclear-weapon-free zone in the appropriate region of Asia should come from the states of the region concerned, taking into account its special features and geographical extent'. The move resulted in the General Assembly adopting both the Indian and Pakistani resolutions without a vote.

The nature of Indian objections did not change even as New Delhi consented to not tabling an alternative draft resolution in 1977. In subsequent years, it continued to raise objections to and even voted against, or abstained from voting, on Pakistani resolutions. Beginning in 1987, however, India's criticism of SANWFZ was subsumed under its philosophical objection to NWFZ anywhere in the world. It argued that the deployment of nuclear weapons around the world could not be reconciled with the idea of establishing NWFZ. Such notions, the Indian representatives began to point out, amounted to 'annual and pointless ritual' which introduced 'unnecessary discordant notes to the process of regional cooperation'.[28] Effectively, therefore, India began to link the possibility of NWFZ, including one in South Asia, with complete and general disarmament.

Notwithstanding these general and specific objections, India's resistance to a SANWFZ can best be understood in terms of other factors as well. On top of the list is its perception of the 'Chinese nuclear threat'. As mentioned earlier, India's nuclear programme was triggered by the Chinese nuclear test of 1964. Since then, New Delhi has perceived the Chinese nuclear programme and its later modernisation with trepidation. In a similar vein to Pakistan, India has focused on its nuclear programme with the view of denying China the ability to drastically alter the regional balance against India and relegating it to a secondary position. These concerns underlie New Delhi's consistent refusal to entertain any notion of declaring South Asia a NWFZ. These concerns were apparent in the initial Indian response to the suggestions of such a zone. In 1974, for example, the Indian representative argued that 'the presence in Asia of countries belonging to military alliances and the existence of nuclear weapon powers would have a vital bearing on the viability of a nuclear weapon free zone' in South Asia. The same concerns have prompted some Indian analysts in the 1990s to argue for an Asian NWFZ instead of one for South Asia.[29]

Within the confines of South Asia only, India's objections have also stemmed from its view that the nuclear issue can only be addressed within the context of a 'comprehensive settlement' of issues bedevilling Indo-Pakistan relations. The 'non-papers' submitted by the Indian government to Islamabad on 24 January 1994, for example, identified the nuclear issue as one of the many that needed to be addressed for improving relations between India and Pakistan.[30]

The Case for a South Asian Nuclear-Weapon-Free Zone   163

Interestingly, despite its proposals for a denuclearised South Asia, Islamabad has also adopted a similar position. It either insists on arriving at a settlement on the Kashmir dispute before tackling the nuclear problem, or often includes nuclear issues in a set of problems that must be addressed to improve Indo-Pakistan relations. In an address to the National Defense University, Washington, for instance, Pakistan's ambassador to Geneva, Munir Akram, stated that 'nuclear proliferation [in South Asia] can be promoted *only* by evolving an approach which can address the inter-related issues – Kashmir, conventional arms and the nuclear threat – *in a comprehensive and integrated way*'.[31]

Indian objections and Pakistan's references to an integrated approach raise a number of questions about the feasibility of establishing a NWFZ in South Asia. Can a SANWFZ be established without improving the general context of Indo-Pakistan relations? Can the linkage between Indian concerns about the Chinese nuclear programme and its position on denuclearising South Asia be ignored in any suggestions for a nuclear-weapon-free South Asia? The answer to the first question can easily be given in the affirmative. Continued hostility between the two South Asian states notwithstanding, India and Pakistan have demonstrated their ability and willingness to negotiate agreements on issues affecting their security. The Indus Water Treaty is a major example of such an agreement, concluded in the non-traditional security arena in the 1960s. In the last decade, the two states have also negotiated on traditional security issues and adhered to these agreements. The agreement not to attack each other's nuclear installations concluded in 1985 and formally signed in 1988 is a significant example of such an attitude. Although the agreement was concluded during relatively calmer days, its formal conclusion, ratification and implementation has proceeded in the last six years of consistent animosity over developments in Kashmir. During the same period, that is, since 1992, India and Pakistan have also concluded agreements on advanced notification of military exercises, manoeuvres and troop movements, on prevention of airspace violations and the declaration on the prohibition of chemical weapons. More recently, with the change of governments in India and Pakistan, the two countries have resumed official dialogue at the highest level. At the South Asian Association for Regional Cooperation (SAARC) summit held in Male in May 1997, Indian Prime Minister Inder Kumar Gujral and his Pakistani counterpart Nawaz Sharif agreed to establish a 'hot line' between prime ministers of the two states.[32] This ability to isolate security issues from the general context of hostility suggests that, despite the claims to the contrary, India and Pakistan can and may be able and willing to negotiate an agreement to denuclearise South Asia.

The linkage between Indian concerns about China and its policy on a SANWFZ are relatively more difficult to answer in the affirmative. As mentioned earlier, India has been concerned about Chinese conventional and nuclear 'threats' to India. The 1990s, however, have witnessed an improvement in relations between the two states. In 1993, the two states began confidence-building measures by signing the Peace and Tranquillity Agreement. During the recent visit to India by the Chinese President, Jiang Zemin, India and China also agreed not to attack each other and to reduce tensions and troops along the Sino-Indian border.[33] These improvements have coincided with the emergence of groups in India that do not subscribe to the notion of China being unconditionally hostile towards India. They also view India as 'using' the 'China card' to justify its nuclear policy which, in their opinion, is really directed towards Pakistan. To say this is not to suggest that those adhering to the notion of Chinese unconditional hostility towards India are in a minority. The balance still favours the latter group. However, the presence of alternative perceptions of China in India suggests that a proposal which takes into account India's concerns *vis-à-vis* China may have a better chance of success in the late 1990s than it did in the past. This raises another question: what does such a proposal need to include?

A Phased Approach to a Nuclear-Weapon-Free South Asia

A proposal for establishing a NWFZ in South Asia requires a mixture of realism and idealism. Realism necessitates acknowledging and accepting the reality of the nuclearisation of South Asia and the dynamics that perpetuate the process. In other words, we need to accept that India acquired nuclear weapons due to a perceived Chinese threat and that Pakistan has opted for this course due to its fear of India. The other reality is the role that public perceptions (which in turn are moulded by the elite) and reactions play in arriving at a settlement in South Asia. Idealism, on the other hand, requires willingness to transcend these limits and explore options that may *ultimately*

The Case for a South Asian Nuclear-Weapon-Free Zone 165

lead to a denuclearised South Asia. Such a combination of realism and idealism suggests that a move towards a SANWFZ will have to be slow and gradual, and in steps that reduce (if not eliminate) misperceptions between the two South Asian nuclear threshold states. Such a move could take place in three phases which are outlined below. The first phase is given more emphasis than the later two primarily because its success would determine the likelihood of the two states entering the next two phases.

Phase I

The first phase would focus on non-*weaponisation*, instead of non-*nuclearisation* of South Asia. It would begin with both India and Pakistan jointly declaring that they would refrain from acquiring nuclear weapons and taking actions that could alter the nuclear strategic balance in South Asia. As in the case of the understanding not to attack nuclear installations declared by India and Pakistan in 1988, the proposed Declaration[34] will merely signal an intent which will be followed by efforts to devise a verification regime.

The first part of the Declaration would commit the two states to not moving from their present status of being nuclear-*capable* to nuclear-weapons states. Such a Declaration of intent is in line with the *declared* Indian and Pakistani positions of not acquiring nuclear-weapons capability. Since testing its nuclear device in 1974, certain factions in the military, academic and scientific community have favoured the 'option' strategy, that is keeping the option of moving from the peaceful to the military uses of nuclear capability.[35] Despite this pressure, and the increased calls in the wake of the debate on the Comprehensive Test Ban Treaty (CTBT) for testing another nuclear device and/or going openly nuclear, New Delhi has avoided committing itself to a nuclear-weapons programme. In September 1996, for example, when asked about weaponising India's nuclear capability, the then Indian Foreign Minister Gujral responded: '*At the moment, the agenda to do so is not there. Whether there will be such an agenda depends on the security threats we face*'.[36] Pakistan has followed a similar policy. Since the late 1980s when Islamabad began to issue direct and indirect acknowledgment of its nuclear capability, the Pakistan government has been careful to avoid suggesting that it intends to acquire nuclear-weapons capability. Instead, it has projected itself as a state willing to enter into an agreement with India on nuclear issues. The first part of the Declaration, therefore, will merely echo the declared positions of the two states.

The second part of the Declaration – a pledge not to alter the nuclear strategic balance – would imply a tacit agreement not to test a nuclear device. Once again, the Declaration would reflect the reality of Pakistani and Indian positions on the nuclear issue. The Indian government has resisted the pressure to test a nuclear device to stress its sovereignty. The Pakistan government has also been cautious not to succumb to the pressure from the 'pro-test lobby' in Pakistan. Essentially the reluctance indicates a realisation on the part of both the states that a nuclear test would change the scenario in the region. Not only would it prompt the other state to openly pursue its own nuclear-weapons programme but it would also elicit negative responses from other states, especially the United States. Despite this realisation, however, the two governments are unwilling to state their reluctance to test nuclear devices due to the expected backlash from their respective people. The proposed second part of the Declaration, therefore, does not categorically state that the parties would not test nuclear devices but implicitly commits them to such a stand.

Following the Declaration of intent, the South Asian regional countries would establish a Preparatory Commission for the Denuclearisation of South Asia, similar to the example of COPREDAL in Latin America (as discussed in chapter 2). The proposed Commission would include representatives from India, Pakistan, Bangladesh, the Maldives, Nepal, Sri Lanka and Bhutan and would be divided into two major working groups. The 'First Group', with representatives from all the member countries, would focus on the peaceful uses of nuclear energy including its possible use in meeting the power generation requirements of the regional states. Such a group would acknowledge that developing countries can benefit from nuclear energy without being classified as 'pariah' states. Indirectly, the presence of scientists from countries other than India and Pakistan would also indicate their interest in preventing the introduction of nuclear weapons in the region. By bringing experts together from the region, the group would also contribute to building confidence among the regional states.[37]

The other working group, the Second Group, would include representatives from India and Pakistan only. Such a group would acknowledge that India and Pakistan are the only two nuclear-capable states, and would work towards a verification regime which could support the Declaration of not acquiring nuclear weapons made by them. To some extent, both India and Pakistan already engage in what may be termed as 'negative verification'; under the agreement not to attack each other's nuclear installations, the two neighbours annually exchange a list of their nuclear facilities. Although the information exchanged by India and Pakistan is not openly available, the likelihood of a nuclear facility being attacked if it was not mentioned in the list operates as an automatic incentive for both sides to provide accurate information on their nuclear installations. Under the proposed Phase I, however, the Second Group would be entrusted with the task of devising a 'positive' regime of verification.

The verification regime would need to acknowledge that the projected number of nuclear weapons that India and Pakistan can acquire is extremely small compared to those present in the US and Russian inventories. Therefore, even a low level of non-compliance with a verification regime could result in extremely significant military-strategic gain for the offending state. Hence, both the states would need to agree upon a verification regime which is more intrusive, stringent and yet flexible than those agreed upon by Moscow and Washington in their arms control agreements. A number of models for verification have been suggested which range from placing all Indian and Pakistani nuclear facilities under the IAEA safeguards to the two South Asian states building their own extensive remote monitoring and support system.[38] While the first suggestion would compromise India's refusal to place all of its nuclear facilities under the IAEA, the latter would cost the two South Asian states $12 billion. A more realistic verification regime, therefore, will be one which is controlled by India and Pakistan while permitting the use of regional and international support networks and facilities to supplement their bilateral efforts. This could take the form of New Delhi and Islamabad agreeing to rely on their national technical means of verification. Given that commercial satellites have been permitted in the US to produce and sell satellite imagery of high resolution, India and Pakistan may be able to arrive at some mutually agreed principles of using these facilities for ensuring compliance with the agreement not to move from nuclear-capable to nuclear-weapons status.[39] They may also draw upon the expertise being developed by the United States and Russia for remote-control monitoring of stocks of weapons-grade nuclear material by using electronic systems.[40]

The issue of on-site inspections will also need to be addressed carefully. The negativity surrounding Indo-Pakistan relations could easily politicise the issue to such an extent that proper verification cannot be ensured. To avoid such an eventuality, it would be advisable to proceed slowly with the idea of on-site inspections. Initially, India and Pakistan could use the help of the IAEA. Some selected nuclear facilities, for example Tarapur reactor in India and KANNUP in Pakistan, are already safeguarded by the Agency. If the two states agree, they could introduce on-site inspections by allowing inspectors from the other country to join the IAEA inspectors for their regular inspections. The process will enable the two sides to build confidence and also establish areas of cooperation between the IAEA, and India and Pakistan. Once enough confidence is built, New Delhi and Islamabad would need to deal with the question of routine and challenge inspections. Once again, the need to protect the verification process from political manipulation would require that the number of these inspections is fixed and not unlimited.

Finally, India and Pakistan could also draw upon the information gathered by the NWS, especially the United States, on nuclear proliferation, or its absence, in South Asia. The information thus gathered – through bilateral, regional and international means – would need to be managed and coordinated by an agency. As in the case of the Treaty of Tlatelolco, an Agency for the Prohibition of Nuclear Weapons in South Asia may be established that performs this task. It could also act as the Standing Committee dealing with complaints of non-compliance. The Agency would need to have two sub-organisations: bilateral and regional. While the regional and enlarged group could be involved in determining if violation of the Declaration has occurred, the primary responsibility and control would rest with India and Pakistan.

Assuming that a verification regime can be devised, the NWS would need to provide negative security guarantees to both India and Pakistan. In view of India's claim that the emergence of new possible nuclear states in Central Asia and Iran also pose potential threats to Indian security, it would be necessary to supplement the guarantees by NWS with negative security assurances from regional states as well. This would effectively result in a two-tiered guarantor system including both regional and global nuclear or potentially nuclear states. China falls within both these categories. The history of its relationship with India would necessitate that China provides more specific security guarantees, especially to India. This would include a pledge not to target Indian sites, and not to supply nuclear weapons or capability to Pakistan.

Once the above-mentioned steps have been completed, the Indian and Pakistani Joint Declaration could be signed as a treaty prohibiting the acquisition of nuclear weapons in South Asia.

Phases II and III

Once the Declaration becomes a treaty, India and Pakistan could begin negotiations on a proportionate reduction in their stocks of fissile material. The Preparatory Commission could perform the role with the help of the proposed Agency. The acquisition of nuclear-weapons capability is often linked by Pakistani analysts to their country's lack of strategic depth and the imbalance in conventional force capability between India and Pakistan. Hence, an agreement dealing with the reduction of fissile material may involve some form of agreement between the two countries on reducing the level of their conventional forces as well. Once completed, India and Pakistan and the region could safely negotiate a treaty for denuclearising South Asia which would meet the traditional criteria of a NWFZ.

Concluding Remarks

The transition from bipolarity to the current state of fluid multipolarity is paralleled by an increase in the types and nature of threats to international stability. Non-military threats and issues faced by the world, including the danger of environmental degradation, drug trafficking and the AIDS epidemic, require new solutions. At the same time, the continued relevance of military issues necessitates creative approaches to deal with threats to stability emanating from the proliferation of all kinds of weapons. Specifically, the threat of horizontal nuclear proliferation requires new or improved solutions which accept the limits imposed by the existing realities while simultaneously attempting to transcend these limits. Within the South Asian context, this translates into finding approaches that acknowledge the continued hostility between India and Pakistan but are not deterred from searching for solutions that assist in 'managing' this hostility. The idea of a phased model for establishing a South Asian Nuclear-Weapon-Free Zone fits into this category. The economic, social and political realities of the region require that such a model be developed and implemented. The process, as outlined in this paper, may be long and tortuous – but is worth the effort.

Notes

1. Cited by Mahmoud Karem, *A Nuclear-Weapon-Free Zone in the Middle East: Problems and Prospects* (New York: Greenwood Press, 1988), p. 2.
2. Ramesh Thakur, 'The Treaty of Raratonga: The South Pacific Nuclear-Free Zone', in David Pitt and Gordon Thompson, eds, *Nuclear-Free Zones* (London: Croom Helm, 1987), pp. 23–45; and Sola Ogunbanwo, 'The Treaty of Pelindaba: Africa is Nuclear-Weapon Free', *Security Dialogue* 27 (February 1996), pp. 185–200.
3. Samina Yasmeen and Aabha Dixit, *Confidence-building Measures in South Asia* (Washington DC: Henry Stimson Center, Occasional Paper No. 24, 1995).
4. US Government, Report to Congress on Progress Toward Regional Nonproliferation in South Asia, (1993), cited by Amitabh Mattoo, 'India's Nuclear Status Quo', *Survival* 38 (Autumn 1996), p. 42.
5. David Albright, William M. Arkin, Frans Berkhout, Robert Norris and William Walker, 'Inventories of Fissile Materials and Nuclear Weapons', *SIPRI Yearbook 1995: Armaments, Disarmament and International Security* (Oxford: Oxford University Press for SIPRI, 1995), p. 321.
6. David Albright, Frans Berkhout and William Walker, *SIPRI World Inventory of Plutonium and Highly Enriched Uranium, 1992* (Oxford: Oxford University Press for SIPRI, 1993), pp. 161–2, cited by Eric Arnett, 'Implications of the comprehensive test ban for nuclear weapon programmes and decision making', in Eric Arnett, ed., *Nuclear Weapons After the Comprehensive Test Ban: Implications for Modernization and Proliferation* (New York: Oxford University Press, 1996), p. 13.
7. W. P. S. Sidhu, 'India's Nuclear Tests: Technical and Military Imperatives', *Jane's Intelligence Review*, April 1996, pp. 171–2.
8. Shafqat Ali Khan, 'Pakistan', in Arnett, ed., *Nuclear Weapons After the Comprehensive Test Ban,* pp. 74–7; and W. P. S. Sidhu, 'Pakistan's Bomb: a quest for credibility', *Jane's Intelligence Review*, June 1996, pp. 278–9.
9. See, for example, Zahid Malik, *Dr A. Q. Khan and the Islamic Bomb* (Islamabad: Hurmat Publications, 1992), ch. 18.

The Case for a South Asian Nuclear-Weapon-Free Zone 171

10. See, for example, Benazir Bhutto's interview on NBC TV, 2 September 1991; General Aslam Beg, *Pakistan Times* (Lahore), 11 December 1993; and Nawaz Sharif's statement, *Nation* (Lahore), 24 August 1994.
11. Arnett, 'Implications of the comprehensive test ban', pp. 16–17; and Albright, et al., *SIPRI World Inventory*, p. 325.
12. See, for example, Devin T. Hagerty, 'Nuclear Deterrence in South Asia: The 1990 Indo–Pakistani Crisis', *International Security* 20 (Winter 1995–96), pp. 79–114; and Najam Sethi, 'Indo–Pak Nuclear Future', *Friday Times* (Lahore), 18–24 April 1996, pp. 6–7.
13. Such an acceptance is reflected in the report prepared by a task force of 28 foreign policy experts under the auspices of the Council on Foreign Relations, issued in January 1997. Cited in *Programme for Promoting Nuclear Non-Proliferation Newsbrief* 37 (First Quarter 1997), p. 10.
14. See, for example, Daniel Goleman, *Emotional Intelligence* (New York: Bantam, 1995); and Anthony Stevens, *The Roots of War: A Jungian Perspective* (New York: Paragon House, 1989).
15. I am indebted to James Trevelyan for bringing this to my attention.
16. Michael Krepon and Mishi Faruqee, *Conflict Prevention and Confidence Building Measures in South Asia: The 1990 Crisis* (Washington DC: Henry Stimson Center, 1994).
17. 'India suspends missile programme', *West Australian* (Perth), 7 December 1996, p. 21.
18. 'Ballistic Missile Capability in the Middle East, Central, South and East Asia Map', *Military Balance 1996–97* (London: International Institute for Strategic Studies, 1996).
19. S. Rashid Naim, 'After Midnight', in Stephen P. Cohen, ed., *Nuclear Proliferation in South Asia: The Prospects for Arms Control* (Boulder: Westview, 1991), pp. 48–58.
20. *From Plan to Market: World Development Report 1996* (New York: Oxford University Press for the World Bank, 1996), pp. 188–222.
21. *Dawn* (Karachi), 4 October 1972.
22. *Dawn*, 29 November 1972.
23. *Dawn*, 21 August 1974.
24. General Assembly, Official Records, Proceedings of the First Committee, 29th Session, 2002nd meeting, 28 October 1974, Document A/C.1/PV.2002, p. 47.
25. Document A/C.1/PV.2002, pp. 43–7.
26. See, for example, Resolution Adopted by the General Assembly: Establishment of a nuclear-weapon-free zone in South Asia, A/Res/50/67, 9 January 1996.
27. General Assembly Official Records, First Committee, 29th session, 2016th meeting, 11 November 1974, Document A/C.1/PV.2016, pp. 26–7.
28. Savita Pande, *Pakistan's Nuclear Policy* (Delhi: B. R. Publishing Corporation, 1991), pp. 139–40.

29. Discussion with Jasjit Singh, Director, Institute for Defence Studies and Analyses (New Delhi), November 1996.
30. J. N. Dixit, *Anatomy of a Flawed Inheritance: Indo–Pak Relations 1970–1994* (Delhi: Konark Publishers, 1995).
31. 'Pakistan for 3-track approach to end nuclear proliferation', *Nation*, 23 November 1996; emphasis added.
32. *Nation*, 14 May 1997.
33. *Hindu* (Chennai), 30 November 1996.
34. Hereafter cited as 'the Declaration'.
35. See, for example, details of the Indian Defence Ministry's Annual Report for 1996–7 in 'India to keep nuclear option open', *Statesman* (Calcutta), 10 April 1997, and 'Gaps in defence', *Hindustan Times* (Delhi), 11 April 1997.
36. Raj Chengappa, '"We had no option": Interview with I. K. Gujral', *India Today*, 15 September 1996, p. 78; emphasis added.
37. The willingness of the new Pakistani government to recognise the need for such regional cooperation is evident in Nawaz Sharif's statements at the Male SAARC Summit. See, for example, 'Nawaz calls for check on military spending', *Nation*, 13 May 1997.
38. Vipin Gupta, 'Sensing the Threat', in Cohen, ed., *Nuclear Proliferation in South Asia*, pp. 225–61.
39. Richard Kokoski, *Technology and the Proliferation of Nuclear Weapons* (Oxford: Oxford University Press for SIPRI, 1995), pp. 209–15.
40. *Programme for Promoting Nuclear Non-Proliferation Newsbrief* 30 (Second Quarter 1995), p. 5.

9
The Obstacles to a South Asian Nuclear-Weapon-Free Zone

Dipankar Banerjee

The 1990s are witnessing a restructuring of the global strategic order, reflecting the realities of the emerging post-Cold War world – an environment that is not necessarily more peaceful, but where major wars between leading nations are less likely than they have been for the last fifty years. The strategic order is in transition, from a bipolar, through temporary unipolarity, to a multipolar world. Yet major powers will still have a dominant voice for some time. A major impact of this has been on the state of weapons of mass destruction (WMD). It had been hoped that after the Cold War, a serious debate would emerge on the role of WMD, and that these could be eliminated over a period of time through international consensus. But the reality has unfolded differently. The nuclear-weapons states (NWS) continue to see these weapons as necessary for their security. Given their ultimate global political authority as permanent members of the UN Security Council, their views are likely to prevail, as long as there is consensus amongst them.

The trend is thus towards arms control, not disarmament, and a perpetuation of the advantages of NWS through sole control over nuclear weapons. It is a move from large stockpiles to smaller but more effective weapons and delivery systems. There are attempts at preventing horizontal proliferation but at the same time consolidating the possession of nuclear weapons in the hands of a select few. Efforts that aim to reduce WMD must surely be welcomed in any environment. Steps that reduce the possibility of conflict, especially nuclear conflict, must be vigorously pursued. But it is also important to understand the context in which these steps are taking place. Only then will they provide a guide to substantial measures that are needed, rather than cosmetic arrangements that do not achieve anything significant.

A number of major and positive steps have indeed been taken in recent years in the sphere of arms control. The Strategic Arms Reduction Treaties (START) I and II are being implemented. The Chemical Weapons Convention (CWC) was signed after long deliberation and came into effect on 29 April 1997. The Nuclear Non-Proliferation Treaty (NPT) has been extended unconditionally and in perpetuity. The Comprehensive Test Ban Treaty (CTBT) was signed at the UN General Assembly in Autumn 1996. The NWS provided negative and positive security assurances on 11 April 1995 prior to the NPT extension, to the signatories of the Treaty. These are indeed major developments and must be welcomed. Yet all these are in response to the compelling new strategic conditions and are not measures for disarmament. They neither challenge the relevance of nuclear weapons in today's world nor their continuance in the hands of a select few.

The START process was an acceptance of two realities and not the result of a change in any strategic thinking. The first reality was the utter mindlessness of the enormous vertical nuclear proliferation of the US and the USSR. Second, it rested on the acceptance by the Soviet Union that it could no longer continue the race. The irrelevance of tactical nuclear weapons in any rational operational scenario had earlier led to the conclusion of the Intermediate-range Nuclear Forces (INF) Treaty and later to the elimination and withdrawal of a large variety of weapons and their delivery means. The CWC, which was long in gestation, became rapidly acceptable only when it seemed likely that it might well emerge as the poor man's nuclear bomb. The discriminatory nature of the NPT is apparent to all. The CTBT will continue to allow modernisation and upgradation through non-explosive means in nuclear laboratories. Actually, the acceptance of a zero-yield CTBT by the US was with major caveats. It permits adequate 'safeguards' in the form of maintaining nuclear-weapons laboratories at high states of readiness, the nuclear test sites ready to resume tests at short notice, and with the US President as the sole arbiter as to whether the nation should 'cease to be bound' by the constraints of the Treaty. Which really makes the CTBT at best a T(emporary)TBT for the US.[1]

The Obstacles to a South Asian Nuclear-Weapon-Free Zone 175

Even these processes are but halting steps. START II is unlikely to be ratified by the Russian Duma in the near future. Elimination of Russian strategic weapons is well behind schedule because of financial constraints. A START III seems to be far too distant. The extension of the NPT without a review process puts it firmly in the status of an arms control arrangement with no compulsions on the nuclear powers for the elimination, or even substantial reduction, of their nuclear stockpiles. The CWC has been triggered for implementation through the 65th ratification in 1996 with major powers out of its fold. There is little possibility of the CWC or even the CTBT being ratified by the US Senate during the next four years under the present administration. China has not reduced a single nuclear weapon – it always puts this off as a distant objective and shifts the goal posts with fresh objections. Beijing is not a party to the INF Treaty. It is presently undertaking a major upgradation of its nuclear weapons and their delivery capability. Serious doubts remain regarding the coming-into-force of the CTBT mainly because of its unique entry-into-force clause and the less-than-wholehearted support extended to it by at least some of the NWS.[2]

It is in the context of the global strategic environment that nuclear-weapon-free zones (NWFZ) have evolved. The motivation of the regions who have declared themselves nuclear-weapon-free is to isolate themselves from superpower nuclear rivalry as well as nuclear-related activities. The Tlatelolco Treaty was a response to the Cuban missile crisis of 1962. The proposal for the African zone was made in the early 1960s as a consequence of French nuclear tests in Algeria. The Rarotonga Treaty came about because of continued French nuclear tests in the South Pacific.[3] The Bangkok Treaty is an attempt at regional solidarity against China's growing nuclear capability and military assertiveness. In all cases they responded to the strategic environment and by themselves could not alter it in a positive way.

The NWFZ have often come into conflict with the strategic interests of the NWS which is the determining factor in their acceptance. As a result NWFZ have to adjust to these requirements, which entail accommodating existing security relationships, respecting the free transit of naval ships and submarines and avoiding direct challenge to the nuclear powers' interests in any way.[4] Even then the actual signing of the protocols may be delayed till their applicability itself may have become redundant. Protocols to the Rarotonga Treaty were acceded to by the three Western nuclear powers only in March 1996. This was achieved after the original purpose of the treaty, to prevent the nuclear tests of France, had ended. The Pelindaba Treaty could be formulated only when South Africa decided to destroy its nuclear arsenal under the changed political condition in the country. The recent treaties may also be seen as a response to the changed strategic realities and the slow progress on global disarmament.

What is a Nuclear-Weapon-Free Zone?

Before proceeding further it is important to briefly consider the nature of a NWFZ. What is it that it seeks to achieve? According to the UN the purpose of a NWFZ is to enhance national and regional security. The UN General Assembly Resolution in 1975 went on to define it as:

> A NWFZ shall as a general rule, be deemed to be any zone, recognised as such by the General Assembly of the UN, which any group of states, in the free exchange of sovereignty, has established by virtue of a Treaty or Convention, whereby:
>
> (a) The status of total absence of nuclear weapons to which the Zone shall be subject, including the procedure for the delimitation of the Zone, is defined.
>
> (b) An international system of verification and control is established to generate compliance with the obligations deriving from that statute.[5]

The first question lies in defining the zone itself. How is it to be delimited? Naturally it has to be large enough to encompass an entire strategic environment. For example the Antarctic, Tlatelolco and Pelindaba treaties include whole continents in their ambit. It is possible to have smaller zones of course as in Rarotonga. But this last treaty area is strategically self-contained and somewhat remote.

The major condition that a zone attempts to achieve is the total absence of nuclear weapons. Members of a NWFZ would usually be signatories to the NPT, unless there were specific objections in principle to the treaty, as in the case of Brazil. The question then is what is it that a NWFZ attempts to achieve that is not provided in the NPT? It is specifically in denying the presence of nuclear weapons in the zone that the NWFZ scores over the NPT. The latter only prohibits the acquisition of a capability. NWFZ ban its deployment by extra-regional parties. This would indeed be a positive step if it were

The Obstacles to a South Asian Nuclear-Weapon-Free Zone 177

possible to achieve it in reality. However, 'nuclear-weapon-free' is entirely misleading. No NWFZ prevents the free movement of warships, nuclear submarines or aircraft with nuclear weapons on board. All NWFZ allow the rights of 'innocent passage'. As long as NWS do not specifically declare these, no questions are asked. By adopting a simple policy of neither confirming nor denying, a NWS can do pretty much as it pleases. It is only rarely and by unilateral action, such as by New Zealand, that more effective exclusion becomes possible. By including the continental shelf within its area, the Southeast Asian Nuclear-Weapon-Free Zone (SEANWFZ) has attempted to widen the zone of ban of nuclear-weapons deployment. This has come under serious opposition from the NWS that are directly affected. The Law of the Sea Convention here conflicts with the strategic requirement of nations. A resolution of this may be a difficult issue to handle.

In any case, the very concept of 'nuclear-weapon-free' is dubious when strategic delivery means permit engagement of targets in a NWFZ from very long distances, indeed from the other end of the world. However, the symbolic value could be of some significance. But even this would lose its relevance if a NWS were to be in the immediate neighbourhood or adjacent to a NWFZ. Its nuclear-weapons capability will directly impinge on the security of nations. It will also perpetuate a definite asymmetry in capability with that nation and others on its borders. In that case the aim of a NWFZ may either be merely to create a buffer, as is being discussed in some quarters for Central Europe, between Russia and an eastward expanding North Atlantic Treaty Organisation (NATO). Or it may be an attempt to dissuade a nuclear neighbour by putting up a symbolic barrier, as in the case of SEANWFZ. Both are of no strategic consequence. Nor do they constitute additional measures of denuclearisation.

An additional feature of a NWFZ is that it adds regional verification measures to the NPT verification structure and the International Atomic Energy Agency (IAEA) safeguards system. This may allow regional pressures to identify violation – a neighbouring country can be expected to have the greatest interest in a possible violation of the treaty. In practice this is hardly a more effective solution. Regional verification mechanisms lack the capability and hence have inadequate assurance. For that matter the IAEA's resources too are inadequate and its inspection mechanism has been enormously stretched. The recent cases of North Korea and Iraq have exposed the IAEA's limitations.

Therefore, NWFZ are unable to prevent deployment and in practice cannot provide assurances higher than that under the NPT. Actually a NWFZ constitutes no panacea. It can neither substitute for a national security policy, nor can it remove the threat of nuclear war. It is primarily a confidence-building measure (CBM) which needs to be tailored to the specific circumstances of the region in question and the links that exists between that region and the international order. It is a possible instrument in support of limited but broader purposes.

The Israeli Foreign Minister Abba Eban compared the NWFZ to neutrality: 'a region declaring itself as nuclear-free is very similar to declaring itself "neutral"'. Therefore, 'nuclear-free zones, like neutrality, are a unilateral hope, not a prescription for safety'.[6]

It is true that a NWFZ does not in itself create a better security environment. It usually follows one. Developing a more conducive security environment may indeed be considered to be a prerequisite for a NWFZ. In the case of Africa, as long as the minority white South African government was in power and hoped to continue, there were no chances of its fruition. Only after it was replaced by a majority black rule and its nuclear-weapons capability was disbanded was it possible to create one. In summation a NWFZ may be considered a palliative, but hardly an antidote.

A South Asian Nuclear-Weapon-Free Zone?

In considering a NWFZ for South Asia, the first issue that arises is one of delimiting the area itself. While South Asia is a geopolitical entity it has never been a geostrategic one. Geographically, its perimeters have been bounded by the Himalayas in the north and the Indian Ocean in the south. Both were major obstacles to movement. This allowed a distinct cultural identity to emerge, but did not define its security parameters. Threats to security always came from outside – from as far as Greece over two millennia ago, to the recent one from the north in the 1960s. The Indian Ocean was crossed by the British Navy for its conquests over three hundred years ago. It was again from the sea that India was challenged by the aircraft carrier *USS Enterprise* with nuclear weapons on board in 1971. The Mughal invasions for over a thousand years originated deep in Central Asia. In recent years the missile capability of nations such as Saudi Arabia and Iran will compel their inclusion as well. Right through history,

Afghanistan has been an extension of the security environment of the region. For the last two decades it has influenced events in the subcontinent even more deeply. Another factor that militates against a too narrow definition of the region is the extra-regional security connections. India was perceived to have a close relationship with the Soviet Union through the Indo-Soviet Friendship Treaty of 1971. Pakistan has, since 1954, been part of the Western alliance. Its links with the US continued until the signing of the Afghanistan accord. Since the 1960s it has had a relationship of strategic cooperation with China. This extended to nuclear and missile technology areas, including the supply of crucial nuclear components and complete missiles. Thus strategic interactions compel a wider view of the region.

At this stage a brief consideration of India-China relations may be helpful. The initial period of friendship in the 1950s soon gave way to tension and conflict. The brief border war of 1962 left a deep mark on the Indian psyche. Relations began to be normalised in 1976 and many positive developments have taken place in the last two decades. Border talks began in 1981 and have continued since then. High-level political visits have helped ease tensions and cooperation has developed in a number of areas. President Jiang Zemin's visit to India in November 1996 was an important milestone in the process. The agreement signed on that occasion renouncing the use of military capability against each other comes as close to a no war pact as is possible between nations.

Yet major problems remain. The actual border is unresolved. Major territorial claims remain outstanding and have not been renounced by China. Significant troop reductions are likely and some have already taken place. But the Line of Actual Control remains militarised. China's relations with Pakistan and Myanmar continue to be of concern to New Delhi. In this environment, an expectation that India should not only lower its guard, but renounce forever any semblance of a deterrent capability, is highly credulous.

Geostrategically Southern Asia, which encompasses these areas, is what will delimit the area of a NWFZ more appropriately. It must then be a continuation of the SEANWFZ, include at least the northern part of the Indian Ocean, and merge with the African NWFZ. While the Pelindaba Treaty could afford to ignore Diego Garcia and leave this out of its limits, a gap such as this cannot be left between two zones. To the west it must include the Arabian peninsula and to its north, Central Asia, Tibet, Xinxiang and southern China.

Any region smaller than this will focus the issue too narrowly on an India-Pakistan framework. Not only will this be an utter travesty of reality, it may actually be a cause of greater instability. Reliance on conventional military capabilities will favour a stronger India. If it is India and Pakistan that are to be considered and security is to be the major issue, a persuasive case can be made to support nuclear-weapons acquisition by both countries. Then by every tenet of Western nuclear doctrine, a state of nuclear deterrence will preclude the chance of conflict. Indeed this is the principal plank of Pakistan's determined effort at acquiring a nuclear-weapons capability for itself. This raises doubts as to whether Pakistan is genuinely sincere about a NWFZ proposal for the restricted South Asian region, or is this merely to 'embarrass' India, knowing full well New Delhi's principled opposition to such an arrangement.

It is this limited focus on bilateral capability in Pakistan's proposal on a NWFZ for the region that India finds difficult to accept. Pakistan has been raising the issue of a NWFZ in South Asia in the UN General Assembly since 1974. It has not abided by the principle of prior consultations among member countries of the wider area. The proposal thus has not emerged as a consensus document from the region but as a unilateral proposal from one country. It is too apparent an attempt at propaganda to merit a response. India's position on this proposal has been that the initiative should emanate from the states of the region and only after considering its special features and geographic extent.

The principal issue in a NWFZ is security. Its goal must be un-diminished and enhanced security for all its members. At the same time the region has to be free of major tensions and conflicts to enable a CBM such as this to be effective. For this to be possible a degree of trust is essential to the process. This alone will allow satisfaction regarding verification systems and procedures and lend credibility to the denuclearisation of the region.

The situation today is still far from conducive to this. There continue to be major outstanding issues. Sino-Pakistan strategic co-operation, its mutual nuclear relationship both in civil power and weapons-related areas and in military weapons development projects cause concern in the region, particularly to India. China's military supply to Myanmar is another area of regional concern. The full dimension and nature of this relationship is unclear, but it has the potential to pose a level of military threat to the region in the future that has to be taken into account. An area of more serious concern is the proxy war by Pakistan in Kashmir and the allocation of a somewhat mystifying role to its nuclear capability in this situation. Finally, there is the range of relationships between India and China. Although this has improved substantially in recent years, there continue to be disturbing elements. Large areas of territory remain disputed. Autonomy of Tibet appears still to be a sore point with China. Large forces remain deployed along the border. In this environment a prudent measure for any nation is not mere cosmetic additional CBM, but the retention of possible options to deal with suddenly developing adverse situations in the future.

Finally, there is the question of verification. The passage of ships carrying nuclear weapons in the Indian Ocean would be of particular concern in the region. A policy of neither confirming nor denying will not suffice. There has to be a more substantive assurance of denuclearisation and a verification system to ensure this. A similar assurance would be needed regarding absence of nuclear deployment in the Tibetan plateau.

SANWFZ Conditionality

It may be interesting to speculate about the conditions that would be necessary to achieve a true and effective NWFZ for Southern Asia that will meet genuine security concerns for all nations of the region. As an important and centrally located country in the region, India's legitimate interests cannot be overlooked in any formulation. The major conditions that will have to be met may be as follows:

- It has to be rooted firmly in the context of global nuclear disarmament. A NWFZ merely as an additional CBM is not worth pursuing.
- It must encompass a Southern Asian region that is wider in its geostrategic context. The northern half of the Indian Ocean is automatically a part of this.
- China has to be included within this region as it is a part of the security environment. At the same time its strategic consideration

vis-à-vis the other major powers needs to be accommodated. The two minimum conditions that China would need to meet are to accept the conditions of the INF Treaty and eliminate delivery systems below 5500km; and eliminate strategic weapons from the Tibetan plateau.

- Await further improvement of India-China relations and perhaps a settlement of the border question.
- Include all WMD in its fold. It is illogical to eliminate only nuclear weapons.
- Eliminate nuclear-weapons passage in the Indian Ocean.

The above are not formidable to achieve. Enough developments have taken place recently that will permit moves along these lines.

A few points to highlight India's approach on disarmament over the years may not be entirely out of place in this regard. As early as 1948, along with the setting-up of the Atomic Energy Commission of India, Jawaharlal Nehru said in Parliament that the country's nuclear energy programme would be for the welfare of the people and other peaceful purposes. In 1957 he was even more explicit:

> No man can prophesy the future. But I should like to say on behalf of any future Government of India that whatever might happen, that whatever the circumstances, we shall never use this atomic energy for evil purposes. There is no condition attached to this assurance, because once a condition is attached, the value of such an assurance does not go very far.[7]

There was considerable moral authority behind this statement which itself was rooted in India's civilisational values. It continues to shape Indian policy today. India did not conduct a nuclear test prior to 1967, which was well within its capability, and one that would have legitimised India's status as a NWS. It did not weaponise after the 1974 peaceful nuclear explosion. It has gone along with all genuine disarmament measures for WMD. It has ratified the CWC even though Russia, China and Pakistan have not yet done so. India is not against either the NPT or the CTBT, but only against their discriminatory provisions and their lack of movement towards disarmament. In the future as well, India can be counted on to adopt policies that are in line with these approaches. This is also largely in line with India's own security interests, which of course cannot be set aside.

Conclusion

A NWFZ is by no means a bad thing. But is it effective? It may be a CBM, but is that meaningful and serving a purpose? These are questions that need to be thought through. Will diversion to a NWFZ deflect us from pursuing substantial and meaningful steps for disarmament and enhancing security? The case in favour is not a strong one. In any case the decision is regional. Freeing the southern hemisphere of nuclear-weapons deployment will by all means be a significant achievement. But this will have to be effective and not merely cosmetic. Surely a stage has come when we need to address the question of restricting these weapons entirely to home countries.

The case for a South Asian NWFZ is not a strong one. But a Southern Asian NWFZ may be an idea worth pursuing. China has adopted a policy of strengthening relations with its neighbours. It needs to be involved in regional disarmament processes. The time now may be right for a beginning.

Notes

1. Mike Moore, 'End the Nuclear Disarmament Shell Game', *Disarmament Diplomacy* 9 (October 1996), pp. 5–6.
2. Ibid., pp. 4–7. Moore, the editor of the *Bulletin of Atomic Scientists*, describes the CTBT process as a shell game.
3. Michael Hamel-Green, 'Nuclear Weapon Free Zone: Peeling the Nuclear Orange from the Bottom Up', *Disarmament Diplomacy* 9 (October 1996), pp. 7–10.
4. Zachary S. Davis, 'The Spread of Nuclear-Weapon-Free Zones: Building a New Nuclear Bargain', *Arms Control Today* 26 (February 1996), p. 15.
5. UNGA Resolution 3472B [30th Session], 11 December 1975.
6. Mahmoud Karem, *A Nuclear-Weapon-Free Zone in the Middle East: Problems and Prospects* (New York: Greenwood, 1988), pp. 53–5.
7. Nehru made this statement while speaking at the inauguration of Apsara, India's first nuclear reactor at Trombay, near Mumbai, 20 January 1957. *Jawaharlal Nehru's Speeches, Vol III, March 1953–August 1957* (New Delhi: Government of India, Ministry of Information and Broadcasting, Publications Division, 1957), p. 507.

10
The Case For a Nuclear-Weapon-Free Zone in the Middle East

Ibrahim A. Karawan

The fact that the Middle East lags behind Latin America, the South Pacific, Southeast Asia and Africa with regard to the creation of a regional nuclear-weapon-free zone (NWFZ) is not surprising. Anyone familiar with the acute complexity of the Arab-Israeli conflict and its protracted nature, as well as its multi-dimensional levels and the historical legacies created by that conflict, will not find it difficult to understand why. The obstacles facing regional actors in reaching a consensus with regard to issues which have been settled in other parts of the developed and less developed worlds are numerous, and the confidence between the parties to overcome these obstacles is seriously lacking.

There are other conflicts in the Middle East that complicate reaching such a consensus. The conflict in the Persian Gulf is one important example of conflicts that influence the political perceptions and interactions not only in that sub-region, but also beyond the boundaries of the Gulf itself. In short, I am aware of the difficulties and the structural and psychological factors that have hindered, thus far, the establishment of a NWFZ in the Middle East. The challenge is so daunting because establishing such a zone in fact, and not on paper, involves two difficult and interrelated tasks: rolling back the Israeli nuclear-weapons programme, and freezing the non-nuclear status of the other regional actors.[1]

Despite the enormous difficulties associated with these tasks, the issue of nuclear weapons and their threatening proliferation is serious enough to warrant reassessing our positions about it. It cannot be ignored just because a breakthrough in the short term is not likely. Rather, regional actors, with the involvement of other powers, should discuss it with the objective of gaining a better understanding of each other's positions.

There is consensus among Middle East observers, as well as policy makers, that the region has one sole nuclear power – Israel. Many use terms, among others, like 'proto-nuclear', opacity and the 'bomb in the basement'.[2] There is little doubt about Israel's possession of a nuclear arsenal and the means of delivering nuclear devices to their intended targets in the extended region, if the Israeli decision makers decided to do so. Regardless of Israel's refusal to acknowledge this nuclear capability, it has become widely recognised regionally and internationally, particularly after information provided by Mordechai Vanunu in 1986. Policy makers in surrounding countries, and their societies, must take this factor into consideration.

The overwhelming majority of discussions about the nuclear factor in the Middle East tend to be quite contentious and polemical in content and style. I would like to make two precautionary points to set the stage for my argument. First, I am not going to argue that the decision by the late Israeli Prime Minister, David Ben Gurion, to acquire a nuclear capability for Israel was at that particular time imprudent. The core features of the regional setting in the late 1950s and early 1960s as they were perceived by the Israeli elite underlined the importance of acquiring a non-conventional deterrence. Israel's demonstration of its own preponderance of conventional might, as well as the widely held perceptions among Arab leaders that it had nuclear capability, put significant constraints on those leaders' conduct *vis-à-vis* the Jewish state. Thus pursuing the nuclear option in that case did not simply result from paranoia. As Henry Kissinger once argued, even paranoid people have enemies at times.

Rather, I argue that one should not minimise the significance of transformations on the regional level, changes that could make the nuclear card or the so-called 'two hundred bombs in the basement' approach reach the outer limits of its strategic utility. What might have been useful two or three decades ago does not remain necessarily so, and may not continue to function that way in the future. Instead, it might accelerate the proliferation of nuclear weapons in the region, because other states are going to perceive the Israeli nuclear monopoly as threatening enough to warrant developing their own nuclear capabilities.

Second, the time frame of any policy restructuring on Israel's part is one of the most important variables that needs to be taken into consideration. A dramatic alteration of Israel's position regarding the Nuclear Non-Proliferation Treaty (NPT), and making the Middle East a NWFZ cannot happen overnight. As the decision to go nuclear was influenced by the protracted state of war in the region, any decision to move in the opposite direction – denuclearisation – has to be tied to the Middle East peace process and its consolidation. Nonetheless, such a move should not be made contingent on having not only Arab but also Islamic countries sign peace treaties and maintain normal relations with Israel for some years before Israel actually agrees to move on the nuclear issue.

For example, the official Israeli position stipulates that all Middle Eastern countries, including the Islamic Republic of Iran, must sign peace treaties and maintain normal relations with Israel for at least two years before negotiating a change in Israel's current policy on the nuclear issue. This can legitimately be viewed as an example of an interest in enjoying nuclear monopoly for a long time to come. One does not necessarily have to be an Arab radical to reach such a conclusion. Even commentators and analysts in the Arab world who accepted putting an end to the conflict with Israel through a historical compromise, such as Mohamed Sid-Ahmed, Abdel Moneim Said, Usama al-Ghazali Harb and Saad Eddin Ibrahim, wonder if this is not an impossible kind of condition. They wonder where the geographical line is going, ultimately, to be drawn by Israel. Would Pakistan, with its so-called Islamic bomb, qualify as a potential source of threat to Israel? If Pakistan has pursued the nuclear option against the backdrop of its conflict with India, who in turn has been worried about China and Pakistan, then would a stable solution to the conflict in South Asia become a prerequisite for any significant modification of Israel's position with regard to nuclear weapons?

Behind the rhetorical component of such questions there is deep concern about the likely strategic and political uses of Israel's own advanced nuclear-weapons programme. The typical Israeli answers about not being the first 'to introduce', whatever that means, nuclear weapons in the Middle East is no longer adequate. Why? Because the very logic of the so-called 'constructive ambiguity' concerning this matter has stretched its usefulness in many respects. By now, Israeli sources talk about nuclear options as military capability, not as an abstract exercise in paradigmatic construction in security studies. Other states in the region look at Israel's nuclear capability as a strategic fact and not as an analytic proposition. Thus, the current Israeli position is neither constructive nor ambiguous. Instead of the desired stabilisation, the current Israeli stand, and the set of interactions resulting from it, are quite likely to lead to greater destabilisation and to a more determined drive on the part of other regional actors to acquire nuclear capability in addition to more chemical and biological weapons. Hence the need for a serious dialogue about the dangers of nuclearisation in the Middle East in a manner that requires all parties, including Israel, to reassess their long-held positions.

Signposts on the Road

What should guide such a reassessment? There are three important questions in this regard. If the parties' answers to these questions are diametrically opposed, there is indeed little hope of a breakthrough. First is the concept of non-discrimination among states regarding our subject matter, and whether establishing one standard of behaviour and verification requirements is a wrong or misguided idea that brings fiction to this discussion. While regions have their own specificity, the recognition of that should not amount to sanctioning two tracks or two sets of standards of what is permissible and what is not permissible: one for democracies and the other for non-democracies. After all, the only country in history that used nuclear weapons against the adversary's cities and civilians has been a democratic country strongly associated with notions of Lockean liberalism.

When it comes to the Middle East, similar arguments about the virtues, even necessity, of discrimination (described by some as differentiation) are used to make the exceptionalist case for Israel. We are told the Middle East is an exceptional case due to structural security dilemmas that involve the Arab-Muslim coalition against Israel. Those who believe so also tell us that Israel is an exceptional case not only because of its identity but also thanks to its political system, which is characterised by democracy and political accountability.

This argument, which I have dubbed 'dual exceptionalism', adds up to the following: Israel has to continue to be the exceptional country in the region in terms of possessing nuclear capability. In short, the Middle East has to become indeed a NWFZ, with one exception: which is more or less what is happening now. Regardless of any intentions, I am not sure that this can be sustained for a long time.

Second, there is the issue of sequencing and priorities, which poses the question of causes and effects. Should the establishment of a NWFZ build regional confidence and security or do they result from consolidated peace, confidence and a sense of security? In the Middle East, this is not merely a theoretical issue. While Egypt argues that clear progress regarding the nuclear issue must precede or be parallel to the progress in achieving a political settlement, Israel argues that security and successful confidence-building measures must come first. This already poses a dilemma, particularly when we take into consideration that the leaders in the two countries have to convince their attentive publics about a change in the intentions and policies of the other before being able to move from maximalist positions towards a compromise.

Third, if the desired outcome is the establishment at some time in the future, and hopefully sooner than later, of a NWFZ in the Middle East, then what is the best approach to bring it about in light of characteristics of the regional situation and lessons learned from successful cases in other regions? How can we assess the merits and demerits of regional vs global approaches; of policy pressure vs political persuasion? These are controversial issues, though it seems the arm-twisting methods when it comes to denuclearisation are not likely to produce more positive results. The record of such tactics in dealing with actors aspiring to join 'the nuclear club' is more ambiguous. It appears also that regional approaches may have a good promise in general because they can actually avoid the charge of international imposition. However, for the regional approaches to be more effective and more legitimate, they should not endorse and perpetuate a privileged position of one regional actor, particularly if that actor, as is the case with Israel, has an acknowledged preponderance of conventional military power and, so far, a monopoly of nuclear power.

Changes in the Regional Setting

For obvious reasons, Israel prefers to focus on the regional approaches and tends to be concerned about international channels or organisations influenced by a pro-Arab 'numerical majority'. Israel argues that it cannot rely on the NPT which was indefinitely extended in May 1995. Moreover it stresses that the verification mechanisms of the International Atomic Energy Agency (IAEA) are dangerously inadequate, as shown by the recent cases of Iraq and North Korea, and hence regional approaches and solutions must be given priority.

An approach that merits the word 'regional' must not ignore important regional transformations. Thus we should have a regional outlook that captures the changes in the regional setting. I would not go as far as those who have concluded that the Arab-Israeli conflict has essentially ended. Rather, for the most important Arab actors the conflict with Israel is no longer about its *wujud* or existence but about its *hudud* or borders. This policy shift did not obviously result from an abrupt normative change of attitudes unconnected to political realities. It has stemmed from experience-driven political learning, the essence of which is that Israel is in the Middle East to stay and that clearly there is no military solution to the Arab-Israeli conflict.

Hafiz al-Assad, Yasser Arafat, King Hussein, King Fahd, President Hosni Mubarak and the leaders of Tunisia, Morocco, Algeria and the Gulf Cooperation Council countries differ in their political reading of regional and international settings. However, they do not differ regarding the futility of any strategy that relies on military power against Israel. Needless to say, if one compares such a position with the famous 'three noes' (no peace, no recognition, and no negotiation with Israel) which were adopted by the Arab summit in Khartoum in 1967, the significance of that alteration of policy should not be that hard to appreciate. In fact, it belongs to the category of what international relations scholars call 'foreign policy restructuring'. The peace process is far from completion and serious difficulties remain, but it would be a major mistake to conclude that nothing of significance has happened in the Middle East or to start from the premise that security threats to Israel do remain unchanged.

Security threats associated with terrorism are obviously not ones that nuclear weapons are useful to deal with. Hizbollah, Hamas and Islamic Jihad leaders did not have doubts about Israel's nuclear capability. But this did not prevent or deter them from launching attacks against Israeli targets, knowing well that Israel could not realistically have used its nuclear weapons against them near its own northern borders. Their links with countries like Syria and Iran are matters of record not speculation. However, Israel could not use the threat of nuclear weapons to compel these two states to stop backing such attacks. Thus, the 'bomb in the basement' is not useful against the most frequent kind of threat or *vis-à-vis* nearby states which give the groups involved some backing through controlling them or via a congruence of interests.

It has been argued that Iraq's behaviour in January–February 1991 demonstrated the utility of having an Israeli nuclear option in forcing Iraq not to use its chemical weapons against Israel. Digging into Saddam Hussein's intentions is a hazardous exercise in crystal ball gazing, to say the least. What remains obvious is that Saddam warned, ahead of time, that if Iraq was attacked, he would launch Scud missiles against Israel and did so despite not having any doubt about Israel's possession of a considerable nuclear arsenal. In other words, he was not deterred. When Israel was reportedly on the verge of a response (search and destroy air missions), it was conventional weapons which were considered then, very much as the US-led coalition against Iraq was doing. It has already been argued that America's threat to use 'unconventional' weapons if Iraq used chemical weapons, had reinforced the Iraqi inclination not to use such weapons unless attacked with weapons of mass destruction.

Iran's intentions have been suspect on the nuclear issue. Estimates vary regarding the time it would need and the conditions necessary for Tehran to develop a nuclear-weapons capability. Many are inclined to see here another experience similar to that of Iraq and to conclude that Iran may display verbal moderation on nuclear issues in front of international organisations while being intent on developing a nuclear-weapons programme. The problem here is that those who may have any credible evidence are not willing to share it. However, if reports about an active nuclear programme by Iran are true, then it would be fair to assume in this case that the Iranians want to succeed. In that regard, their model would be Israel, which succeeded, not Iraq, that failed, and had as a result of its defeat some of the most intrusive inspection regimes in its important military sites and bases.

What Is To Be Done?

Everyone agrees that there is no short cut to deal with this subject matter. But the talk about obstacles should not lead to immobilism and inaction. The price of such a position is unaffordable by regional parties concerned and even beyond. The idea of a NWFZ has to be evaluated and compared with other courses of action. While it cannot be agreed upon and actually implemented immediately, I am not sure there are other and possibly better options to pursue.

As alternatives, one can identify two. The first favours the status quo. Israel has to remain the only regional nuclear power for the foreseeable future. It is argued by advocates of this view that it is good not only for Israel but also for the region. Here we have a regional version of the theory of hegemonic stability. Some argue this would be welcome by the Arab countries in the Gulf who are concerned about Iraq or Iran. Israel's nuclear umbrella can provide unlimited security goods for these states and the regional stability would be enhanced as a result.

There are many holes in this argument. The most important is that it ignores completely the impact of domestic politics in Arab countries. Even authoritarian regimes have domestic politics to contend with. There are already strident discussions in Arab political life about Israel's assured monopoly of nuclear weapons and the strategic risks involved in allowing such a monopoly to continue. In fact, retired generals who belong to or sympathise politically with opposition forces provide the general membership and readers of opposition newspapers with alarming accounts of the expansion of Israel's nuclear arsenal. They argue that Israel behaves on the assumption that its long conflict with the Arabs is continuing while Arab regimes act as if that conflict has become a thing of the past. This can be seen in Egypt and Jordan and other Arab countries where the mass media, whether official or oppositional, denounce the American insistence on denying the Arabs nuclear options while de facto sanctioning Israel's possession of a large nuclear arsenal.

The more the degree of political liberalisation in the Arab world, the greater the likelihood that more segments of public opinion will refuse to accept Israel's nuclear monopoly. This means that regimes will be pressured to take a stronger stand against this monopoly, to refrain from signing treaties banning chemical weapons, or even to pursue the nuclear option themselves. Advocacy of such courses of action may not come only from the ranks of the opposition. They may actually come from within the institutional structure of the state itself. The case of the Egyptian Foreign and Defence Ministries, when it comes to dealing with Israel regarding the 'nuclear file', is an example. While they may accept that Israel is a democracy, they argue that democratic elections can bring extremist parties and leaders to state power and they see Likud and Binyamin Netanyahu in Israeli politics as a confirmation of that outlook.

Pro-Western Arab regimes will not venture to rely on an Israeli nuclear umbrella while they can avail themselves of protection by the United States in case of extreme situations. If that happens, they will again try to make sure, as they did during the war to liberate Kuwait, that Israel does not intervene militarily and thus greatly complicate matters for them politically on domestic and regional levels.

The other alternative is based on the Waltzian notion of 'the more the better' for regional stability. To put it crudely, from such a perspective, it is better to have a Middle East with nuclear weapons on all sides of the region's conflicts, than to have an area ridden with recurrent wars but with no nuclear weapons. I am not going to address the many weaknesses of this argument here. Suffice it now to point to the inapplicability of the Soviet-American model to the case of the Middle East, to the serious risks involved in nuclear proliferation, and to the fact that the chances of a general war in the region have been reduced fundamentally after Egypt and Israel opted out of the war equation in the late 1970s.

For a long time now the Egyptian policy has been one of advocating the establishment of a NWFZ in the Middle East. As Egypt embarked on a settlement with Israel starting in 1974, it raised this issue before the General Assembly of the United Nations. President Mubarak suggested in 1990 the establishment of a zone free of weapons of mass destruction in the Middle East.[3] Egypt accepted the notion that this process would require several years for confidence-building and institution-building purposes and a verification regime that would go beyond procedures described in the NPT to ensure strict compliance by the member states which should have equal rights and responsibilities.[4]

To conclude, the threat of nuclear proliferation remains real in the Middle East. But it is not likely to be a proliferation that leads to more stability or more prudence of policy. Rather, it can generate more fears and insecurity in the region, possibly with some disastrous consequences. Even countries that have made peace with Israel, as in the case of Egypt, do not want to be reduced to helpless entities under

Israel's nuclear dominance. Even if their leaders were ready to accept that, many in state institutions, particularly in the military, are likely to continue to see relations with Israel generally in competitive terms. Their societies and attentive elites will find Israel's nuclear capability threatening and will pressure their governments for confronting Israel's nuclear monopoly.

While abolishing immediately, with no exceptions, nuclear weapons in the Middle East is far-fetched, moving seriously in the direction of eliminating nuclear threats in the region is absolutely necessary for regional security and stability. There is no better alternative indeed.

Notes

1. John Brook Wolfsthal, 'Nuclear-Weapon-Free Zones: Coming of Age?', *Arms Control Today* 23 (March 1993), p. 7.
2. See Shai Feldman, *Israeli Nuclear Deterrence* (New York: Columbia University Press, 1982); Benjamin Frankel, *Opaque Nuclear Proliferation* (London: Frank Cass, 1991); and Etel Solingen, 'The Domestic Sources of Regional Regimes: The Evolution of Nuclear Ambiguity in the Middle East', *International Studies Quarterly* 38 (June 1994), pp. 305–37.
3. On the Egyptian position see Mahmoud Karem, *A Nuclear-Weapon-Free Zone in the Middle East: Problems and Prospects* (New York: Greenwood, 1988), as well as Mohamed Shaker, *Prospects for Establishing a Zone Free of Weapons of Mass Destruction in the Middle East* (Lawrence Livermore National Laboratory, October 1994).
4. See some interesting ideas in Efraim Karsh and Yezid Sayigh, 'A Cooperative Approach to Arab–Israeli Security', *Survival* 36 (Spring 1994), pp. 121–5.

11
The Obstacles to a Middle East Nuclear-Weapon-Free Zone

Gerald M. Steinberg

It is increasingly clear that progress towards the goal of a nuclear-weapon-free world, as outlined in the Report of the Canberra Commission on the Elimination of Nuclear Weapons,[1] will require a series of regional agreements and frameworks that go beyond the scope of existing frameworks. The nuclear-weapon-free zones (NWFZ) that have been negotiated and implemented in Latin America, the South Pacific, Southeast Asia and, most recently, Africa, provide examples. Other areas in which multifaceted regional approaches will be required include South Asia, the Korean peninsula and the Middle East.

The examination and analysis of the requirements and conditions for the creation of a functioning NWFZ in these conflictual regions demonstrate that this will require the settlement of intense and ongoing conflicts. In cases in which nuclear deterrence in some form (deployed or virtual) is viewed as essential for national security, without the settlement of these conflicts, the deterrence requirement will remain. In addition, the nuclear potential or capability is seen as a response or deterrent to non-nuclear threats, both conventional and un-conventional. Thus in such cases a NWFZ must also be linked to a wider set of agreements and limitations encompassing chemical and biological weapons, ballistic missiles and other long-range delivery systems, and massive conventional forces. A regional arms control system, including a NWFZ, must also include stringent and reliable verification systems, in order to meet the concerns of all the parties regarding possible cheating, undetected preparations for 'breakout' (in which one party secretly creates the basis for a rapid development of prohibited weapons, and when the 'breakout' occurs, this does not leave sufficient time for a response). Together, these three sets of requirements present a major challenge or, until these challenges can be met, obstacles to the creation of zones free of nuclear weapons and other weapons of mass destruction (WMD).

Background

Since 1980 the United Nations General Assembly has supported, by consensus, annual resolutions calling for the creation of a Middle East NWFZ (MENWFZ) All the states in the region have supported this consensus, including Egypt, Israel and Iran. In addition, the leaders of these states have consistently voiced support for a MENWFZ in public statements.

However, this consensus has masked a number of fundamental differences in approach and substance. Initially, and throughout the 1980s, Israel and the Arab states were divided on major issues of process. While Israel insisted that the negotiations take place through direct face-to-face talks as part of a regional peace process, the continuing refusal of the Arab states (with the notable and very important exception of Egypt) to end the state of war with Israel created an impasse. This basic obstacle was reduced, to some degree, in 1991 following the Middle East Peace Conference in Madrid in which many of the parties participated (with the exception of Iraq, Iran and Libya). The conference led to the establishment of a number of multilateral working groups, including one on Arms Control and Regional Security (ACRS) which, for the first time, provided a format for direct negotiations on such issues. However, the refusal of Syria to participate, as well as the absence of Iran, Iraq and Libya (which reject the peace process and, in the case of Iran, actively support rejectionist terror groups such as Hamas and Hizbollah) have limited the ability of ACRS to consider regional security issues such as the MENWFZ in any detail. Without the active participation of all of these states in this or a similar forum, it is difficult to proceed towards significant regional agreements.

Beyond the procedural issues, there are a number of substantive differences and conflicts that will be difficult to resolve. The first issue in the consideration of a NWFZ in any region is the scope of the areas to be included. In conflictual regions, such as the Middle East, the core sector is defined in terms of potential or actual states that might be involved in military confrontation in which nuclear capabilities or threats could play a role.

In comparison with the other areas in which regional NWFZ have been created, the Middle East is particularly complex.[2] This is an area plagued by a long history of intense and overlapping ethno-national and religious conflict, and there are many obstacles and difficulties to reaching agreement on a MENWFZ. To be effective, a zone would have to include the 22 member states of the Arab League, as well as Iran and Israel, and stretch from Algeria in North Africa to Iran and the Persian Gulf.[3] There are specific issues regarding some peripheral states, such as Turkey which is a member of the North Atlantic Treaty Organisation (NATO) alliance. As part of an organisation that has a nuclear component (through its nuclear-weapons states members), Turkey is an anomaly for a MENWFZ that must, at some point, be considered. The large number and diversity of necessary participants, in itself, is a significant obstacle to agreement.

In addition, there are wide differences between the various conceptions and mechanisms that have been proposed. These primary differences result from conflicting perceptions of the security requirements and threats posed to the states in the region, and the link between the establishment of a NWFZ and the regional peace process in the region. There are also related disagreements on the implementation of a wide network of confidence-building measures (CBM), the link between changes in the status of Israel's ambiguous nuclear deterrence option and limitations on conventional as well as other military-strategic capabilities, the relation of a MENWFZ to the global regime centred on the Nuclear Non-Proliferation Treaty (NPT) and the International Atomic Energy Agency (IAEA), and the nature of verification.

Nevertheless, in terms of long-term goals the concept of a MENWFZ, as part of a wider zone free of WMD, is the best option for creating and maintaining long-term stability, and for progressing towards the goals of the Canberra Commission. Despite the opposing interests and positions on other issues, all the states in the region, including Israel and Egypt, have signed the Comprehensive Test Ban Treaty (CTBT), and this could serve as a basis for gaining experience in regional cooperation. As will be demonstrated in this paper, efforts

The Obstacles to a Middle East NWFZ

to find 'short cuts' that fail to meet the essential security requirements of the key states in the region, including Israel, in the attempt to create a MENWFZ, and that do not address the basic factors that are necessary for such a zone, are unlikely to succeed. Indeed, such pressures could, in themselves, become sources of additional conflict and will actually set back the achievement of this goal.

The MENWFZ at the United Nations

The concept of a MENWFZ was introduced in the UN General Assembly in 1974 by Egypt and Iran. Until 1980, Israel abstained in the annual votes on this issue but, since then, Israel has joined the consensus, and has thereby also had a voice in shaping the language and in determining the fate of various changes that Egypt and other states sought to introduce over the years. [4]

The emphasis on this issue increased in the wake of the United Nations Special Session on Disarmament (UNSSOD) in 1988. A number of leaders in the region, including Israeli Prime Minister Yitzhak Shamir and Egyptian Foreign Minister Ismat Abdel Meguid addressed this Special Session, and presented their views on disarmament in general and proposals for the region in particular.[5] Egypt also proposed that the Secretary-General create an expert group to consider the 'Establishment of a Nuclear-Weapon-Free Zone in the Region of the Middle East', and this group issued its report in 1990. This highly detailed report explicitly examined the terms required for 'effective and verifiable measures' which would facilitate the establishment of a MENWFZ, as well as the necessary conditions and preliminary steps, including CBM and balanced reductions in conventional arms.[6] The authors also noted that even under the most favourable conditions, the process would take several years. The Israeli position on this concept has been favourable and was most recently reiterated by Foreign Minister David Levi in the 1996 UN General Assembly. In his statement, Levi declared that:

> After peaceful relations and reconciliation have been established among all states in the region, Israel will endeavour to establish in the Middle East a zone free of chemical, biological and nuclear weapons, as well as ballistic missiles, based on mutual and effective verification. Negotiations to establish such a zone will commence following the signing of bilateral peace accords between Israel and all states in the region.[7]

Since then, the issue has been discussed and debated annually in the First Committee of the United Nations and discussed in other forums, including the meetings of the IAEA Board of Governors, the meetings of the ACRS multilateral working group, and in the context of the 1995 NPT Review and Extension Conference. Examination of the positions taken by the various parties at these meetings and in other settings provide a basis for examining the differing positions in detail, and for analysing the obstacles to the establishment of a MENWFZ. The intense political conflicts and efforts to obtain minor political and public relations advantages in the wording of declarations and resolutions, particularly in the First Committee of the United Nations and the meetings of the Board of Governors of the IAEA, are indications of the long period which will be necessary to overcome the substantive and political obstacles.[8]

The Central Issues and Conflicts

Links Between a MENWFZ and the Global NPT/IAEA Regime

The question of whether and how to link a regional NWFZ to the existing global regime is a central and perhaps the most conflictual issue facing the parties. The global system is based on universality (except for the five recognised nuclear-weapons states); differences in geography, demography and regional threat situations (both conventional and unconventional) are irrelevant. In contrast, a regional approach emphasises precisely these specific issues, allowing for the development of a complex and tailor-made framework, as seen in the case of Latin America.[9]

In general, the Arab states, and Egypt in particular, demand that a regional zone be integrated within the global structure, while for Israel this is unacceptable and would defeat the purpose of the NWFZ. The Egyptian position on this issue was clearly stated in the 1990 Mubarak initiative (formally presented in a letter to the UN Secretary-General in July 1991). This proposal emphasised the demand that all states in the region accept the NPT and adopt IAEA safeguards on all nuclear facilities. In his letter, Mubarak also included a broad call for the major powers 'to step up their efforts to ensure that all Middle East nations which have not yet done so adhere to the Treaty'.[10] This position is stressed frequently. For example, the final communique of the June

1993 summit meeting of the Arab League in Cairo stated 'The Arab leaders stress the need for Israel to join the Nuclear Non-Proliferation Treaty and to subject all their nuclear facilities to the inspection regime of the International Atomic Energy Agency. They also renew their call for establishing a zone free of weapons of mass destruction, especially nuclear weapons, in the Middle East'.[11]

The institutional question is also linked to broader conflicts regarding the role of international organisations, such as the United Nations, in enhancing or guaranteeing regional security. Although the NWFZ concept is ostensibly regional, Cairo's position stresses the centrality of the global regime and the role of global institutions such as the UN. In policy statements, the Egyptian leaders demand that 'any regional arrangement or measure of disarmament' be consistent with 'the purposes and principles enshrined in the Charter of the United Nations' and with 'the revitalisation of the United Nations' role in the fields of disarmament and international security'.[12] Mohamed Nabil Fahmy, a prominent official of Egypt's Foreign Ministry, called on the Security Council and General Assembly to take active measures to pressure states to 'relinquish and not acquire' nuclear weapons.[13] This position was repeated, with some minor variations, in the annual meetings of the UN General Assembly, the sessions of the First Committee and in the meetings of the Board of Governors of the IAEA.

The problems raised by efforts to incorporate a MENWFZ within the NPT/IAEA also include the fact that, while the IAEA deals only with limitations on nuclear weapons, security threats are multifaceted and, in the Israeli case, are addressed by the nuclear deterrence option. Israel's deterrence policy is a response to the threats posed by other weapons systems and technology, including massive conventional forces that threaten national survival, as well as chemical and biological warheads. (These threats will be examined in greater detail below.)

The ACRS working group, in which Israel, Egypt and Jordan are active participants, provided a framework that overcame many of these differences. ACRS is not linked to the UN, IAEA or any international organisation. In addition, this mechanism is not limited to any specific weapon or technology and allows for discussion of the links between such capabilities and the threats that they pose. Thus ACRS can be used for the eventual discussion leading to the establishment of a MENWFZ, in connection with widespread peace agreements.

However, the effort to produce an agreed framework or declaration of principles for the next stage of ACRS broke down in 1994 precisely over the differences on the role of the NPT. While Egypt insisted on obtaining explicit Israeli agreement to language linking the NWFZ to the NPT, Israel rejected this linkage. Since then the ACRS process has been stalled, reflecting both the importance attached to this issue and the degree to which it constitutes a fundamental obstacle to progress in negotiating a MENWFZ. (It should, however, be noted that the 1994 Jordanian-Israeli Peace Treaty calls for a Middle East free from WMD, 'both conventional and non-conventional', without specific reference to nuclear weapons or the NPT and IAEA.)[14]

Verification and Safeguards

Any arms limitation regime, whether global, regional or bilateral, is only as strong as the verification and safeguards systems that are implemented. For example the 1972 Biological Weapons Convention has been ineffective, reflecting the absence of any verification system. The NPT has failed in areas where verification and safeguards were too weak to deter violations, as in the case of Iraq and North Korea, and, it is increasingly feared, Iran. The IAEA in general, and the safeguards and verification system in particular, are vulnerable to political influence, allowing states to exclude inspectors from some areas and to manipulate the system in a way which would prevent or delay the 'timely detection of violations' and allow states to produce weapons before an international response. The IAEA Board of Governors, which appoints IAEA officials and must consider whether to report cases of suspected safeguards violations for action to the UN Security Council, is a political body, with representation based on politically defined groups. Some states, such as Israel, are systematically excluded from these groups and therefore from representation on the Board of Governors.

The Middle East poses some very difficult verification requirements. There are a number of diverse political systems ranging from open democracies to closed and tightly controlled dictatorships. In the case of closed societies, particularly those with relatively large territorial boundaries, it is possible to hide weapons development and production programmes from international inspectors. This has been clearly demonstrated in the case of Iraq, where both IAEA and the UN

Special Commission (UNSCOM) inspectors have been attempting to determine the extent of the Iraqi capability since 1991. For over five years, the Iraqi government has been able to keep significant capabilities and information hidden from the international inspectors despite the agreement guaranteeing access and cooperation as specified in Security Council Resolution 687.

For these reasons, there is a strong argument for creating a system of safeguards based on a dedicated regional system of mutual verification, negotiated and implemented by the parties, without the political aspects of the IAEA or other international body. This is the Israeli position, and it was underlined in 1993 when Israel did not send an official participant to the IAEA workshop on 'The Modalities for the Application of Safeguards in a Future Nuclear-Weapon-Free-Zone in the Middle East'. (An unofficial observer, however, was present.)

In contrast, the formal Arab position has consistently stressed placing regional verification under the control of the IAEA. Ambassador Mohammed Shaker placed primary emphasis on adherence to the NPT and to giving the IAEA a 'major role' in safeguarding nuclear activities in the region and in the verification of a MENWFZ.[15] This is also consistent with the overall Egyptian emphasis on linking the MENWFZ to the global structure and subordinating the regional regime to the global framework, as discussed above.

The development of a regional and mutual inspection system is also dependent on some form of recognition and cooperation among all the parties, including Syria, Iran, Iraq and Libya. This requirement has two driving factors. First, the failures and lack of reliability of third-party verification on an issue critical to national survival lead individual states that might be threatened by a clandestine nuclear programme to have their own sources of information and verification with respect to the other states in the zone. If any one state was able to violate the agreement and suddenly 'break out' from the limitations by producing nuclear weapons, this would pose a grave threat. From this perspective, the best way to reduce and limit this possibility is through mutual verifications.

Secondly, mutual acceptance and recognition of legitimacy is a necessary requirement for peaceful relations on which a NWFZ is predicated and in the context of which mutual inspection and verification can take place. If some states are not ready for mutual inspection, it can be argued that they are not really ready for regional peace, and the conditions necessary for a regional NWFZ do not yet exist. (See the detailed analysis of the links between the peace process and a MENWFZ below.)

The experience in Latin America suggests that a regional monitoring system is feasible. The 1967 Treaty of Tlatelolco (which took almost 30 years to become operable) and the Argentina-Brazil Accounting and Control Commission (ABACC) provide a model that has been studied in the Middle East. Although there are many differences between the conditions in each of these two regions, and regional verification systems addressed to the needs of the Middle East would be quite different, the concepts are similar.

Conflicts, Threats and Last-Resort Deterrence

As widely noted, Israel is not a signatory to the NPT, and operates a nuclear reactor at Dimona which is reportedly capable of producing plutonium for the production of nuclear weapons. Since the 1960s Israel has followed a policy of deliberate ambiguity and Israeli leaders have consistently refused to acknowledge or deny the possession of nuclear weapons.[16] For many years, they have simply repeated the ambiguous formula that 'Israel will not be the first nation in the region to deploy nuclear weapons' (and sometimes, with the addition that it will also not be the second state.)

The Israeli position is primarily based on deterrence considerations. Responsible for the security of a small state lacking strategic depth and threatened by very large conventional forces, the Israeli leadership views the ambiguous deterrent as providing a weapon of last resort against existential attacks. The threat of nuclear retaliation has been and continues to be seen as the key to national survival, and the ambiguous capability, option, or potential provided by Dimona has provided this deterrence. This policy is supported by a consensus of the Israeli decision makers and by the vast majority of public opinion, and is linked to the perception that this option is necessary for national survival. The late Shalheveth Freier, who served as the head of the Israeli Atomic Energy Commission, described the nuclear deterrent option as providing 'a sense of reassurance to Israelis in times of gloom' and 'as possible caution to states contemplating obliterating Israel by dint of their preponderance of men and material'.[17] More recently, in January

1996, former Foreign Minister and Israeli Defence Force Chief of Staff Ehud Barak declared that, in the absence of proven and reliable regional peace agreements, 'Israel's nuclear policy, as it is perceived in the eyes of the Arabs, has not changed, will not change and cannot change, because it is a fundamental stand on a matter of survival which impacts all the generations to come'.[18]

This policy is widely supported across the Israeli political spectrum and is based on a national consensus. There are no differences between parties, ideologies or perspectives on the peace process. On this issue, there is little to distinguish the public statements of late Prime Minister Yitzhak Rabin, former Foreign Ministers Shimon Peres and Ehud Barak, and leading politicians in the Left such as Yosi Beilin and Yosi Sarid. This position is also supported by a consensus in the Israeli public, and polls showed that close to 90 per cent explicitly approve of the continuation of Israeli nuclear policy and, unless and until there is a fundamental change in the threat environment, this public support is unlikely to change.[19]

The Israeli position is that any change in the status of Dimona through international inspection would reduce or end this ambiguity, thereby weaken or destroy the deterrent, and thus make the country vulnerable to renewed existential attacks. Israel has consistently rejected pressures that it accede to the NPT and accept inspection. At the same time, Israel has not tested any weapons or taken any steps that would turn the ambiguous capability into an acknowledged and visible capability.[20]

The policy of deterrence is inherently not susceptible to empirical testing (except after it has failed), and there is always a great deal of uncertainty in any deterrence situation.[21] However, Israelis will argue that although deterrence may be flawed, no better and realistic alternative is available short of comprehensive peace agreements and fundamental political changes in the region. This position is also supported by recent examples in which deterrence and the threat of massive retaliation has been seen to have induced restraint. For example, some analysts argue that the Egyptian decision not to exploit initial breakthroughs in the Sinai in 1973 was due to the Israeli nuclear deterrent. In addition, it can be argued that while Iraq possessed and had tested Scud missiles and chemical warheads prior to the 1991 war, it did not use the chemical weapons against Israel in response to the potential Israeli retaliatory capability. In other words, from the Israeli perspective, this form of ambiguous threat of massive retaliation against existential threats or the threat to use WMD seems to be effective. Under such conditions Israeli leaders have declared that they will maintain this capability as long as the threats remain. On the other hand, the Israeli policy also emphasises the long-term goal of banning all WMD when this form of deterrence is no longer necessary.

Links with Other Forms of Arms Limitation and Regional Security

As noted above, in the Middle East the development of nuclear weapons or options is not isolated from other security-related factors and sources of military threats and capabilities. When there are fundamental asymmetries in land area, population and large scale conventional capabilities, as continue to exist in many states in the region, as well as chemical and biological agents, the nuclear option designed in response as a deterrent is closely linked to the non-nuclear sources of this perceived deterrence requirement. In other words, in this particular case the proposed limitations on nuclear capabilities are inseparable from the development and implementation of limitations on other military capabilities, both conventional and non-conventional. As numerous UN reports and related studies have concluded, a MENWFZ must be linked to or include such broad limitations, each of which is, in itself, complex and difficult to implement. The development of an acceptable and stable level of conventional weapons, limited in terms of both quantity and quality, in order to prevent any state or group of states from threatening the survival of any other state, is a complex process. However, precedents from the Conventional Forces in Europe (CFE) agreements and from the UN conventional arms register (with which only Israel has complied in the Middle East) provide a basis for negotiations and, indeed, a first step towards a comprehensive weapons-limitation agreement in the Middle East.

The threat from wars and attacks involving conventional weapons in the Middle East has always been significant and, in spite of recent progress towards historic peace agreements, this threat remains and in some ways has even increased. The Israeli strategic situation is essentially unique. In the Arab-Israeli conflict zone, Israel is a small state and geographic, demographic, military and economic asymmetries have played a central role in the development of security policies and strategic culture. In area, Israel consists of less than 21 000km^2 (ex-

The Obstacles to a Middle East NWFZ

cluding the Judea and Samaria regions of the West Bank and the Golan Heights), compared to 1 million km^2 for Egypt and 186 000km^2 for Syria. This small size and the extremely narrow area between the Eastern border and the Mediterranean (15km in the pre-1967 borders), leave Israel without the strategic depth necessary for absorbing armored and air attacks, and without the ability to recover and respond. Israel's vulnerability to conventional attack was made clear in 1948 when forces from a number of Arab states (Egypt, Jordan, Syria and Iraq) advanced rapidly and came close to destroying the nascent state. In May 1967 the preparations for war by the Arab states were seen as threatening national survival, and the combined Egyptian and Syrian attacks in October 1973 (the Yom Kippur War) also highlighted Israel's extreme vulnerability.

The massive conventional forces that can be fielded by Syria, Egypt and Iraq (after the lifting of the international embargo) are seen, particularly through the lenses of history, as a continued existential threat to Israel. Although the Soviet Union no longer exists to provide low-cost and technologically advanced weapons, Syrian ground forces are continuing to grow and include 4800 main battle tanks (1400 of which were acquired in the past four years). The Syrian standing army is twice as large as Israel's and a surprise attack, based on forces in place and supported by combat aircraft and missiles armed with chemical warheads, could prevent mobilisation of Israeli reserves. Three-quarters of the Israeli ground forces are in the reserves and unhampered mobilisation takes from 48 to 96 hours.

Although Egypt signed a peace treaty with Israel in 1979, the Egyptian military has continued to devote billions of dollars in US military aid to the purchase of modern M-1 A-1 main battle tanks and F-16 aircraft, as well as tactical missiles and related systems. In September 1996 Egyptian forces held their largest combined exercises (Badr 96) since the 1973 war, in an area near the Sinai desert. Egyptian officials announced that these exercises included simulated canal crossings. From an Israeli perspective, these exercises served as a reminder of the continued potential for an Egyptian surprise attack.[22]

Similarly, it has become increasingly recognised that nuclear-weapons limitations must be linked to limits on other forms of WMD (chemical and biological warheads). Indeed, in his 1990-1 initiative, President Hosni Mubarak included all forms of WMD, and Israeli Foreign Minister Levi also stressed the link between a ban on nuclear and other WMD as well as ballistic missiles. Israel was among the first signatories of the Chemical Weapons Convention (CWC) and has participated actively in the preparatory committee meetings towards the implementation of the CWC.

The Relationship to the Peace Process

In any region of the world, arms control agreements and regional limitation zones are dependent on the resolution and amelioration of existing conflicts. In the case of Europe, the success of the Helsinki process that contributed to the Stockholm agreement and the development of the Organisation for Security and Cooperation in Europe (OSCE) resulted from the end of the Cold War and the breakup of the Soviet Union. In Latin America, the entry-into-force of the Treaty of Tlatelolco was delayed for thirty years, due to a series of low-level conflicts involving Argentina, Brazil and, to a lesser degree, Chile. In the case of the Treaty of Rarotonga, the absence of significant conflict was also a major factor in allowing the process to go forward.

In the Middle East, security, arms control and the peace process are closely interrelated and progress towards a MENWFZ is dependent on the establishment and implementation of peace agreements with all states in the region, from Algeria to Iran. In his address to the UN in 1996, Israel's Foreign Minster reiterated the long-standing Israeli position that the establishment of peaceful relations and reconciliation and bilateral peace agreements with all states, including Iran and Iraq, is a fundamental condition for beginning negotiations. In contrast, the Egyptian and Syrian position is that the sequence should be reversed, with the negotiation of a MENWFZ and/or Israeli accession to the NPT and the ending of the Israeli nuclear option or potential coming before major new steps towards a regional peace agreement.

After more than 70 years of violence in the form of both fullscale war and continued terrorism, it is unrealistic to expect that the establishment of a stable Middle East peace can be accomplished in the span of a few years. To have any chance of success, this process must take years and even decades. The process began with the historic visit of President Anwar Sadat to Jerusalem in 1977 and continued with the 1979 Egypt-Israel Peace Treaty, the 1991 Madrid Conference, the 1993 Oslo Agreement, the 1994 Israel-Jordan Peace Treaty and the 1995 Oslo II agreement.

However, it is important to recognise that this is only the beginning of the process. No agreement has been reached between Israel and Syria and war is still considered to be a serious possibility. A war of attrition and terrorism continue in the areas of northern Israel and southern Lebanon and include Iranian forces working with Hizbollah to attack Israeli positions, settlements and forces. Tensions continue between Israel and Egypt, and while these can be explained in terms of jockeying for position and playing to domestic audiences, particularly in Egypt, in the Middle East events can often assume an independent path, pushing decision makers to take action over which they lose control (as occurred in 1967). The series of brutal terrorist attacks and suicide bombings in Israel during February and March 1996, in which over 100 were killed, brought the Israeli-Palestinian peace process to a halt, and it has not yet recovered. In summary, as Leonard and Prawitz note, 'There is . . . a great deal of skepticism in Israel about the ultimate intentions of others with regard to a true peace'.[23]

The essential factor in the establishment of a MENWFZ is the progress towards comprehensive regional peace and security. In the absence of peace and an alternative security framework, the obstacles to a NWFZ will remain. Failure of the peace process will mean an end to any possibility of a regional zone. With continued progress, the process must be extended with the participation of Syria, Iran and Iraq. A new structure for regional security will have to be established to replace the existing conventional and unconventional forces on all sides. This will require time and the development of a series of increasingly substantive confidence-building measures, including steps to prevent surprise attack, thinning out zones for conventional weapons, the exchange of information and, most importantly, continuous exchanges of views, ideas and perceptions. Efforts to rush this process by pressing for the establishment of a MENWFZ in the absence of these necessary conditions will be self-defeating.

Notes

1. *Report of the Canberra Commission on the Elimination of Nuclear Weapons* (Canberra: Department of Foreign Affairs and Trade, 1996).
2. See, for example, Jan Prawitz and James F. Leonard, *A Zone Free of Weapons of Mass Destruction in the Middle East* (Geneva: UNIDIR, 1996).

3. Ibid., pp. 63–5. These issues are also considered in Shalhevet Freier, 'A Nuclear-Weapon-Free Zone in the Middle East and Effective Verification', *Disarmament: A Periodic Review by the United Nations* 16:3 (1993), pp. 66–91.
4. For a detailed history of the role of the United Nations in this issue, see Mahmoud Karem, *A Nuclear-Weapon-Free Zone in the Middle East: Problems and Prospects* (New York: Greenwood, 1988); Avi Beker, *Disarmament Without Order: The Politics of Disarmament in the United Nations* (Westport: Greenwood, 1985); and Avi Beker, 'A Regional Non-Proliferation Treaty for the Middle East', in Louis Rene Beres, ed., *Security or Armageddon: Israel's Nuclear Strategy* (Lexington, MA.: Lexington Books, 1985).
5. Address of Israeli Prime Minister Yitzhak Shamir, UN General Assembly, 7 June 1988, and Address of Egyptian Foreign Minister Ismat Abdel Meguid, 13 June 1988, reprinted in Dore Gold, ed., *Arms Control in the Middle East* (Tel Aviv: Jaffee Center for Strategic Studies, 1990).
6. 'Establishment of a Nuclear-Weapon-Free Zone in the Region of the Middle East: Study on effective and verifiable measures which would facilitate the establishment of a nuclear-weapon-free zone in the Middle East', *Report of the Secretary-General* (New York: United Nations General Assembly document A/45/435, 10 October 1990). This report was the result of a study by James Leonard, Ben Sanders and Jan Prawitz.
7. Statement of Foreign Minister David Levi, United Nations General Assembly, 3 October 1996.
8. The political conflicts in these international organisations in the effort to obtain support from other participants are similar to the type of activity that took place in the UN during the 1950s and 1960s, between the US and the USSR.
9. Se Gerald M. Steinberg, 'Non-Proliferation: Time for Regional Approaches?', *Orbis* 38 (Summer 1994), pp. 409–24.
10. Letter from the Minister of Foreign Affairs of Egypt to the Secretary General of the United Nations, UN document A/46/329,S/22855, 30 July 1991.
11. Text of 'Final Communique' issued by the Arab Summit Conference in Cairo on June 23, read by Egyptian Foreign Minister Amr Musa; FBIS-NES-96-122, 23 June 1996.
12. Statement by Dr Mounir Zahran, Permanent Representative of Egypt to the United Nations Office and Other International Organisations in Geneva on Regional Disarmament, at the UNIDIR Regional Conference of Research Institutes in the Middle East, Cairo, 18 April 1993, pp. 1, 6.
13. Mohamed Nabil Fahmy, 'Egypt's disarmament initiative', *Bulletin of the Atomic Scientists* 46 (November 1990), p.10.
14. Bruce Jentleson, 'The Middle East Arms Control and Regional Security (ACRS) Talks: Progress, Problems, and Prospects' (San Diego: University of California, IGCC Policy Paper 26, September 1996).

12
A Nuclear-Weapon-Free Southern Hemisphere

Terence O'Brien

Nuclear-weapon-free zones (NWFZ) are regionally derived initiatives. In this regard they are qualitatively different from other parts of the international nuclear weapons and arms control agenda where the initiative derives substantially from the acknowledged nuclear-weapons states (NWS). For all practical purposes this means that the lion's share of the nuclear security discourse and agenda is promoted, indeed defined, by those acknowledged NWS. The stage reached on the international agenda – with the indefinite renewal of the Nuclear Non-Proliferation Treaty (NPT) in 1995, and the adoption of the Comprehensive Test Ban Treaty (CTBT) and the International Court of Justice (ICJ) Advisory Opinion on the legality of nuclear weapons in 1996 – has refocused attention on NWFZ and their utility in advancing matters further down the twin tracks of genuine non-proliferation and real nuclear disarmament.

There are shifts discernible in the context of the nuclear disarmament and arms control debate. The end of the Cold War, the unremitting efforts of individual governments and non-government agencies at the level of the UN, regionally and elsewhere, and the contribution of various blue-ribbon expert groups, including the 1996 Canberra Commission, have succeeded, as we stand at the threshold of a new century, in bestowing respectability on the discussion of issues that in the recent past might have been carefully and deliberately side-stepped. As the new century opens, the very utility of nuclear deterrence in the

15. Mohamed Shaker, 'Prospects for Establishing a Zone Free of Weapons of Mass Destruction in the Middle East', Director's Series on Proliferation, Lawrence Livermore National Laboratory, 6 (1994), p. 22.
16. Although a flood of books and articles, both journalistic and academic, have been published on the Israeli nuclear option or potential, the technical nature of the capability is highly ambiguous. Estimates of this capability range from 50 weapons to over 200, and these are all based on guesses (some more educated than others) regarding the capacity and operations of Dimona, and efforts to sift fact from fiction in the claims of Mordechai Vanunu. In comparison, India had detonated a nuclear device, making it a defacto nuclear power (although India claimed this to be a 'peaceful nuclear explosion' and not a test of a weapon).
17. Shalheveth Freier, 'A Nuclear-Weapon-Free Zone (NWFZ) in the Middle East and its Ambiance', unpublished manuscript (1992). An edited version of this paper was published as 'A Nuclear-Weapon-Free Zone in the Middle East and Effective Verification', in *Disarmament: A Periodic Review by the United Nations* 16:3 (1993), pp. 66–91.
18. Aluf Benn, 'Barak: Nuclear Policy has not and will not change' *Haaretz*, 31 December 1995, p. 10a. A recent advisory ruling by the International Court of Justice on the legality of nuclear weapons stated that while in most cases the threat or use of such weapons would be illegal, this would not necessarily be the case when the deterrent threat was in a situation of use as a weapon of last resort.
19. Asher Arian, 'Israel and the Peace Process: Security and Political Attitudes in 1993', Tel Aviv University, Jaffee Center for Strategic Studies, Memorandum No. 39, February 1993, p. 12.
20. For analyses of the NPT issue in Israeli–Egyptian relations, see Gerald M. Steinberg, 'The 1995 NPT Extension and Review Conference and the Arab–Israeli Peace Process', *NonProliferation Review* 4 (Fall 1996), pp. 17–30; and Fawaz A. Gerges, 'Egyptian–Israeli Relations Turn Sour', *Foreign Affairs* 74 (May/June 1995), pp. 69–78.
21. There is a vast literature debating the role of deterrence, particularly during the Cold War. For one of the most comprehensive critiques, see Richard N. Lebow and Janice G. Stein, *We All Lost the Cold War* (Princeton, NJ: Princeton University Press, 1994).
22. In the past, Iraqi forces have joined in attacks on Israel and, despite the reduction of the Iraqi military capability, the capability to intervene in the Arab–Israeli theatre continues and may grow following the end of the embargo against Saddam Hussein.
23. Prawitz and Leonard, *A Zone Free of Weapons*, p. 78.

A Nuclear-Weapon-Free Southern Hemisphere 211

world has itself become part of the mainstream debate. Such developments are central to informed discourse and policy change.

The basic bargain of the NPT – according to which non-NWS committed themselves not to acquire nuclear-weapons capability in return for a commitment by the NWS to disarm – is still unconsummated. The 1996 ICJ Advisory Opinion substantially amplifies the obligations of the five acknowledged NWS[1] in international law to commence collectively serious nuclear disarmament which only two (the US and Russia) have, until this point in time, undertaken. China has committed itself, under a 1996 UN General Assembly resolution, to support commencement of negotiation of a UN convention on nuclear disarmament. France and the UK have accepted no obligation to commence actual negotiation.

In the course of the last thirty years the conclusion of NWFZ treaties for the regions of Latin America (Treaty of Tlatelolco, 1967), the South Pacific (Treaty of Rarotonga, 1985), Southeast Asia (Treaty of Bangkok, 1995) and Africa (Treaty of Pelindaba, 1996) has had the effect of transforming the greater part of the southern hemisphere into an area covered by separate pieces of international law that designate it to be nuclear-weapon-free. If Antarctica is added to this aggregate of treaty areas (Antarctica is not covered by a NWFZ as such, but under the 1959 Antarctic Treaty, it is demilitarised to exclude nuclear weapons), then more than 50 per cent of the globe's surface is so designated.

The idea for a southern hemisphere-wide nuclear-weapon-free area is not entirely new. It was first spoken of in the 1960s. The idea has recently, however, become the object of renewed attention by governments collectively,[2] as well as in academic quarters. There is no doubt more than one reason for this. But a UN resolution sponsored by Brazil and adopted in 1996 by 129 votes to 3 with 38 abstentions,[3] invited states parties to the four existing NWFZ treaties to explore 'means of cooperation . . . including the consolidation of the status of the nuclear-weapon-free southern hemisphere and adjacent areas'. (The 'adjacent areas' refers to those parts of the northern hemisphere which are covered in all four treaties, but in particular under Pelindaba and Tlatelolco.) The United Nations, for its part, was called upon to urge the full recognition of the southern hemisphere and other areas covered by the four zones by all relevant states, to encourage further

NWFZ establishment, and to provide assistance, through the UN Secretary-General, to facilitate the accomplishment of these goals. In a subsequent meeting of the UN Disarmament Commission on 22 April 1997, a number of delegates strongly supported the initiative and the contribution that NWFZ could make to disarmament. In particular, the New Zealand delegate, Peter Rider, noted that while the creation of formal links between the four zones might be 'complex and difficult', there was scope for developing 'political links', and that the Brazilian initiative would lead to increased cooperation between the zones.[4] Nevertheless, other than generalised endorsement for the idea, at the level of political leadership there appears to be no detailed proposition yet about how to attain this objective.

The Context

Denuclearisation commands wide assent south of the equator as well as to its north. The near universality of approval in 1995 for the renewed NPT itself[5] provides substantial proof of the repudiation of the nuclear option by a majority of states – not just the eligible signatories of the four existing NWFZ treaties – both above and below the equator.

The three essential aims of NWFZ, as they concern nuclear weapons, are non-possession, non-deployment and non-use. The provisions of the four existing NWFZ, especially in respect of non-deployment and non-use, in fact go further than the NPT itself. The four NWFZ are thus indeed constituent parts of the global nuclear non-proliferation regime; and are companion pieces for other nuclear disarmament treaties (the Sea Bed Treaty, the Outer Space Treaty, the Comprehensive Test Ban Treaty) as well as other parts of international law which cover weapons of mass destruction (WMD) – notably chemical and biological weapons.

By their very existence, NWFZ reinforce the conclusion that nuclear weapons are indeed becoming less relevant to the security calculations of all but a few countries.[6] They add substantially to normative behaviour (norms) in the world. Common to all NWFZ is an evident belief amongst signatories that they would be more secure if their regions were free from nuclear weapons.[7] The NPT, underpinned by the 1995 decision to make it permanent, rejects nuclear weapons and is committed to their complete elimination. That is crystal clear as a matter of international law. The effect is to delegitimise nuclear weapons. The NPT does not provide a legal basis for the maintenance by NWS of their weapons. It does not provide a basis for those states either to argue that disarmament or arms control can be deferred, or that all the international effort must be first or exclusively applied against horizontal proliferation of nuclear weapons to states that do not possess them.

The 1996 Advisory Opinion of the ICJ, with the question mark it places over nuclear weapons as a legitimate instrument of national power, underscores delegitimisation. As direct extensions of the NPT, the NWFZ as well reinforce the effect of delegitimisation. The question is, can the norms and law be strengthened or new instruments devised that are more vigorous in their design and impact for achieving the basic NPT bargain between genuine nuclear non-proliferation and disarmament?

There is no one authorised international definition of what precisely constitutes a NWFZ.[8] The motives behind and the details of the four separate southern hemisphere zones vary from region to region. The differences are, in some measure, the product of different negotiations, at different times, in different circumstances. The South Pacific and Latin American treaties were negotiated in times of the Cold War, and Tlatelolco predates even the NPT itself. The African and Southeast Asian treaties are post-Cold War products. They derive from a time when impatience and concern in the international community mounts at the failure by NWS to live up to the nuclear disarmament obligations of the NPT, and when anxieties about proliferation continue to resonate in many places.

Nuclear Deterrence

The end of the Cold War has not produced an in-depth examination, by any nuclear-weapons state, of the intrinsic rationale or utility of nuclear deterrence. The circumstances in which the doctrine of nuclear deterrence was first conceived and developed have passed into history with the end of the Cold War.[9] Deterrence is logical when confronted with the likelihood of unambiguous and unprovoked aggression. In its absence, and under different geostrategic circumstances, the unchanged promotion of nuclear deterrence may help provoke the very instability and conflict it is intended to prevent.[10] Deterrence, which resides in the jealously guarded and stringently enforced nuclear monopoly, may induce the very nuclear proliferation to countries in whose hands such weapons or capability would indeed be more dangerous. It is hardly logical to envisage a system of global security management continuing into the twenty-first century that is based unalterably on nuclear-weapons monopoly by five countries, with no serious collective effort by *all* five to constrain that monopoly, negotiate cuts in nuclear arms, reduce the impact and salience of nuclear weapons on and for international relations, devise effective systems of international control over warhead stocks and ultimately dismantle all nuclear weapons. Time, together with the power of freely circulating ideas and knowledge, will surely defeat the obstinate attachment to the status quo.

The 1994 in-house US Nuclear Posture Review concluded in effect that the US continues to require nuclear deterrence 'just in case'.[11] The Review advocated a cautious hedge strategy resting upon an indispensable nuclear-weapons capability, even though the likelihood of nuclear or other war between major powers is improbable. In 1990 members of the North Atlantic Treaty Organisation (NATO) decided that the alliance could reduce its reliance upon nuclear weapons, 'making nuclear weapons truly weapons of last resort'.[12] But NATO is an alliance that remains grounded in nuclear deterrence and first strike capability. And the basic definition of deterrence is now conceived as a doctrine to include prevention of WMD from falling into the hands of states or groups whose motivation is suspect (in many instances, rightly so). That is a quite different rationale for nuclear deterrence from what went before. Then it was to deter nuclear *attack*. Now it includes prevention or deterrence of actual weapons *acquisition* (by unacceptable hands). That rationale has never been substantively debated.[13] It is what lies behind the examination of doctrines of 'counter-proliferation' that have now entered the lexicon of security planners. The actual employability of nuclear weapons as a deterrent against nuclear-weapons acquisition, especially in the case of terrorists, must remain highly conjectural.

The utility, indeed relevance, of nuclear deterrence is affected too by the 'revolution in military affairs' (RMA). The new technologies of sophisticated, smart sub-nuclear weapons and the unassailable US superiority in such conventional weaponry affect the utility of nuclear weapons in security calculations. American superiority would, for all practical purposes, be unaltered, indeed reinforced, were nuclear weapons excluded (or severely reduced) from the post-Cold War security strategy.[14] In a nuclear-weapon-free (or largely free) world, US deterrence grounded in 'smart' conventional weapon superiority alone would be formidable and in itself constitute a severe constraint upon proliferation of any or all types of WMD, including to terrorist groups. In professional military circles inside the US, there is evidence of agnosticism about the true utility of nuclear deterrence and a preference for developing sophisticated conventional capabilities. Amongst retired professionals there is open disavowal of the utility of nuclear deterrence.

Principles and Guidelines for a Possible Southern Hemisphere NWFZ

Nuclear-Weapons States

The five NWS have signed the relevant protocols of the Latin American, South Pacific and African treaties. The process of final acceptance in the cases of Tlatelolco and Rarotonga was a lengthy one. This is explicable with reference to the perceived constraints that NWFZ treaties impose upon NWS strategic options for mobile nuclear deployment and development (vertical proliferation). For a long period, these constraints were judged by the NWS to offset potential benefits of the zones in containing the spread of nuclear capability (horizontal proliferation). There is indeed still basic NWS ambivalence about whether further denuclearisation objectives, evident in the southern hemisphere and beyond, should be encouraged or resisted. And for some NWS, their signatures on the NWFZ protocols are largely symbolic. The signatures do not, in their eyes, commit their governments to do anything additional by way of disarmament. For some, indeed, signature justifies an assertion that they are abiding by Article 6 of the NPT (which commits the NWS to effective disarmament) and therefore honouring pledges made at the time of its indefinite extension in 1995.

At the time of writing the NWS have not signed the protocols with respect to the Southeast Asian NWFZ treaty. SEANWFZ includes the 200 mile exclusive economic zone (EEZ) and continental shelf within its definition of the nuclear-weapon-free zone. This encompasses islands which are in dispute with China, as well between the member states of the Association of South-east Asian Nations (ASEAN) themselves. Beijing has declined to sign the protocol. The US, which perceives ambiguity about high seas freedoms with the establishment of the EEZ as the limit of a security zone, has withheld support. The other NWS have followed suit.

At the time of writing it is not clear whether the SEANWFZ protocol can be amended to accommodate satisfactorily the interests of the NWS; or indeed whether ASEAN states would be agreeable to amending it so. Negotiations between the signatories and the NWS are continuing. While the conventional wisdom of the Cold War NWFZ (Tlatelolco and Rarotonga) was that the endorsement of the NWS was of course an essential purpose of the NWFZ, Southeast Asian states by their actions to date may be reinforcing a larger message to all NWS (and in particular to China and the US) that the utility of extended nuclear deterrence is now contestable in the context of regional security management.[15] The adherence of the NWS to treaty protocols is highly desirable but not indispensable. Such a view, if shared by the eligible regional signatories of existing NWFZ that cover the southern hemisphere, will expand the margin for action to extend to the law, or (more likely) to the norms, more vigorous impact; and will lend a more purposeful air to action intended to consolidate a nuclear-weapon-free southern hemisphere.

Freedom of Navigation

The southern hemisphere is predominantly a maritime environment. The issue of high seas navigation and rights of innocent passage are manifestly relevant here. Such rights are enshrined in the UN Convention on the Law of the Sea (UNCLOS) and in other documents that predate UNCLOS. In all essential strategic respects, nuclear weapons in the post-Cold War are weapons of the high seas. This accounts for the central importance attached by NWS to high seas freedoms in an international security context, and in the southern hemisphere in particular. Further consolidation of a nuclear-weapon-free southern hemisphere and its adjacent zones by the regional signatories, if it is to be more than just symbolism, may necessarily entail constraints, at least of a declaratory kind. The effective absence of strategic weapons like intercontinental ballistic missiles (ICBMs) from the southern hemisphere should theoretically make it easier for the NWS to accept constraints upon the (submarine) passage of ICBMs in the southern hemisphere. But the issue of setting a precedent would surely be paramount in determining NWS views.

The rights of freedom of navigation and innocent passage are already limited in law by the principle of peaceful purposes and the requirement for due regard for other states' interests. One question here is whether the 1996 ICJ Advisory Opinion, which concluded that the threat or use of nuclear weapons is generally illegal (although the Court could not reach a decision on this in the extreme circumstances of self-defence), creates a fresh and sufficient basis to support a further case through the ICJ, to constrain the rights of freedom of navigation and of innocent passage, in cases where nuclear weapons are deployed.

In the absence of considered legal assessment it is impossible to predict what likelihood there is that such a case could be sustained in international law, or what the practical effects would be if an opinion in favour of restraining high seas freedoms were delivered. While there is growing recognition with regard to maritime freedoms that linkages between national security and environmental degradation and resource depletion are real and destabilising (and should therefore constitute potential constraints upon those freedoms),[16] all NWS would be concerned over nuclear-weapons constraints on high seas and their rights of legitimate defence. Without profound rethinking about the utility of nuclear deterrence, such an ICJ opinion adverse to perceived NWS interests would be vigorously contested and surely ignored by the NWS, and probably other non-NWS as well for whom high seas freedoms are also paramount. Such an opinion would, on the other hand, palpably strengthen the basis of normative structure that is intended to be an influence on international behaviour.

The four existing NWFZ uphold high seas freedoms. The treaties of Rarotonga, Pelindaba and Bangkok affirm however the right of each signatory to decide about actual port or aircraft visits in territorial waters. This provision, first included in Rarotonga, covers the position of New Zealand, whose national Nuclear Free Zone law (1987) prohibits visits by nuclear-armed or nuclear-powered vessels. Some other countries (the Philippines, the Solomon Islands and Vanuatu) constrain passage of nuclear weapons in their territorial sea because they are not judged to be 'innocent'. No other southern hemisphere or adjacent country has taken national restrictions beyond NWFZ treaty provisions. Nevertheless, the option of course remains available to each individual government.

Approaches to Treaty Consolidation

The differences between the four existing treaties (and with the Antarctic Treaty) plus the fact that the various zones are not wholly contiguous, manifestly diminish the prospects for blending the various treaties into one composite legal instrument, which declares the southern hemisphere and adjacent areas to be nuclear-weapon-free. It would not entirely defeat the prospects. A complex process of negotiation, or renegotiation, would however be entailed – involving all the eligible signatories of all the treaties (over 110 countries in total) plus the five NWS (and, possibly, Antarctic Treaty members who would be European states for the great part). Of the more than 110 countries situated in the geographical areas designated in the four treaties, (excluding Antarctica), less than half, 47, are situated in the southern hemisphere.[17]

The task of blending all the current treaties into one bumper legal instrument would be herculean and, almost inevitably, doomed to infinite disappointment. One possibility would be a new uniform protocol to existing treaties, drawn up by southern hemisphere and adjacent governments themselves, that invites the NWS to accept voluntary restraint on the deployment and transit of nuclear weapons through the southern hemisphere. The NWS would see a danger in such a development and would almost certainly decline to accept such voluntary restraint. But that is not a necessarily sufficient reason for the southern hemisphere and adjacent areas to abandon the idea of a voluntary restraint protocol. If the aim is to limit any new initiative to what is immediately achievable, things will not go far. As experience to this point proves, it is necessary to take the long and patient view on nuclear disarmament. The exercise of building normative behaviour in international relations is, by definition, protracted. The idea of voluntary restraint protocols could, with time, gain weight as anti-nuclear sentiment consolidates further and as stocks of nuclear weapons diminish because of bilateral nuclear or other arms reduction agreements.

Consolidation of a nuclear-weapon-free southern hemisphere and adjacent areas could also be sought through political rather than juridical means. A high-level political statement, declaration or resolution by regional countries which are eligible signatories of the existing NWFZ treaties, signifying collective disavowal of nuclear weapons, constitutes the outer limit of what is attainable. But something which is not more than a symbolic reaffirmation of existing treaty provisions may not be useful or meaningful. Such a statement could of course call for action by the NWS in respect of key outstanding elements on the nuclear agenda, such as those identified, for instance, by the Canberra Commission[18] (for example, taking nuclear weapons off alert in the southern hemisphere and adjacent areas, applying effective verification safeguards, at least in the southern hemisphere and adjacent areas and so on). But the principal requirement for any such political statement of consolidation should be something more than exhortation and should go further than the existing treaties' provisions, including those in the protocols.

As they exist, the NWFZ which embrace the southern hemisphere and adjacent areas prohibit acquisition, testing, manufacture and stationing of nuclear explosive devices; and establish compliance and verification systems. They serve, as suggested earlier, to reinforce NPT norms, the non-proliferation consensus and the effective delegitimisation of nuclear weapons. They are thus an important component of the overall mosaic of international action on denuclearisation. The de facto consolidation of southern hemisphere nuclear-weapon-free status would however be enhanced by a political statement that included a collective declaration that the southern hemisphere and adjacent areas no longer wish to be defended by nuclear weapons.

This would be a political statement of consequence. It would represent the logical extension of the creation and consolidation of the zones and of the delegitimisation of nuclear weapons implicit in the zone treaties and NPT. Whether individual treaty signatory governments would decide, as a consequence of such a statement, to take further action in terms of the statement would be a matter of individual choice. Countries which have operational security alliances with individual NWS could only sign up presumably with an explicit proviso that the statement represents the ideal; but in prevailing circumstances, they remain attached to existing political-security relationships. A disavowal of nuclear deterrence by the southern hemisphere and adjacent governments (even with a proviso for countries still in alliance relationships) would, nonetheless, on its own and in the absence of any new NWS undertakings, mark, by most standards, a significant political act.

Until the recent past strategic security realism would have repudiated such a suggestion as radical, unjustified and dangerous. For various reasons touched upon in this chapter, including the shift in mainstream opinion about the international nuclear disarmament agenda (notably about the intrinsic relevance of nuclear deterrence itself), the leap, from what now exists in the substance of the renewed NPT and the existing NWFZ to a political statement as proposed here, is not as great for eligible regional NWFZ signatories to contemplate as it may once have been. There are precedents. In the conventions negotiated by the international community on chemical and biological weapons, the stipulations and safeguards about non-use add up to the disavowal of any wish on the part of signatories to be defended by such WMD. That disavowal could now be extended to nuclear weapons, in the form of an autonomous political declaration or statement by the eligible regional signatory states of southern hemisphere NWFZ treaties in the first instance.

The political statement suggested here would be one both for southern hemisphere countries which are members, variously, of the four negotiated NWFZ treaties, as well as northern hemisphere signatories of those treaties. Significant diplomatic preparation would be needed if such a course of action were deemed, in principle, to be worthy of pursuit. It would certainly require the active support of a collection of individual southern hemisphere countries from each of the existing treaty zones, upon whom responsibility for the carriage of the initiative would fall; and actual carriage should be exercised at a political, not bureaucratic, level.

The convening of an inter-governmental conference of all signatories of all four of the existing NWFZ treaties (a distinction should here be drawn between signatories of the full NWFZ treaties and of their protocols), in order to lend effect to consolidation of the southern hemisphere's nuclear-weapon-free status, would send a powerful message. In effect it would be a meeting (desirably at the political level) of all states that supported the UN resolution on a nuclear-weapon-free southern hemisphere. But the critical need for careful preparation, including of the desired outcome (does the conference pursue a juridical or political approach along the lines distinguished in this paper?), would require judicious preparation by a small group of initiating countries. The five NWS could be expected to lobby conference participants actively for an outcome that did not infringe their perceived vital security interests. But the southern hemisphere states (and other NWFZ signatories) will need to be resolute if their initiative is to produce an outcome that is meaningful on the threshold of the new millennium.

Conclusion

The above proposal represents the upper limit of what consolidation of the nuclear-weapon-free southern hemisphere and adjacent areas could entail in terms of political commitment. The statement would not, as indicated above, necessarily lead to specific action by individual governments to lend effect to the statement. But it could do so if individual governments so decided.

At the other end of the scale, a straightforward resolution at the UN General Assembly would be the very least that consolidation would require. In the General Assembly the need would be for a unanimously supported resolution, (including by the NWS) if consolidation was not to appear qualified, even contested. That requirement would almost certainly necessitate in its turn a generalised, non-contentious, lowest common denominator text that could be little more than symbolic in content. A more ambitious formula is required if the consolidation of a nuclear-weapon-free southern hemisphere and adjacent areas is intended to be an action of substance, and not just a gesture of symbolism.

Notes

1. China, France, Russia, the United Kingdom and the United States of America.
2. See, for example, the South African–New Zealand (Mandela–Bolger) joint Memorandum on Cooperation in Disarmament and Arms Control, 8 August 1996.
3. UN Document A/C 1/51/L.4/Rev 1 of 7 November 1996.
4. United Nations, *Press Release DC/2580*, 22 April 1997.
5. As of the end of 1996, more than 180 countries had signed the NPT.

6. Zachary S. Davis, 'The Spread of Nuclear-Weapon-Free Zones: Building a New Nuclear Bargain', *Arms Control Today* 26 (February 1996), p. 15.
7. Jon Brook Wolfsthal, 'Nuclear-Weapon-Free Zones: Coming of Age?', *Arms Control Today* 23 (March 1993).
8. Certain general characteristics have been defined. See for example United Nations Conference on Disarmament, *Comprehensive Study of the Question of Nuclear-Weapon-Free-Zones in All its Aspects*, UN General Assembly, 30th Session, Supplement No.27A, A/10027/Add.1, 1975.
9. Paul Keal, 'Nuclear Weapons and the New World Order', in Richard Leaver and James L. Richardson, eds, *Charting the Post-Cold War Order* (Boulder: Westview, 1993), p. 96.
10. Andrew Mack, 'Key Security Issues in the Asia–Pacific', in Leaver and Richardson, eds, *Charting the Post-Cold War Order*, p. 155.
11. *1994 U.S. Nuclear Posture Review* (Washington: Office of Assistant Secretary of Defense for Public Affairs, Department of Defense, News Release 546-94, 22 September 1994).
12. See the London Declaration on a Transformed North Atlantic Alliance: NATO, July 1990.
13. The UN Security Resolution of February 1995 underscored the paramount importance of halting proliferation of weapons of mass destruction and described it 'as a threat to international peace and security', which implies that a military response may be in order. See Alton Frye, 'Banning Ballistic Missiles', *Foreign Affairs* 75 (November/December 1996), p. 108. By no stretch of the imagination does such a resolution add up to the justification of nuclear deterrence for preventing proliferation.
14. Davis, 'The Spread of Nuclear-Weapon-Free Zones', p. 19.
15. Ibid., p. 17.
16. As attested to by the example of French–Japanese nuclear waste shipments through the southern Pacific and the strong adverse reaction of regional states.
17. Of the 53 eligible signatories of Pelindaba, 24 are in the southern hemisphere; of the 34 in Tlatelolco, 9; of the 10 in Bangkok, 1; of the 16 in Rarotonga, 13.
18. *Report of the Canberra Commission on the Elimination of Nuclear Weapons* (Canberra: Department of Foreign Affairs and Trade, 1996).

Index

Abubakar, Iya, 95
Adeniji, Olu, 112
Advena, 94, 115
Afghanistan, 154, 178
African Commission on Nuclear Energy (AFCONE), 17, 113, 115
African National Congress (ANC), 103, 105, 106
African NWFZ, *see* Pelindaba, Treaty of
Agency for the Prohibition of Nuclear Weapons in Latin America and the Caribbean (OPANAL), 17, 36, 42–6, 49, 74, 168
Agu, Benson, 116
Akram, Munir, 163
Albright, David, 105
Algeria, 95, 175, 189, 196, 206
Andaman and Nicobar Islands, 21
Angola, 101, 102, 106
Antarctic Treaty, 4, 63, 141, 176, 211, 218
Antigua and Barbuda, 54 n22
ANZUS, 15–16
Arab-Israeli conflict, 184, 189, 204
Arab League, 196, 199
Arafat, Yasser, 189
Argentina
 and Brazil, 46–50, 52, 56 n33, 206
 and Islas Malvinas, 20
 and NPT, 45
 nuclear aspirations of, 26, 35, 38, 48, 52, 54 n18, 55 n29
 and Nuclear Suppliers Group, 57 n35
 and Tlatelolco Treaty, 39–40, 53 n6, n10
Argentina-Brazil Accounting and Control Commission (ABACC), 36, 43, 46, 48–50, 51, 58 n39, n43, 124, 202
Argentine-Brazilian Committee on Nuclear Policy, 57 n37
Arms Control and Regional Security (ACRS), 9, 195, 198–200
ASEAN, *see* Association of South-east Asian Nations
ASEAN Free Trade Area (AFTA), 82
ASEAN Regional Forum (ARF), 9, 144
Asia–Pacific Economic Cooperation (APEC), 144
Asiatom, 18
Assad, Hafiz al, 189
Association of South-east Asian Nations (ASEAN), 69
 Declarations: Bali, 82; Bangkok, 82; Kuala Lumpur, 82; Manila, 85
 and conflict management, 10, 81
 High Council, 83
 membership, 83
 and Southeast Asian NWFZ, 81–4, 124, 142, 216
 summits: Kuala Lumpur, 83; third, 83; fourth, 82; fifth, 83
Australia, 63, 77, 84
 and ANZUS, 16
 and Indonesia, 69, 86
 and Pacific Islands, 66
 peace movements in, 60

Australia (cont'd)
 and SPNFZ, 16, 62–3, 74, 142
 and USA, 16, 29, 63–4, 68, 69, 74
 Australian Scientific Advisory Group, 80 n24

Bahama, 54 n22
Bamako Convention, 111
Banerjee, Dipankar, 10, 27
Bangkok, Treaty of, 5, 21, 72, 82–92, 124, 175, 177, 211, 213
 background, 84–6
 critique of, 88–91
 and delivery systems, 87
 and disarmament, 87
 and EEZ, 7, 19, 87, 90, 215
 and entry-into-force, 10
 and existing security arrangements, 84–6, 89
 and freedom of the seas, 19, 89–90, 217
 and IAEA, 17, 87–90
 and ICJ, 18
 and innocent passage, 89
 membership, 5, 11
 and negative security assurances, 88, 90
 and non-proliferation, 87, 91
 and nuclear-ship visits, 88
 and nuclear testing, 90
 and nuclear waste, 89–90
 and nuclear-weapons states, 215
 and peaceful nuclear development, 85, 87, 89–90
 and peaceful nuclear explosions, 6
 protocols, 23
 and Rarotonga Treaty, 70, 73, 86
 and regional security & stability, 86–91
 review of, 10
 and South Asian NWFZ, 179
 and Tlatelolco Treaty, 86
 and UN, 17, 88
 and verification, 17–18, 88
 withdrawal clauses, 11, 88

Bangladesh, 154, 166
Barak, Ehud, 203
Barbados, 43, 54 n22
Beg, Aslam, 171 n10
Beilin, Yosi, 203
Belize, 45, 53 n10
Bell, Robert, 66
Bhaba, Homi, 153
Bhutan, 166
Bhutto, Benazir, 171 n10
Bhutto, Zulfiqar Ali, 154, 158
Biological Weapons Convention, 77, 200, 220
Bolger, James, 221 n2
Bolivia, 9, 53 n6, 54 n22
Brazil, 100
 and Argentina, 46–50, 52, 56 n33, 206
 military coup (1964), 37
 and NPT, 26, 55 n27, 176
 nuclear aspirations of, 26, 35, 48, 52, 54 n18, 55 n29
 and Nuclear Suppliers Group, 57 n35
 and southern hemisphere NWFZ, 211–2
 and Tlatelolco Treaty, 9, 26, 35, 37, 39–40, 45, 53 n6, n10
Britain
 and Diego Garcia, 20
 and Falkland Islands, 20
 and nuclear testing, 77
 and nuclear weapons, 4, 211; on ships, 32 n19
 and NWFZ: African, 113; Latin American, 39–40, 44; South Pacific, 22–3, 60, 66–7
 and South Africa, 103
Brunei, 84
Bush, George, 32 n19, 132
 Administration, 66

Cam Ranh, 85–6
Cambodia, 83–6

Index

Canberra Commission on the Elimination of Nuclear Weapons, 194, 196, 210, 219
Cartagena, 52 n3
Carter Administration, 22
Castro, Fidel, 38
Center of International Strategy, Technology and Policy, 124, 132, 138 n2
Central Asia, 168, 178, 180
Chemical Weapons Convention, 77, 174, 175, 182, 206, 220
Chile, 9, 41, 45, 53 n6, 206
China, 15, 182–3
  and disarmament, 211
  and India, 20, 153, 164, 169, 179–82, 186
  and Japan, 147
  and Myanmar, 179, 180
  and North Korea, 13
  and nuclear tests, 13, 37, 134, 153, 162
  and nuclear weapons, 4, 130, 132, 144, 162–3, 175, 182
  and NWFZ: African, 113; Latin American, 44; Northeast Asian, 12, 23–4, 29, 128, 131, 133–8, 141, 143–50; South Asian, 12–13, 20, 23, 161, 164, 169, 180–2; South Pacific, 22–3, 66–7, 73; Southeast Asian, 23, 216
  and Pakistan, 13, 157, 169, 179–82, 186
  and Russia/USSR, 24–5, 85
  and Taiwan, 10, 29
  and Tibet, 23, 182
  and USA, 24–5
Christmas Island, 77
Clark, Roger, 80 n24
Clinton, W., 114
  Administration, 66–7
Cold War, 3, 4, 29, 64, 70, 73, 74, 81, 94, 97–100, 123, 128, 135, 140–3, 145, 149, 155–6, 213, 216
  end of, 60, 86, 106, 108, 128, 129, 206, 210, 213
  post-Cold War, 14–15, 22, 49, 73, 75, 77, 81, 86, 89, 123, 129, 134, 136, 142, 144, 147, 160, 173, 213–14, 216
Colombia, 53 n6
Commission for SEANWFZ, 17–18, 88
Communist Party of the Soviet Union (CPSU), 129–30
Comprehensive Test Ban Treaty (CTBT), 15, 18, 60, 67, 123, 149, 165, 174–5, 196, 210, 212
Conference on Disarmament, 24, 97
Contadora, 52 n3
Convention on Conventional Weapons, 77
Conventional Forces in Europe Treaty (CFE), 143, 204
Coordinating Committee on Export Controls (COCOM), 94
COPREDAL, *see* Preparatory Commission for the Denuclearisation of Latin America
Costa Rica, 35, 53 n6
Council on Foreign Relations, 171 n13
CTBT, *see* Comprehensive Test Ban Treaty
Cuba, 5, 22, 38–9, 44–5
Cuban missile crisis, 15, 22, 52 n2, 117 n12, 125, 134, 141, 142, 175
Cunningham, William, 131
Czechoslovakia, 4

Davinic, Prvoslav, 100
de Klerk, F. W., 104–5, 107
de la Torre, Enrique, 57 n36
de Villiers, J. W., 105–6
Declaration on Denuclearisation of Africa, 98–9, 109
deterrence, 3, 213–15, 219
  in Africa, 106
  and disarmament, 94

deterrence (cont'd)
    extended, 140, 216
    in Latin America, 41
    in the Middle East, 196, 199, 202–4
    NATO and, 214
    non-conventional, 185
    in Northeast Asia, 129, 132, 140, 144–5, 148
    and 'nuclear allergy', 23–4
    and NWFZ, 194
    in South Asia, 152, 180
    in the South Pacific, 69
    and terrorism, 214–15
    theory of, 155
    US, 215
    utility of, 210, 213–17, 220
    and WMD, 214–15
Dhanapala, Jayantha, 8
Diego Garcia, 20–1, 119 n42, 179
Dimona, 202–3, 209 n16
disarmament, 4, 15, 24, 94, 107, 128, 149, 173, 213, 220
Dominican Republic, 53 n6

Eban, Abba, 178
Economic Commission for Africa (ECA), 109, 115–16
Economic Community of West African States (ECOWAS), 115–16
Ecuador, 9, 53 n6, 54 n22
Egypt, 97, 109, 188, 191–2, 195–201, 203, 205–7
Egypt-Israel Peace Treaty, 205, 206
Eigtheen Nations Disarmament Committee, 41
El Salvador, 53 n6
Endicott, John E., 138 n2
Epstein, William, 38
Equatorial Guinea, 96
Esquipulas, 52 n3
Ethiopia, 97
Europe: Central, 4, 141, 177; Eastern, 143, 160
European Atomic Energy Community (Euratom), 18, 123

Fahd, King, 189
Fahmy, Mohamed Nabil, 199
Fangataufa, 77, 142
Federated States of Micronesia (FSM), 5, 11, 20, 63, 70, 75
Fiji, 62
Five Power Defence Arrangements (FPDA), 84
Foz de Iguacu, 49, 56 n33, 57 n37
France, 104
    nuclear tests, 3, 20, 22, 59, 60–1, 66–9, 71–2, 77, 97–8, 142, 175
    and nuclear waste, 222 n16
    and nuclear weapons, 4, 211; on ships, 32 n19
    and NWFZ: African, 113; Latin American, 40, 44, 54 n22; South Pacific, 22, 60, 66–7
    and South Africa, 103, 105
Freier, Shalheveth, 202
French Polynesia, 20
Fry, Greg, 69

Georgia Institute of Technology, 124, 132, 138 n2
Germany, 4, 57 n36, 103
Golan Heights, 205
Gorbachev, Mikhail, 32 n19, 67, 130
Greece, 178
Grenada, 54 n22
Guadalajara agreement, 49
Guantanamo, 22, 38, 45
Guatemala, 53 n10
Guinea-Bissau, 102
Gujral, Inder Kumar, 163, 165
Gulf Cooperation Council, 189
Gulf War (1990–1), 24, 48, 203
Gurion, David Ben, 185
Gurtov, Mel, 145
Guyana, 45, 53 n10

Halperin, Morton, 131
Hamas, 189, 195
Hamel-Green, Michael, 16
Harb, Usama al-Ghazali, 186

Index

Hashimoto, Ryutaro, 150
Hawke, R. G., 62
Hayasi, Maeda, 131
Hayden, W., 80 n21
Helsinki process, 206
Hernandez, Carolina, 16
Hiroshima, 150
Hizbollah, 189, 195, 207
Hochstein, Manfred, 80 n24
Honduras, 53 n6
human security, 108
Hussein, King, 189

IAEA, *see* International Atomic Energy Agency
Ibrahim, Saad Eddin, 186
ICJ, *see* International Court of Justice
Ihonvbere, Julius, 16
IMF, *see* International Monetary Fund
India, 18
  Atomic Energy Commission of, 182
  and China, 20, 153, 164, 169, 179–82, 186
  and CTBT, 15, 165, 182
  and missiles, 156–7
  and NPT, 12, 18, 93, 182
  and nuclear weapons, 4, 13, 29, 94, 152–5, 160, 165, 180, 182
  and Pakistan, 25, 26, 94, 152–70, 180–2, 186
  'peaceful nuclear explosion' by, 153, 158, 160, 165, 182, 209 n16
  and South Asian NWFZ, 21, 29, 152–83
  and USA, 13
  and USSR, 179
Indian Ocean, 178, 179, 181, 182
Indo-Soviet Friendship Treaty, 179
Indonesia, 69–70, 73, 81–2, 85–6
Indus Water Treaty, 163
Inter-American Conference, 53 n10
Intermediate-range Nuclear Forces (INF) Treaty, 174–5, 182
International Atomic Energy Agency (IAEA), 94, 116, 158
  Board of Governors, 198–200
  and Israel, 200–1
  and NWFZ, 17–18, 110, 196–201
  and OPANAL, 44–6
  safeguards, 11, 19, 22, 31 n11, 40, 44–6, 49–51, 65, 87, 113, 123–4, 167–8, 177, 198, 201
  and South Africa, 103
  and verification, 7, 38, 189
International Court of Justice (ICJ), 18, 44, 209 n18, 210–1, 213, 217
International Monetary Fund (IMF), 108
Iran, 168, 178, 186, 189–91, 195–7, 200–1, 206–7
Iran-Iraq War (1980–8), 25
Iraq, 190–1
  and Israel, 203–6, 209 n22
  and Middle East NWFZ, 201
  and Middle East peace process, 195, 207
  and NPT, 200
  and nuclear weapons, 18, 24–5, 93–4, 105, 146, 177, 189, 200
  and UNSCOM, 200–1
Israel, 16, 26, 76
  area of, 204–5
  and arms register, UN, 204
  Atomic Energy Commission of, 202
  and Egypt, 192, 195, 205–7
  exceptionalism, 187–8
  and IAEA, 200–1
  and Iraq, 203–6, 209 n22
  and Jordan, 200, 205
  Likud Party, 192
  and Middle East NWFZ, 29, 184–209
  and NPT, 186, 189, 202–3, 206
  and nuclear weapons, 4, 16, 24, 29, 94, 102, 184–93, 196, 199, 203–4, 206, 209 n16
  and Palestinians, 15, 25, 207
  and South Africa, 99, 105
  and Syria, 205–7

Jamaica, 38, 54 n22
Japan, 94
　and China, 147
　constitutional restraints on, 147
　and Korea, 146–9
　Liberal Democratic Party, 150
　New Party Sakigake, 150
　nuclear programme of, 128, 130, 135, 136, 138, 146–7
　and nuclear waste, 222 n16
　and NWFZ, 12, 85, 128–9, 131, 133–8, 141–50
　Social Democratic Party, 150
　Socialist Party, 131
　and UN, 147
　and USA, 13, 15, 134–5, 140, 143, 147–9
Jiang Zemin, 164, 179
Jordan, 191, 199–200, 205
Jordan-Israel Peace Treaty, 200, 206
Judea and Samaria, 205

Kalahari Desert, 104
Karachi Nuclear Power Plant, 158, 168
Karawan, Ibrahim, 16, 27
Kashmir, 153, 156, 157, 160, 163, 181
Kenya, 95, 108
Khan, Abdel Qadir, 154
Khrushchev, Nikita, 129
Kim Il Sung, 15, 130
Kiribati, 76
Kissinger, Henry, 185
konfrontasi, 81–2
Koo, Bon-Hak, 25, 27
Korea, North, 86
　and China, 13
　and Northeast Asian NWFZ, 12, 124, 128, 130–1, 133, 141
　and NPT, 12, 128, 200
　and nuclear weapons, 12, 29, 89, 94, 128, 136, 138, 144, 146, 177, 189
Korea, South, 86
　and Northeast Asian NWFZ, 12, 131, 134, 136–7, 141–9
　and nuclear option, 145–6
　and USA, 13, 130, 134, 136, 143–5, 148–9
Korean peninsula, 6, 25, 86, 124, 128–31, 136–7, 143, 145, 148, 194
Kuwait, 192

Lagos Plan of Action, 108
Lakshadweep Islands, 21
Lange, David, 59, 70, 78
Laos, 83
Latin American NWFZ, *see* Tlatelolco, Treaty of
Lebanon, 207
Leonard, James, 23, 207, 208 n6
Levi, David, 197, 205–6
Liberia, 109
Libya, 93, 95, 105, 107, 117 n3, 195, 201
Lome, 99
London Declaration on NATO, 222 n12

McCloy-Zorin Statement, 97
Mack, Andrew, 71
Madagascar, 5, 11, 109
Mahathir bin Mohamad, 142
Malawi, 108
Malaya, 81
Malaysia, 81–2, 84, 85
Maldives, 166
Male, 172 n37
Mandela, Nelson, 106, 114, 221 n2
Manhattan Project, 118 n27
Marshall Islands, 5, 11, 20, 63, 66, 75
Martinique, 5, 11
Mauritius, 20
Meguid, Ismat Abdel, 197
Mexico, 35, 39, 41, 53 n6
Middle East NWFZ, 184–209
　and 'breakout', 195, 201
　and confidence-building measures, 188, 196, 207
　geographic scope of, 196
　and IAEA, 196–201
　and NPT, 192, 196–200

Index

Middle East NWFZ (cont'd)
  and peace process, 206-7
  and proliferation, 192
  regional vs global approaches, 188-201
  and regionalism, lack of, 9
  and terrorism, 206-7
  and Tlatelolco Treaty, 9
  and Turkey, 13-14
  UN report on, 6
  and verification, 192, 196-7, 200-2
  and WMD, 195-200, 204-6
Middle East peace process, 186, 206-7
  Madrid Conference (1991), 195, 206
Missile Technology Control Regime (MTCR), 57 n34, n35, 94, 114
Moon Agreement, 4, 141
Moore, Mike, 183 n2
Morocco, 189
Mororoa, 59, 72, 77, 80 n24, 142
Mozambique, 102
Mubarak, Hosni, 109, 189, 192, 198, 205
Musa, Amr, 208 n11
Myanmar, 83, 179, 180

Nagasaki, 150
Naim, Rashid, 157
Namibia, 101, 102, 106
negative security assurances, 22-3, 36, 39-40, 59, 68, 71, 77, 88, 90, 113, 125-7, 132, 137, 138, 159, 168, 174
Nehru, Jawaharlal, 182
Nepal, 166
Netanyahu, Binyamin, 15, 192
New Zealand, 84, 177
  and ANZUS, 15
  Nuclear Free Law of, 217
  and Pacific Islands, 66
  peace movements in, 60
  and South Africa, 221 n2
  and southern hemisphere NWFZ, 212
  and SPNFZ, 62-5, 74, 142

and USA, 15-16, 63-4
Nigeria, 95-7, 104, 107-9, 114
Nixon, Richard, 31 n14
non-government organisations (NGOs), 6, 60, 62, 75, 76, 106
non-proliferation, 3, 94, 97. *See also* proliferation
Non-Proliferation Treaty (NPT), 4, 28, 30, 67, 83, 85, 87, 94, 148
  Article 6, 32 n18, 215
  Article 7, 7
  bargain, 18-19, 32 n18, 211, 213
  and disarmament, 8, 25, 91, 182, 213
  discriminatory nature of, 174, 182
  indefinite extension of (1995), 8, 15, 60, 87, 104, 113, 174-5, 189, 210, 212
  and non-proliferation norm, 21, 32 n18, 123-4, 213, 219
  and nuclear apartheid, 32 n18
  and NWFZ, 7, 12, 74, 123, 125, 176-8, 192, 196-200, 212-13
  Review and Extension Conference (1995), 8, 198
  safeguards, 19, 87, 146, 177, 200
  and Taiwan, 31 n11
nonalignment, 97-8, 100
Non-Aligned Movement, 97
North Atlantic Treaty Organisation (NATO), 13, 22, 60, 160, 177, 196, 214, 222 n12
Northeast Asian NWFZ, 12, 123-51
  bilateral Japan-Korea NWFZ, 149
  and China-Taiwan relations, 10, 150 n2
  and confidence-building, 128, 136, 147
  and existing security arrangements, 13, 134
  and innocent passage, 148
  limited NWFZ, 124, 132, 136-7
  membership, 12
  and negative security assurances, 132, 138

Northeast Asian NWFZ (cont'd)
  and non-proliferation, 129, 136, 150
  and NPT, 130
  obstacles to, 133–5, 143–5
  positive trends for, 135–7
  proposals for, 129–32
  rationale, 127–9
  scenarios for, 148–9
  as strategic option, 145–8
Nuclear Suppliers Group, 45, 57 n35, 94, 114
nuclear-weapon-free zones (NWFZ)
  and arms control/disarmament, 3, 13, 15, 21, 26–30, 91, 97, 126, 183, 210, 212, 215
  characteristics of, 141–3
  as confidence-building measures, 14, 15, 21, 27–30, 127, 178, 183
  and delivery systems, 7, 28, 177, 194
  and EEZ, 7, 19
  entry-into-force clauses, 10
  and existing security arrangements, 13–16, 175
  and freedom of the seas, 21–2, 28, 137, 175
  geographic scope of, 19–21
  goals of, 6–8, 212
  and IAEA, 7
  and innocent passage, 62, 137, 177
  limitations and utility, 23–9, 126–7
  meaning, 6–8, 124–7, 176–8, 213
  and negative security assurances, 23, 125–7, 137
  and non-proliferation, 13, 21, 26, 152, 210, 212, 215
  and norm, anti-nuclear, 24–5, 212–13, 216
  and NPT, 7, 12, 125, 176–8, 212–13
  and nuclear waste, 7
  and nuclear-weapons states, 14, 18, 22–3, 30, 91, 125, 137, 175, 215–21
  and peaceful nuclear development, 18–19
  and peaceful nuclear explosions, 7, 62
  regional initiatives for, 8–10
  and smoke-free zones, 30
  symbolic value of, 177
  and testing, nuclear, 8
  and 'thinning out' of nuclear weapons, 23
  and treaty requirement, 10–1
  and UN, 61–2
  and USA, 61–2
  and verification, 16–18, 177, 194–5
  and withdrawal clauses, 11
  see also Bangkok, Treaty of; Middle East NWFZ; Northeast Asian NWFZ; Pelindaba, Treaty of; Rarotonga, Treaty of; South Asian NWFZ; southern hemisphere NWFZ; and Tlatelolco, Treaty of
nuclear weapons
  and anti-nuclear 'allergy', 22–4, 145
  'black bomb', 95, 101, 107
  and negative security assurances, 23, 159, 174
  proliferation, 4, 16, 60
  and terrorism, 16, 189–90
  tests, 24, 149
nuclear-weapons states (NWS)
  and disarmament, 4, 14, 94, 99, 173, 211, 213–14
  'neither confirm nor deny' policy of, 28, 177, 181
  and NPT, 18–19, 25, 211
  and NWFZ, 14, 18, 22–3, 30, 91, 125, 137, 150, 175, 215–21

O'Brien, Terence, 24
Ogawa, Shinichi, 146
OPANAL, *see* Agency for the Prohibition of Nuclear Weapons in Latin America and the Caribbean

Index

Operation Brasstacks, 156
Organisation for Security and
  Cooperation in Europe (OSCE),
  206
Organisation of African Unity (OAU),
  98–9, 105, 115
  and African NWFZ, 9, 17, 86, 98,
    101–2, 109–12, 115–16, 142
  and apartheid, 97
  Cairo conference, 98
  Council of Ministers, 99, 109
  and Southern Africa, 101
Organisation of American States
  (OAS), 9, 17, 39, 41, 52 n3
Organisation of Petroleum Exporting
  Countries (OPEC), 95
Oslo accords, 15, 206
Outer Space Treaty, 4, 141, 212

Pacific Islands, 60–2, 66
Pakistan
  Atomic Energy Commission of, 154
  and China, 13, 157, 169, 179–82,
    186
  and India, 25, 26, 94, 152–70, 180–
    2, 186
  and Israel, 186
  and missiles, 156–7
  and NPT, 12
  and nuclear weapons, 4, 29, 105,
    152–5, 160–1, 180, 186
  and South Asian NWFZ, 29, 152–
    83
  and USA, 154, 161, 179
Palau, 5, 11, 20
Panama, 53 n6
Panama Canal, 38
Panama declaration (1939), 41
Papua New Guinea, 60, 62–3
Paraguay, 53 n6
Paris, Stempel, 45
Partial Test Ban Treaty, 44, 98
peaceful nuclear explosions (PNE), 6,
  7, 19, 39–41, 46–7, 62, 65, 110–
1, 153, 158, 160, 165, 182, 209
  n16
Pelindaba, Treaty of, 5, 20, 86, 93–
  120, 124, 142, 175–6, 211, 213,
  217
  background, 96–100, 109
  and Chagos Archipelago/Diego
    Garcia, 20, 179
  and disarmament, 110–1, 115
  entry-into-force, 10–1
  evaluation, 109–14
  future, 114–16
  and IAEA, 112–13
  impediments to, 100–2
  imperatives for, 102–4
  membership, 11, 109
  and negative security assurances, 113
  and non-proliferation, 110, 114–15
  and nuclear facilities and research, 7
  and nuclear testing, 111, 113
  and nuclear waste, 7, 111
  and nuclear-weapons states, 110
  and peaceful nuclear development,
    110, 112–13, 115–16
  and peaceful nuclear explosions, 6,
    110–1
  and Rarotonga Treaty, 71–3
  and South African challenge, 104–8
  and South Asian NWFZ, 179
  and UN, 17
  and verification, 17, 113
  withdrawal clauses, 11
Peres, Shimon, 203
Persian Gulf, 184, 196
Peru, 53 n6
Philippines, 5, 84–6, 104, 217
Portugal, 102–3, 110
Prawitz, Jan, 23, 74, 79 n11, 207, 208
  n6
Preparatory Commission for the
  Denuclearisation of Latin
  America (COPREDAL), 36–42
Pressler Amendment, 154

Principles and Objectives for Non-proliferation and Disarmament, 8, 113
proliferation, 4, 12, 16, 97–8, 107, 123, 129, 145–6, 155, 168–9, 173–4, 184–5, 213–14. *See also* non-proliferation
Puerto Rico, 38, 45

Rabin, Yitzhak, 203
Rapacki, Adam, 4, 141
Rarotonga, Treaty of, 5, 59–81, 109, 123, 135, 137, 141–2, 175, 206, 211, 213
  and ANZUS, 15, 63
  as confidence-building measure, 70, 74, 78
  Consultative Committee, 17, 75
  and delivery systems, 28–9, 59, 73, 76
  entry-into-force, 10
  and environmental controls, 72–3
  and existing security arrangements, 63–4, 134
  features, key, 61–8
  and freedom of the seas, 64–5, 67, 217
  and French nuclear testing, 15, 134
  future directions, 74–8
  geographic scope of, 19–21, 63, 176
  and IAEA, 65
  impact: global, 71–2; regional, 68–71
  and innocent passage, 64–5, 67
  membership, 5, 11, 20, 63
  and missiles, 60, 73, 76
  as model, 73–4
  and negative security assurances, 59, 68, 71, 77
  and nuclear testing, 68–9
  and nuclear waste, 7
  and nuclear-weapons states, 66–8, 74, 215–16
  and peaceful nuclear explosions, 6, 19, 65
  and Pelindaba Treaty, 65, 76
  and regionalism, 9, 62
  and Russia/USSR, 22
  and Tlatelolco Treaty, 59, 62, 65, 73, 74, 76
  and UN, 76
  and USA, 11, 22, 59, 63–4
  utility, 68–74
  and verification, 17, 65–6, 76
  withdrawal clauses, 11, 62
Reagan Administration, 22, 66
regional security complex, 10
revolution in military affairs (RMA), 214
Rider, Peter, 212
Rio Group, 52 n3
Rio Treaty, 41
Roy, J. Stapleton, 66
Russia, 128, 177, 182
  and China, 24–5
  and nuclear weapons, 144, 167, 175, 211
  and NWFZ: African, 119 n42; Northeast Asian, 12, 23–4, 29, 124, 128–30, 133–8, 141, 143–4, 146, 149; South Asian, 161
  and USA, 24–5, 130
  see also Soviet Union

Sadat, Anwar, 206
Saddam Hussein, 190, 209 n22
Sahara, 97
Said, Abdel Moneim, 186
St Lucia, 45
St Vincent & Grenadines, 45
Sajima, Naoko, 25
Sanders, Ben, 208 n6
Sarabhai, V. A., 153
Sarid, Yosi, 203
Saudi Arabia, 178
Savimbi, Jonas, 106
Seabed Treaty, 4, 141, 212
Selassie, Tilahun W., 108
Senegal, 108
Serrano, Monica, 9, 26

Index

233

Seychelles, 109
Shagari, Shehu, 95
Shaker, Mohammed, 201
Shamir, Yitzhak, 197
Sharif, Nawaz, 164, 171 n10, 172 n37
Sid-Ahmed, Mohamed, 186
Singapore, 82, 84, 85
Singh, Jasjit, 172 n29
Smith, Ian, 102
Solomon Islands, 60, 217
Somalia, 101, 109
South Africa, 178
  and African NWFZ, 102, 109, 176
  and Angola, 102, 106
  and apartheid, 97, 101, 103-7
  Atomic Energy Corporation of, 105-6, 109
  and IAEA, 107
  and Israel, 99, 105
  and New Zealand, 221 n2
  and NPT, 102, 104, 106-7
  and nuclear test, 103-4
  and nuclear weapons, 7, 94-6, 99-108, 111, 114, 176
  and OAU, 107
  and Portugal, 102-3
  and USA, 101-3, 105, 114
South Asian Association for Regional Cooperation (SAARC), 9, 10, 163, 172 n37
South Asian NWFZ, 152-83
  and comprehensive security, 157-8
  conditionality, 181-2
  as confidence-building measure, 166, 168, 180-1
  and disarmament, 162, 181
  geographic scope of, 20-1, 179-81
  and India-Pakistan rivalry, 10, 152-72
  and negative security assurances, 159, 168
  and peaceful nuclear development, 166
  phased approach to, 164-70
  principles, 159
  proposals, 158-64
  rationale, 153-8
  and regionalism, lack of, 9
  and verification, 167-8, 180-1
South Pacific Environment Ministers Meeting, 80 n24
South Pacific Forum, 59, 67
  membership, 11, 70, 75-6
  and Rarotonga Treaty, 9, 17, 20, 62, 65, 68, 86, 142
  Secretariat, 65
South Pacific Nuclear Free Zone, see Rarotonga, Treaty of
South Pacific Regional Environmental Programme (SPREP), 72-3
South West African People's Organisation (SWAPO), 102
Southeast Asian NWFZ, see Bangkok, Treaty of
Southern Africa, 101, 109
southern hemisphere NWFZ, 62, 74, 77-8, 152, 183, 210-22
  and arms control/disarmament, 218
  and delivery systems, 216-17
  and existing security arrangements, 219-20
  and freedom of the seas, 216-17
  and innocent passage, 216-17
  and norm, anti-nuclear, 218-19
  and nuclear-weapons states, 215-17, 221
  and political declaration/statement, 219-21
  principles & guidelines, 215-21
  UN resolution on, 211-2, 220-1
  and voluntary restraint protocol, 218
Soviet Union, 95, 104, 205
  and Afghanistan, 154
  breakup of, 14, 15, 45, 143, 206
  and China, 85
  and India, 179
  and nuclear weapons, 4, 160, 174; on ships, 23, 32 n19
  and NWFZ: Latin American, 39-40, 44; Northeast Asian, 124, 129-

Soviet Union (cont'd)
31; South Pacific, 22, 66–7, 142;
Southeast Asian, 85
and USA, 102, 125, 140, 155–6
see also Russia
Spain, 110
SPNFZ, *see* Rarotonga, Treaty of
Spratly Islands, 85–6, 216
Sri Lanka, 166
Steinberg, Gerald, 13, 27
Stockholm International Peace Research Institute (SIPRI), 154–5
Strategic Arms Reduction Treaties (START), 174–5
Sweden, 104
Syria, 189, 195, 201, 205–7

Taiwan, 10, 12, 29, 31 n11, 150 n2
Tarapur reactor, 168
Tarhunah, 117 n3
Thailand, 84–5
Thakur, Ramesh, 74
Tibet, 23, 180, 181, 182
Tlatelolco, Treaty of, 4–6, 8, 20–1, 35–58, 63, 71, 109, 118 n16, 134, 135, 142, 152, 176, 211, 213
  creation, 37–43
  Cuban missile crisis and, 15, 125, 133–4, 141, 142, 175
  entry-into-force, 11, 41, 206
  and IAEA, 11, 22, 38, 44
  implementation, 43–7
  and Islas Malvinas/Falkland Islands, 20, 39
  membership, 11
  and negative security assurances, 36, 39–40
  and non-proliferation, 26, 35–6, 41–2, 46–8, 50–2, 123
  and NPT, 44, 213
  and nuclear-weapons states, 215–16
  and peaceful nuclear development, 46, 48–9, 51
  and peaceful nuclear explosions, 7, 39–41, 46–7
  and regionalism, 9, 36, 42
  title, change of, 11, 54 n22
  and transport of nuclear weapons, 40–1
  and UN, 17, 41, 44
  and USA, 22, 35, 52 n4
  and verification, 17, 168, 202
  withdrawal clauses, 11
Tobago, 38
Togo, 96, 99
Tonga, 5, 60, 61, 63
Törnudd, Klaus, 31 n7
Treaty of Amity and Cooperation, 82–3
Trinidad, 38
Tunisia, 189
Turkey, 13–14, 196

Uganda, 96
United Kingdom, *see* Britain
United Nations (UN)
  arms register, 204
  and CTBT, 174
  and disarmament, 197, 199, 211
  and Iraq, 201
  and NWFZ, 6, 102, 109–10, 115–16, 119 n36, 197–9, 204
  and South Africa, 104
UN Charter, 87, 89, 199
UN Convention on the Law of the Seas (UNCLOS), 19, 67, 89, 91, 177, 216
UN Disarmament Commission, 212
UN General Assembly
  and African denuclearisation, 100, 104, 109
  and NWFZ, 7, 17, 41, 61–2, 65, 87, 109, 126, 152, 159, 161, 176, 180, 192, 195, 197–9, 211, 220–1
  Resolutions: anti-testing, 71; on disarmament, 211; 16/1652, 98; 20/2033, 99; 45/56A, 109

Index   235

UN Institute for Disarmament Research
    (UNIDIR), 208 n12
UN Secretary-General, 159, 197, 212
UN Security Council, 17, 65, 104,
    173, 199, 200, 201
UN Special Commission on Iraq
    (UNSCOM), 200–1
UN Special Session on Disarmament
    (UNSSOD), 197
United States
    and Angola, 101
    and Australia, 29, 63–4, 68, 69, 74
    and China, 24–5
    and CTBT, 174, 175
    and Diego Garcia, 21
    and disarmament, 18, 211
    and France, 22, 69
    and Japan, 13, 15, 134–5, 140, 143, 147–9
    and Latin America, 36, 49
    and Namibia, 101
    'neither confirm nor deny' policy of, 15–16, 89
    and non-proliferation, 18, 145, 160, 168
    Nuclear Posture Review, 214
    and nuclear weapons, 119 n44, 132, 167, 174; on ships, 23, 32 n19
    and NWFZ, 61–2, 128, 134;
        African, 101, 113–14, 117 n3;
        Latin American, 22, 35, 38–40, 44, 52 n4; Middle East, 191–2;
        Northeast Asian, 23–4, 29, 128–9, 131, 133–8, 141, 143–9;
        South Asian, 161, 166; South Pacific, 11, 22, 59–69; Southeast Asian, 11, 85, 90, 216
    and Pakistan, 154, 161, 179
    and Philippines, 84–6
    and Russia/USSR, 24–5, 140; and nuclear rivalry, 4, 101–2, 125, 128–30, 155–6, 192
    and Somalia, 101
    and South Africa, 101–3, 105, 114
    and South Korea, 13, 130, 134, 136, 143–5, 148–9
    and Zimbabwe, 101
Uruguay, 53 n6, n10, 54 n22
USS Enterprise, 13, 178

Valindaba, 103
Vanuatu, 60, 61, 63, 217
Vanunu, Mordechai, 76, 185, 209 n16
Venezuela, 53 n6, n10, 54 n22, 104
Vietnam, 85–6
Virgin Islands, 38, 45

Waltz, Kenneth N., 192
Warsaw Pact, 4
weapons of mass destruction (WMD),
    70, 73–5, 77, 93–4, 96, 100,
    112, 114, 173, 182, 190, 192,
    195–200, 204–6, 212, 214, 220
West Bank, 205
Whiting, Allen, 131
World Bank, 108

Xinxiang, 180

Yasmeen, Samina, 27
Yeon Hyong-mook, 131
Yom Kippur War, 205

Zahran, Mounir, 208 n12
Zaire, 96
Zambia, 108
Zangger Committee, 114
Zimbabwe, 101, 102
zone of peace, freedom and neutrality
    (ZOPFAN), 82, 84, 85, 87, 89, 142